From the Assumption to Advent

From the Assumption to Advent

Daily readings and meditations
to pray alone or as a family

Fr. Patrick Troadec, SSPX

Translated by Ann Marie Temple

Angelus Press

PO Box 217 | Saint Marys, KS 66536

Original edition, *De L'Assomption à L'Avent au Jour le Jour,* published by Via Romana, 2016

Translated from the French by Ann Marie Temple.

Cover: *The Immaculate Conception.* Guido Reni (1575-1642). The Metropolitan Museum of Art, New York.

Library of Congress Cataloging-in-Publication Data

Names: Troadec, Patrick, 1960- author.
Title: From Advent to Epiphany : daily readings and meditations to pray alone or as a family / Fr. Patrick Troadec, SSPX.
Other titles: De l'avent áa l'âepiphanie. English
Description: First English edition. | Kansas City : Angelus Press, 2018. | Includes bibliographical references and index.
Identifiers: LCCN 2018039468
Subjects: LCSH: Advent--Prayers and devotions. | Christmas--Prayers and devotions. | Epiphany--Prayers and devotions. | Catholic Church--Prayers and devotions.
Classification: LCC BX2170.A4 T7613 2018 | DDC 242/.33--dc23
LC record available at https://lccn.loc.gov/2018039468

© 2022 Angelus Press
All rights reserved.

ANGELUS PRESS
PO Box 217
Saint Marys, Kansas 66536
Phone (816) 753-3150
Fax (816) 753-3557
Order Line (800) 966-7337
www.angeluspress.org

ISBN: 978-1-949124-78-1
FIRST PRINTING—October 2022

Printed in the United States of America

Table of Contents

A Note to Our Readers _____ 1

August 15th _____ 3

9th Sunday after Pentecost _____ 5
Monday of the 9th Week after Pentecost _____ 7
Tuesday of the 9th Week after Pentecost _____ 9
Wednesday of the 9th Week after Pentecost _____ 11
Thursday of the 9th Week after Pentecost _____ 13
Friday of the 9th Week after Pentecost _____ 15
Saturday of the 9th Week after Pentecost _____ 17

10th Sunday after Pentecost _____ 20
Monday of the 10th Week after Pentecost _____ 22
Tuesday of the 10th Week after Pentecost _____ 25
Wednesday of the 10th Week after Pentecost _____ 27
Thursday of the 10th Week after Pentecost _____ 29
Friday of the 10th Week after Pentecost _____ 31
Saturday of the 10th Week after Pentecost _____ 33

11th Sunday after Pentecost _____ 35
Monday of the 11th Week after Pentecost _____ 37
Tuesday of the 11th Week after Pentecost _____ 39
Wednesday of the 11th Week after Pentecost _____ 42
Thursday of the 11th Week after Pentecost _____ 44
Friday of the 11th Week after Pentecost _____ 46
Saturday of the 11th Week after Pentecost _____ 49

12th Sunday after Pentecost _____ 51
Monday of the 12th Week after Pentecost _____ 53
Tuesday of the 12th Week after Pentecost _____ 56
Wednesday of the 12th Week after Pentecost _____ 58
Thursday of the 12th Week after Pentecost _____ 60
Friday of the 12th Week after Pentecost _____ 62
Saturday of the 12th Week after Pentecost _____ 64

13th Sunday after Pentecost _____ 66
Monday of the 13th Week after Pentecost _____ 68
Tuesday of the 13th Week after Pentecost _____ 70
Wednesday of the 13th Week after Pentecost _____ 72
Thursday of the 13th Week after Pentecost _____ 74
Friday of the 13th Week after Pentecost _____ 77
Saturday of the 13th Week after Pentecost _____ 80

From the Assumption to Advent

14th Sunday after Pentecost — 82
Monday of the 14th Week after Pentecost — 84
Tuesday of the 14th Week after Pentecost — 86
Wednesday of the 14th Week after Pentecost — 88
Thursday of the 14th Week after Pentecost — 90
Friday of the 14th Week after Pentecost — 92
Saturday of the 14th Week after Pentecost — 94

15th Sunday after Pentecost — 97
Monday of the 15th Week after Pentecost — 99
Tuesday of the 15th Week after Pentecost — 102
Wednesday of the 15th Week after Pentecost — 104
Thursday of the 15th Week after Pentecost — 106
Friday of the 15th Week after Pentecost — 108
Saturday of the 15th Week after Pentecost — 110

16th Sunday after Pentecost — 112
Monday of the 16th Week after Pentecost — 114
Tuesday of the 16th Week after Pentecost — 116
Wednesday of the 16th Week after Pentecost — 118
Thursday of the 16th Week after Pentecost — 121
Friday of the 16th Week after Pentecost — 124
Saturday of the 16th Week after Pentecost — 127

17th Sunday after Pentecost — 129
Monday of the 17th Week after Pentecost — 131
Tuesday of the 17th Week after Pentecost — 133
Wednesday of the 17th Week after Pentecost — 135
Thursday of the 17th Week after Pentecost — 137
Friday of the 17th Week after Pentecost — 139
Saturday of the 17th Week after Pentecost — 141

18th Sunday after Pentecost — 143
Monday of the 18th Week after Pentecost — 145
Tuesday of the 18th Week after Pentecost — 147
Wednesday of the 18th Week after Pentecost — 149
Thursday of the 18th Week after Pentecost — 151
Friday of the 18th Week after Pentecost — 153
Saturday of the 18th Week after Pentecost — 155

Table of Contents

19th Sunday after Pentecost 157
Monday of the 19th Week after Pentecost 160
Tuesday of the 19th Week after Pentecost 162
Wednesday of the 19th Week after Pentecost 165
Thursday of the 19th Week after Pentecost 168
Friday of the 19th Week after Pentecost 170
Saturday of the 19th Week after Pentecost 172

20th Sunday after Pentecost 175
Monday of the 20th Week after Pentecost 178
Tuesday of the 20th Week after Pentecost 181
Wednesday of the 20th Week after Pentecost 184
Thursday of the 20th Week after Pentecost 186
Friday of the 20th Week after Pentecost 188
Saturday of the 20th Week after Pentecost 191

21st Sunday after Pentecost 193
Monday of the 21st Week after Pentecost 195
Tuesday of the 21st Week after Pentecost 198
Wednesday of the 21st Week after Pentecost 200
Thursday of the 21st Week after Pentecost 202
Friday of the 21st Week after Pentecost 204
Saturday of the 21st Week after Pentecost 206

22nd Sunday after Pentecost 208
Monday of the 22nd Week after Pentecost 210
Tuesday of the 22nd Week after Pentecost 212
Wednesday of the 22nd Week after Pentecost 214
Thursday of the 22nd Week after Pentecost 216
Friday of the 22nd Week after Pentecost 218
Saturday of the 22nd Week after Pentecost 220

23rd Sunday after Pentecost 223
Monday of the 23rd Week after Pentecost 225
Tuesday of the 23rd Week after Pentecost 228
Wednesday of the 23rd Week after Pentecost 230
Thursday of the 23rd Week after Pentecost 233
Friday of the 23rd Week after Pentecost 235
Saturday of the 23rd Week after Pentecost 237

From the Assumption to Advent

24th Sunday after Pentecost — 239
Monday of the 24th Week after Pentecost — 242
Tuesday of the 24th Week after Pentecost — 244
Wednesday of the 24th Week after Pentecost — 247
Thursday of the 24th Week after Pentecost — 249
Friday of the 24th Week after Pentecost — 251
Saturday of the 24th Week after Pentecost — 253

The Last Sunday of October — 255

November 1st — 257

Addenda — 259

Spiritual Communion — 260
The Mysteries of the Rosary — 261
    Joyful Mysteries — 261
    Sorrowful Mysteries — 261
    Glorious Mysteries — 261
Creed — 262
Confiteor — 263
Glory Be to the Father — 263
Act of Faith — 263
Act of Hope — 264
Act of Charity — 264
Act of Contrition — 264
Prayer to the Holy Ghost — 264
Act of Confidence in God — 265
St. Claude de la Colombière — 265
Prayer to St. Michael Archangel — 266
Invocations to St. Michael the Archangel — 266
Litany of the Sacred Heart — 267
Litany of the Holy Guardian Angels — 269
Litany of Humility — 271
Latin Hymns — 272
Magnificat — 272

Table of Contents

    The Seven Penitential Psalms 273
        Psalm 6 273
        Psalm 31 274
        Psalm 37 275
        Psalm 50 (*Miserere*) 276
        Psalm 101 278
        Psalm 129 (*De Profundis*) 280
        Psalm 142 281
    Psalm 90 282
    Salve Regina 283
    Soul of Christ (*Anima Christi*) 283
    Hymn *Soul of My Savior* 284

Bibliography 285

A Note to Our Readers

Dear Readers,

This little volume, sixth of the series, draws the liturgical year to a close.[1] Each of these booklets has been designed to slip easily into a briefcase or a handbag, as nourishment for the spiritual life at any time of the day.

Each day offers two pages of text: a meditation based on Holy Scripture, two prayers, two thoughts, and three resolutions.

The meditations seek to shed light on the word of God. They cover different aspects of the life of Jesus and of the Christian life, addressing our duties toward God, toward our neighbor and toward ourselves. August 15th brings us already in sight of the season of Autumn. It is the time to renew our fervor by good resolutions before school begins again, or before returning to work after a summer holiday. With this goal in view, a certain number of meditations focus on the life we are leading now on this earth and the meaning of the trials we endure, encouraging us to confidence in Divine Providence; others invite to the practice of faith, hope and charity—charity toward God and neighbor; still others bring us before the questions surrounding the four last things: questions about death, about hell, purgatory and Heaven; finally, other meditations remind us that we are children of God and help us live daily in the company of God and His angels and saints.

The wealth contained in the prayers and the thoughts for the day can be a strong help in maintaining our morning fervor throughout the day.

The prayers are taken from the book *Divine Intimacy* by Fr. Gabriel of St. Mary Magdalen, from Fr. Emmanuel's *Meditations for Every Day of the Year*, from St. Alphonsus Liguori in the collection *Holiness Day by Day*, but also from the writings of many other saints.

The thoughts are most often the words of saints, and saints from every time period: starting with Fathers of the Church like St. Ambrose, St. Augustine, St. John Chrysostom, St. Gregory the Great; Medieval

---

[1] Easter is a moveable feast, and as a result the Assumption can fall anywhere from the 9th to the 13th week after Pentecost depending on the year. For this reason, weeks 9 to 13, which were included in the previous volume, are reproduced here.

saints and saints of the Renaissance; all the way through to saints of our modern times.

We have tried to offer a wide variety of resolutions in order to help our readers apply their meditations very concretely, so that every day brings a new commitment to becoming better. Parents can help their children see the best efforts for each one of them to make, according to age and temperament.

Finally, the end of the volume contains prayers and hymns in the spirit of the meditations, to continue nourishing our piety.

This little book on the Christian life is spiritual but simple and also practical and may therefore be of use to the entire family. Every member may find something here to help him advance. Parents may need to simplify certain meditations even further, depending on the maturity of their children. The prayers of the day could be recited as a family.

Whatever a person's state in life, all may find matter for spiritual progress in this daily reading. If we foster our Christian life every day by a few words of love, little by little we will enter a continual heart to heart conversation with Jesus Christ.

With joy, therefore, do I offer you this new booklet. May it help you move forward with steps of love toward the beautiful Heaven that awaits us.

Remembering all of my readers in my priestly prayers, especially during the Holy Sacrifice of the Mass, I ask that you also pray for me, and I extend to you already my heartfelt gratitude.

Fr. Patrick Troadec

THE ASSUMPTION OF OUR LADY

August 15th

God speaks to us:

A great sign appeared in Heaven: A woman clothed with the sun, and the moon under her feet, and on her head a crown of twelve stars.

Introit: Apocalypse 12:1

Meditation

Let us contemplate the triumphal rise of our Lady into Heaven. Let us watch her enter the blessed homeland. Let us imagine the ineffable joy of the angels and saints who admire for the first time the Queen of Heaven, the woman blessed among all women, the Immaculate, the most beautiful of all creatures. What a cry of joyful delight rises from all of the elect! And with what respect, what veneration, do they approach her, to congratulate her and greet her: *Salve Regina, Mater Misericordiae*, "Hail, O Queen, Mother of Mercy." The angels and saints receive a new flow of happiness in contemplating her who is both our queen and our mother.

Once these first marks of love and veneration had been expressed, our Lord certainly came up to her to lead her to her throne set over all creatures.

If it is true that "eye has not seen nor ear heard, nor has it entered into the heart of man, what things God has prepared for those who love Him" (I Cor. 2:9), then what must have been the welcome reserved by our Lord for His most holy mother! We will have to wait to reach Heaven ourselves before we know just how great were the honors that Jesus bestowed on His mother.

To help us picture the magnificence of our Lady's triumph, the Church applies to her these words from the book of the Apocalypse: *"A great sign appeared in Heaven: A woman clothed with the sun, and the moon under her feet, and on her head a crown of twelve stars."* This woman is the Blessed Virgin. She has the moon under her feet to show her constancy, her evenness of temper, her fidelity. Her head is crowned with twelve stars.

St. Bernard writes that these stars symbolize her twelve prerogatives: her immaculate conception, the salutation by the angel, the coming of the Holy Ghost in her and the conception of our Lord, then her virginity, her immaculate maternity, her childbirth without pain, and her assumption; finally, her discretion, her humility, her extraordinary faith and the martyrdom of her heart.

Prayer

O most Blessed Virgin Mary, assumed into heaven, I beg you to purify my senses so that I may begin to enjoy God even while I am on earth.
— Fr. Gabriel, DI, p. 1115

Or else:

From this earth over which we tread as pilgrims, comforted by our faith in the future resurrection, we look to you, [O our Lady], our life, our sweetness, and our hope.
— Fr. Gabriel, DI, p. 1117

Thoughts

- The Blessed Virgin is without stain, adorned with all the virtues that render her so beautiful and pleasing to the Holy Trinity.
  — Curé of Ars, TD2, August 15
- I will do everything for Heaven, which is my homeland; there I will find my mother in all the splendor of her glory, and with her I will rejoice with perfect security in the happiness of Jesus Himself.
  — St. Bernadette, R, p. 35

Resolutions

1. To recite the fourth glorious mystery, meditating on this beautiful mystery of the Assumption.
2. To meditate for ten minutes on the happiness of Heaven.
3. To practice one of the virtues represented by the stars of the Virgin of the Apocalypse. (Specify which one.)

THE TEARS OF JESUS
9th Sunday after Pentecost

God speaks to us:

When [Jesus] drew near, seeing the city, He wept over it.
Gospel of Sunday: St. Luke 19:41

Meditation

What a striking image, to see Jesus weeping before the great city of Jerusalem! A short time before, the calm and peace of Heaven shone in His eyes; now those eyes are filled with tears. In the days just previous, His lips spoke only words of life and consolation; now those lips utter complaints and lamentations! And this hand which was raised only to bless is now lifted threatening and terrible against the city of Jerusalem!

Why these threats and lamentations? Does Jesus not love His fellow countrymen? Has He not showered them with benefits? Has He not blessed, embraced and caressed their children, healed their sick, raised their dead, passed among them doing good? Where do these tears come from? These tears are His love, weeping over them all. He sees the sins of this blind and ungrateful people, and He already perceives the future destruction of the guilty city; He deplores above all the loss of souls and cannot keep from shedding tears.

To understand these tears, we must look at the initial plan of God. God created man free, and He desires that man answer *yes* to the divine plan of love. God did everything He could to help this happen, going beyond anything we could have imagined. He took on a human nature like our own and accepted to carry the weight of our sins Himself, expiating them by horrific sufferings. Despite all this love, man with incomprehensible blindness very often prefers nothingness over being, ugliness over beauty, evil over good. Our Lord does not will the death of the sinner and He weeps to see man refuse His repeated advances, His outstretched hand, His pressing invitations. These tears therefore show that God, though deploring evil, yet respects the freedom of man, for better or for worse. They reveal that our Lord wills man's salvation, but they also show how man by a mysterious blindness often refuses the offered salvation and stubbornly remains in his wickedness.

Lord Jesus, as I contemplate the tears that flow down Your face at the sight of the city of Jerusalem, I measure the greatness of the sorrow You felt when You were here on earth, seeing the blindness of so many souls. Help me to share Your sorrows and heal me of my own blindness.

Prayer

Weep, Lord; weep, Lord Jesus: Your tears will not all be lost; I give You my soul to let them fall and bear fruit; by Your tears, Lord, save my soul.
— Fr. Emmanuel, M, p. 251

Or else:

O most gentle Lamb, weeping and dying for us, be our salvation!
— Fr. Emmanuel, M, p. 253

Thoughts

- It may be literally true that some of those tears of our Lord were for me, so much has He loved me.
  — Fr. Emmanuel, M, p. 253
- How compassionate is the heart of Jesus, how precious are His tears! Let us adore His heart, His eyes, and His tears.
  — Fr. Emmanuel, M, p. 248

Resolutions

1. To read with attention the Gospel of the day in order to weep over our sins alongside our Lord.
2. To receive communion in reparation for the sufferings that we have caused our Lord.
3. To console a person who is suffering, by taking the time to listen and to understand.

AN ELASTIC CONSCIENCE

Monday of the 9th Week after Pentecost

GOD SPEAKS TO US:

He who follows Me will not walk in darkness but will have the light of life.

St. John 8:12

MEDITATION

Let us consider today that blindness which is willed and even deliberate, and is therefore culpable.

This is any blindness that we maintain in ourselves and that we do not want to have healed, because of the constraints that truth would put on us.

This willful blindness makes us fear to see clearly the evil that we do, or the good that we do not do, because seeing clearly would oblige us to change, and change is what we absolutely do not want. We prefer to remain in our blindness because it is more convenient, and we refuse the light because it bothers us. Unfortunately, there is no guarantee that we ourselves are totally free of this sin. We may well have an upright conscience on many points of Catholic doctrine, but still there are certain areas of shadow that we avoid investigating because we are attached to a freedom that is not of God.

It can even happen that we have a very strict conscience on certain points of morality, and on other points, a conscience that is elastic, more or less broad, and not in accord with a just measure.

Thus, for example certain people do not fulfill the duty of restitution when they have acted against the virtue of justice. Others fall quite easily into a sin against justice by making personal use of company goods, on the pretext that everybody does the same. Still others make false declarations on the argument that we live in a dog-eat-dog world. In all these ways, we ourselves become part of the system by acting in a dishonest manner. Some people, who tend to speak ill of others, neglect to repair the damage they may have caused by their calumnies. Others, again, neglect to instruct themselves on certain points of Christian morality and so remain in ignorance as to the gravity of certain sins. Still others fulfill perfectly their duties toward God and neglect their duties as spouses or their duties toward their children. And the list goes on…

Lord Jesus, help me to eliminate once and for all the areas of shadow which still remain in me, and which prevent me from being totally Yours.

Prayer

St. Michael Archangel, enlighten me by your light; St. Michael Archangel, protect me under your wings; St. Michael Archangel, defend me with your sword.

— Invocations to St. Michael

Or else:

O Lord my God, enlighten my eyes that I never sleep in death
— Ps. 12:4

Thoughts

- We will live well when we make an examination of conscience every night.
  — Curé of Ars, TD2, September 4
- We will be judged on the good we could have done and did not do, and on the sins of others which we have caused.
  — Curé of Ars, TD2, September 18

Resolutions

1. To read attentively an examination of conscience in a missal.
2. To examine with our spiritual guide the points on which our conscience may be too broad or too narrow and make a resolution in consequence.
3. To help a person who lives in sin by enlightening his conscience and encouraging him to change his life.

CULPABLE IGNORANCE

Tuesday of the 9th Week after Pentecost

GOD SPEAKS TO US:

Master, that I may see.

St. Mark 10:51

MEDITATION

The blindness of the soul can come from ignorance and still be a cause of sin.

We speak of invincible ignorance and vincible ignorance.

Invincible ignorance is an ignorance that we cannot conquer because we do not have the means to do so.

Thus, we sometimes fail in certain of our duties, not because we are refusing to know what they are, but because in fact we simply do not know them. Our failings are due not so much to bad faith as to simple ignorance: in that case, we are not culpable.

On the other hand, vincible ignorance can be overcome; we are guilty of it.

Let us see a few examples.

When the members of the Sanhedrin put our Lord to death, they killed Him, says St. Peter, out of ignorance (Acts 3:17), because passion and hatred were blinding them.

Likewise, we ourselves sometimes make hasty judgments about people and fail in justice and charity, because we judge on appearances, or we lack information. This is certainly due to our ignorance, but we are not thereby cleared of all guilt, because we could have informed ourselves better or simply suspended our judgment and held our tongue.

In case of doubt, when we do not know if a thing is a sin or not a sin, if it is grave or not grave, we have the duty to enlighten our conscience and not act in doubt (unless we know we suffer from scruples, which creates a different situation).

Moreover, this duty of eliminating doubt concerns not only ourselves but also those under our charge. Thus, parents have the duty to enlighten their children as to what they should do and what they should avoid, so their children will know the truth and not fall into the trap of blindness.

Lord Jesus, enlighten me so that I may not fall into guilty ignorance but may accomplish courageously all the good that You expect of me.

Prayer

Cleanse me, [Lord], of my secret sins, and preserve Thy servant from the greatest sin [the sin of pride].

— Ps. 18: 13-14

Or else:

Help us, my God, in this cleansing of our minds, our souls, and our hearts; turn us truly into Your temples, truly into houses of prayer where all is pure, and all glorifies Your name.

— Charles de Foucauld, TD, January 18

Thoughts

- Jesus weeps over the blind soul. He says to her, as to Jerusalem: If you only knew! But she does not want to know. The light wearies her, the light is a burden.

  — Fr. Emmanuel, M, p. 251

- Let us work constantly toward our conversion, because as long as we are only half good, half bad, we are going to be very fragile.

  — Charles de Foucauld, TD, April 10

Resolutions

1. To say a prayer to the Holy Ghost that He enlighten us to see our failings.
2. When we do not know whether a given act is a sin or not, let us go to a priest in order to enlighten our conscience.
3. To avoid making hasty judgments.

BLINDNESS: A DIVINE PUNISHMENT

Wednesday of the 9th Week after Pentecost

God speaks to us:

And Jesus said: "For judgment have I come into this world, that they who do not see may see, and they who see may become blind."

St. John 9:39

Meditation

There is willful blindness and blindness that proceeds from ignorance, and there is also a blindness that is sent by God as a punishment for sin. This blindness is a sign of malediction. May God spare us this chastisement, the most rigorous punishment that we can suffer on this earth, because it is the most opposed to the path of our conversion.

How can God, who is Light, produce darkness? Does He actually impress error upon the soul? Certainly not! God is Truth and cannot infuse error or deceit. Consequently, if God blinds us, He does not do so positively but negatively, that is, by way of privation. God, who had been giving the soul graces of light and conversion, takes them away, ceases to offer them, leaving the soul to its own light, which is often only darkness.

Let us not imagine that God goes so far as to push the soul to sin: to believe such a thing would be a blasphemy. But when He sees that a soul abuses His graces and takes no account of them, He sometimes takes those graces away and leaves that soul to its own strength. God gave man freedom and He does not force us to love Him. He wants man to choose Him freely. How many men—alas!—prefer to yield to their evil tendencies rather than listen to the voice of their conscience! How many men never dare to admit their sins humbly in the confessional! How many men spend their life silencing and stifling the voice of conscience instead of turning back toward God!

For our part, when God enlightens us on the aspects of our life that need reforming, may we listen to His voice and not stifle it, lest we find ourselves in the night of blindness, foretaste of the night of hell. Let us therefore always have an openness of mind and heart that will allow us to recognize what in our life displeases God in one manner or another.

Lord Jesus, give me Your grace, so that I might walk with an eager step on the path of perfection, letting myself be guided by Your divine light, and thus may I come to glory in the blessed eternity of Heaven.

Prayer

O my Savior and my God, grant us the grace to look at things with the same eye as You do!

— St. Vincent de Paul, TD2, January 19

Or else:

I fly unto thee, sweet Virgin of Virgins, my mother; to thee do I come, before thee I stand, sinful and sorrowful, mourning and weeping in this valley of tears. Mother of the Word Incarnate, despise not my petitions, but in thy clemency hear and answer them.

— *Memorare*

Thoughts

- When a sinner consents to a grave sin, with deliberation, in a way he is saying to God: "Lord, go away; I no longer want to have anything to do with You."

    — St. Alphonsus Liguori, HDD, p. 150

- We must ask God that He Himself enlighten us and inspire us to do what is pleasing to Him.

    — St. Vincent de Paul, TD2, August 30

Resolutions

1. To regret profoundly our past sins.
2. To read Psalm 50 as a sign of repentance (see page 276).
3. To give up today the principal obstacle to our state of grace: a particular person, or book, or form of leisure… and then to schedule a time with a priest so we can go to confession.

THE FALSE PEACE OF THE DEVIL

Thursday of the 9th Week after Pentecost

God speaks to us:

They healed the breach of the daughter of My people disgracefully, saying: Peace, peace: and there was no peace.

Jeremiah 6:14

Meditation

The devil reassures the man who habitually lives in sin. He tells him, "Don't worry, none of that matters, everyone does it. You can always go to confession on your deathbed. You are certainly in better shape than most people. God is merciful." So many false arguments whose end result is to leave the sinner in his sin! Unfortunately, society today makes itself the servant of the devil in many domains, seeking to silence man's conscience, telling him that the sting of his conscience is tied to a complex of guilt, or societal taboos, or else to the Church of the past which used to threaten people with eternal hellfire to keep them in a state of fear. Thus, our postmodern Western society puts all its energy into stifling forever the voice of man's conscience.

Here is a very timely example. A woman who had been abandoned by her spouse ended up after a few years moving in with another man. As a Catholic, she knew she was not supposed to do so. She admitted that it had been very difficult for her at first. "But after a while, things got easier," she said. Little by little, she had silenced the voice of her conscience. There could be no greater misfortune. There is nothing more dangerous than peace in sin, because the sinner runs a very great risk of being lost.

Many reassure themselves by comparing their way of living with that of their contemporaries. But it would be wiser to see themselves through the lens of God, remembering also all the graces that we have received.

We would then be more modest in our judgments about ourselves and more ardent in drawing the best out of our talents.

Lord Jesus, help me not to become bogged down in a mediocre life, but to take myself in hand, seeking constantly to do all the good You expect of me, in order to give my life its greatest possible fruitfulness.

Prayer

Eternal source of light, Holy Ghost, scatter the darkness that hides from me the ugliness and malice of sin. My God, make me conceive so great a horror of sin that I hate it, if it were possible, as much as You Yourself hate it, and that I fear nothing so much as to commit it in the future.

— Evening prayer

Or else:

Behold me, Lord, covered in confusion, and seized with sorrow at the sight of my sins. Here before You, I detest them, with true unhappiness at having offended a God so good, so lovable and so worthy of being loved.

— Evening prayer

Thoughts

- There is nothing more dangerous or more to be dreaded than peace in sin.

  — Bourdaloue, CW, II, p. 261

- Let each one of us know that we must never settle into a peaceful laziness: we have to struggle always.

  — St. Francis de Sales, TD, July 5

Resolutions

1. Never to stifle the voice of our conscience.
2. To judge our actions in the light of God; to believe that we can do so, and that it will bring us peace.
3. Not to react angrily when a person living in sin makes a derogatory remark about our own life, but to offer these humiliations for their conversion.

THE GRACE OF REMORSE

Friday of the 9th Week after Pentecost

God speaks to us:

My sin is always before my sight.

Psalm 50:4

Meditation

Our good angel does the opposite of the devil and needles our conscience, while God Himself offers us light to show us the ugliness and gravity of sin. Conscience then torments the sinner. It says to him, "What will happen if God calls you when you are in this state? Aren't you ashamed to be wallowing in your sin? Do you realize what you have done? Are you truly happy?" This unpleasant feeling weighs on the soul. By no means is it a malediction; on the contrary, it is a divine benediction. God desires the salvation of His children and does not leave their souls in peace when they have closed Him out of their heart. The pangs of conscience which torment the sinner and pursue him night and day are a grace, a blessing from God. These interior reproaches can be cruelly painful, but we must see in them the hand of God, who is using them as a means of pressure to win back a rebel heart. When God torments the sinner, it is a sign that He loves him and is attached to him and that He is anxious for the sinner's conversion.

Above all, the sinner must never consider his pangs of conscience as a sign of reprobation, but on the contrary as a blessing from God.

Look at King David. His life was holy in many ways but on one occasion he strayed from the path. His eyes led him into sin; he committed adultery and then murder. What means did God use to bring him back to an upright life? He sent David His prophet Nathan, who made him realize the gravity of his crime. And King David acknowledged what he had done: "I have sinned—*peccavi*" (II Kings 12:13). Overcome by his own flesh, he had shed the blood of a just man. And so, his heart broken with remorse, he composed the magnificent psalm *Miserere*. This grace of repentance is all the greater, the more it is constant. It pursues the sinner wherever he goes. Wherever he finds himself, the sinner is there with his sin. This is the meaning of David's words: *My sin is always before my sight.*

O Jesus, grant that I listen always to the voice of my conscience when I have the unhappiness to fall into sin, and help me to have recourse to the sacrament of Penance.

Prayer

My God, what treasures in a single grace, and how much the sinner owes to Your mercy for bringing him thus to his duty!

— Bourdaloue, CW, II, p. 261

Or else:

Stir up, O Lord, stir up our conscience, and do not allow it to fall into a slumber from which it never awakes.

— Bourdaloue, CW, II, p. 266

Thoughts

- Remorse of conscience is the first of all the graces which God gives to a sinner to begin the work of his conversion.
— Bourdaloue, CW, II, p. 257

- Hold yourself firmly at the side of God when your conscience reproaches you, because it is an infallible proof that God is thinking of you, and that He is still gazing on you with the eyes of salvation.
— Bourdaloue, CW, II, p. 264

Resolutions

1. To have sincere regret after falling into a sin and give up some kind of food as penance or offer alms.
2. To arouse in our soul a profound contrition, thinking over the gravity of the offense committed against God by sin.
3. As circumstances permit, to object and correct when people make insulting comments about faith or morals.

DEEP CONTRITION

Saturday of the 9th Week after Pentecost

God speaks to us:

And [Peter] went out and wept bitterly.

St. Matthew 26:75

Meditation

There exist holy, Christian tears, which are a gift from God and which call down blessings on those who shed them. These are tears of compassion toward those who suffer.

But there are others even more precious. These are tears of remorse and penance: the tears of King David, of St. Mary Magdalene, of St. Peter, of St. Augustine. Let us ask Heaven for this gift of tears which purify the soul and make it ready for the joys of eternity. To obtain this gift, let us rouse a deep contrition in our soul.

Contrition is "a deep sorrow and detestation for sin committed, with a resolution of sinning no more."[2]

It is first a sorrow, the sorrow of a child who has misbehaved for a moment and caused pain to his mother, whom he loves. Truly, God's affection for us has all the tenderness of the most loving mother.

This sincere regret leads to a detestation of sin. To detest sin means to hate it. And how can we not hate sin when we consider it in itself and in its disastrous consequences? Sin offends God who is so good, and delights the devil, who wants only our destruction. How can we do anything but detest this thing that is sin?

Finally, this detestation leads to a firm resolve no longer to commit sin in the future. The sign that the soul truly has this good disposition is the

---

[2] Council of Trent, Session XIV, ch. 4, DZ 1676 (897), in *The Church Teaches*, p. 308.

avoidance of occasions of sin: be they companions, reading, entertainment...

And so, if today we hear the voice of God, let us not harden our hearts. On the contrary, let us open them to repentance and let us answer the tenderness of God with a generous fidelity, attentive to every grace He offers.

In this way we will console the wounded heart of Jesus; He will no longer weep over us because we ourselves will be shedding the tears that expiate everything and lead to the joys of the blessed eternity of Heaven.

Prayer

You are good, my God, to tell us that we must weep seriously for our sins, from the bottom of our heart... We easily forget this truth, that when we love, we suffer at having offended the one we love, and we ask for forgiveness.

— Charles de Foucauld, TD, September 3

Or else:

My God, please give us that contrition which breaks our hearts, which eats away at our hearts—ah, that beautiful contrition which gives us so quickly back the friendship of God!

— Curé of Ars, R, p. 29

Thoughts

- Alas! how often do we weep over the loss of an object worth a handful of coins, ... and for our sins—often for mortal sins—we shed not a tear, we give not even a sigh of regret! My God, how little man knows what he does, when he sins!

    — Curé of Ars, R, pp. 28-29

- We ought to spend more time asking God to give us contrition than we spend making our examination of conscience... We need to ask for the grace of regret.

    — Curé of Ars, TD2, December 10

Saturday of the 9th Week after Pentecost

Resolutions

1. To recite an act of contrition from the bottom of our heart.
2. To flee near occasions of sin, particularly those related to our cellphone, the internet, television, or magazines and newspapers.
3. To tell the children the story of St. Peter or of St. Mary Magdalene.

THE PRIDE OF THE PHARISEE

10th Sunday after Pentecost

God speaks to us:

The Pharisee stood and began to pray thus within himself: "O God, I give Thee thanks that I am not as the rest of men, extortioners, unjust, adulterers."

Gospel of Sunday: St. Luke 18:11

Meditation

The Pharisee looks like an honest member of the faithful, one who to all appearances fulfills the Law of God. He "fasts twice a week and pays tithes of all that he possesses" (*cf.* Lk. 18:12). He is neither a thief nor a man of loose living. In a word, his conduct is irreproachable; his works are good. Yet there is a shadow over him. He has a failing which he does not suspect, and it appears when he comes to pray. His defect is to think he has no defects. His weakness is that he thinks he is better than other people. His prayer expresses it clearly: *O God, I give Thee thanks that I am not as the rest of men.* Plus, not content with condemning the rest of men as a group, he focuses on the publican who is also there in the Temple, a man who is known for his disordered life. In a word, the Pharisee is full of himself; he is completely self-satisfied, completely self-sufficient. For this reason, when he prays, he has nothing to ask. The only thing he does is thank God for his own qualities. There is an application of this parable to ourselves: whatever our good actions and our degree of union with God, pride is able to destroy the value of our good works. Whether it be the practice of temperance, perfect chastity, disdain for riches: without humility, these are all sullied.

Moreover, as St. John Chrysostom says, "the pirates who lurk upon the sea are not going to attack a boat just leaving the port—what good would it do them to sink it when it is still empty? They only go in for the attack when the boat is returning with a rich cargo. That perverse spirit lies in wait especially for men who have gathered great riches, fasts, prayers, alms, and all kinds of virtues."[3] The devil does not often attack the sinner but focuses his energy on the just man.

Lord Jesus, help me to avoid the trap of self-complacency and vainglory, which so often make me lose the merit of my good actions.

Prayer

Lord, how I need to realize the great damage that pride wreaks in my soul. But how can I see clearly, if You do not give me the grace?

— St. Vincent de Paul, TD2, March 27

Or else:

Help me, O Lord, to triumph over this pride which… steals Your gifts and makes my life sterile by preventing me from receiving the abundance of Your graces.

— Fr. Gabriel, DI, p. 306

Thoughts

- Alas! it is hard to imagine how and over what so small a creature as us can be prideful. A pinch of dust the size of a walnut: that is what we will become after our death. We certainly have reason to be proud!

    — Curé of Ars, TD1, July 30

- The Lord reveals to us only gradually and partially who we really are. Truly, it is hard for me to grasp how anyone with intelligence or common sense can be prideful.

    — Padre Pio, TD, August 1

Resolutions

1. To meditate for ten minutes on our Lord's crowning with thorns and recite the third sorrowful mystery.
2. To humiliate ourselves inwardly when a thought of vanity or pride arises in us.
3. To avoid all self-complacency.

---

[3] St. John Chrysostom, *Complete Works*, V, p. 480.

THE HUMILITY OF THE PUBLICAN

Monday of the 10th Week after Pentecost

God speaks to us:

But the publican, standing afar off, would not so much as lift up his eyes to heaven.

Gospel of Sunday: St. Luke 18:13

Meditation

In contrast to the Pharisee, yesterday's Gospel presented us with the publican, a sinner, a man bent beneath the weight of his sins. This man could very well take the commandments of God one by one and realize that he had violated all of them. He is therefore a great sinner. However, as bad as his works are, he knows his misery, unlike the Pharisee; he recognizes his state as a sinner and comes to beg God to have pity on him. Hearing the insults which the Pharisee proclaims against him, he does not even answer. He does not seek to justify himself. He simply humbles himself before God and implores His mercy. Then comes the conclusion: "I tell you," declares our Lord, "this man went back to his home justified rather than the other; for everyone who exalts himself shall be humbled, and he who humbles himself shall be exalted." (Lk. 18:14)

To help us understand the situation of these two men, St. John Chrysostom chooses the image of two chariots. "One is drawn by justice and pride, the other by sin and humility; you will see the chariot of sin pull ahead of the chariot of justice, certainly not because of its own lightness, but thanks to the vigor of humility which accompanies it; likewise, the other chariot fails not because of any weakness of justice but because of the weight and volume of pride."[4] This comparison gives us food for thought.

---

[4] St. John Chrysostom, *Complete Works*, I, p. 423.

Monday of the 10th Week after Pentecost

Our Lord in the Gospel is teaching us to fear pride, but at the same time He is showing us the power of humility over the heart of God. Indeed, if we look closely at the situation of the two men, we observe that one of them accomplishes good works, and the other comes with empty hands, having nothing to present to God but his misery. And what do we see? We see that words have more weight than works. O, the mystery of God's plan! In spite of his works, the Pharisee falls from justice and, by his words alone, the publican attains to the justice of sanctity.

Encouraged by the example of the publican, I, too, acknowledge my state as a sinner. Lord Jesus, have mercy on me!

Prayer

My God, here I am, a very poor soul who has nothing and can do nothing. Grant me the grace to love You, to serve You, and to know that I am nothing.

— Curé of Ars, TD1, July 27

Or else:

Help us, O Blessed Virgin, you who were so filled with this holy humility; obtain that virtue for us from your dear Son. This is the prayer that I offer you with all my heart.

— St. Vincent de Paul, TD2, May 29

Thoughts

- The moment we are empty of ourselves, God will pour Himself into us, because He always fills an emptiness.
— St. Vincent de Paul, TD2, February 27

- Remember your sins with deep sorrow and displeasure, and never think yourself to be anything because of your good deeds.
— *Imitation of Christ*, III, ch. 4

Resolutions

1 To remember our past sins in order to acquire humility and in order to thank God for having forgiven them.

2 To consider sinners with great mercy and avoid any disdainful judgment. To love them as Jesus does.

3 To know how to acknowledge our mistakes and ask forgiveness.

THE NATURE OF HUMILITY

Tuesday of the 10th Week after Pentecost

GOD SPEAKS TO US:

John answered and said, "[Jesus] must increase, but I must decrease."
St. John 3:27, 30

MEDITATION

Humility is a virtue which leads man to correct his disordered love of self by moving him to perform actions contrary to his natural leaning. St. John the Baptist understood this well, when he said in announcing the Messiah, *[Jesus] must increase, but I must decrease."*

Like St. John the Baptist, I must disappear little by little and give place to Jesus. I must be small in my own eyes in order to give God all the space due to Him in my life. I must become again like a little child, recognizing my fundamental dependence on my Creator and my Savior.

The first lesson that our Lord gives us in coming into this world is that a man begins to be great when he becomes small in his own eyes. This does not mean that he has to be trampled underfoot by other people and never be "fulfilled." When our Lord asks us to be small in our own eyes, when He asks us to have a humble opinion of ourselves, He is simply asking that we stand in our proper place before God and before men.

Our Lord simply wants us to abandon the illusion where we too often find ourselves, in which we take ourselves for what we are not; in which we are all imbued with our own self.

We live in a world that gives more credit to what appears than to what is; a world that gives more credit to appearances than to reality. Man judges based on the outside and not on the inside; he judges based on what he perceives and not what *is*. What makes his judgment even more flawed is the acuity with which he discovers the defects of others, his ease in noticing the failings of his neighbor, and on the contrary his blindness when it comes to recognizing his own failings, his own limits. Almost unconsciously, we compare our qualities to other people's defects, thus proving and fostering a disordered love of ourselves.

Strong with the example of John the Baptist, I, too, wish to decrease in my own eyes to allow You to live in me, O Jesus.

Prayer

O Jesus, You who were so humiliated for us, teach me how to practice true humility.
— Fr. Gabriel, DI, p. 301

Or else:

O God, who resist the proud and bestow graces upon the humble: increase in us the virtue of true humility, the pattern of which Thy only-begotten Son exhibited in Himself to the faithful, that we may never provoke Thy indignation by our pride, but submissive to Thee we may receive ever more the gifts of Thy mercy.
— Collect of the Mass to obtain humility

Thoughts

- Humility is like a weighing scale: the more it goes down on one side, the more it goes up on the other.
— Curé of Ars, TD1, August 5

- What could be higher than humility? In bringing itself down very low, humility unites itself to the Creator, who dwells above all that is highest.
— St. Gregory the Great, TD, August 27

Resolutions

1. To recite the first joyful mystery in meditating on the incredible self-abasement of the Son of God.
2. To spend the day under the gaze of Jesus by making Him our confidant, our support, our friend.
3. To efface ourselves before others, considering them as higher than us, and looking at ourselves in the mirror the least often possible.

HUMILITY AND MAGNANIMITY

Wednesday of the 10th Week after Pentecost

God speaks to us:

Let your light shine before men, in order that they may see your good works.

St. Matthew 5:16

Meditation

Some people think that humility consists in thinking oneself incapable of doing anything at all. That is a pitfall to be avoided. While it is true that the humble man affirms that he is nothing of himself, that he is pure nothingness, still he does not deny the capacities and talents and gifts which he has received from God. Jesus gave us a good lesson about this realism in the parable of the talents. The man who had five talents gained five others, the man who had two gained two, but the man who only had one buried it in the ground. Our Lord rewarded the first two but condemned the third for not earning money on his capital, meager as it was. The lesson is that humility should not lead us into weakness or laziness.

Here we see why the humble soul is magnanimous. The humble man yearns to develop his talents in order to spread the kingdom of Christ and to do as much good as possible, convinced of the shortness of this life and of the need to conquer Heaven and lead there as many souls as possible. Magnanimity therefore implies a noble soul, with high ideals; a courageous soul, whose life is in harmony with his convictions. Magnanimity finds expression not only in noble sentiments but in noble actions. Our Lord said, "*Let your light shine before men, in order that they may see your good works* and give glory to your Father in heaven" (Mt. 5:16); "in this is My Father glorified, that you may bear very much fruit, and become My disciples" (Jn. 15:8).

Humility and greatness of soul are therefore not opposed to one another. The magnanimous man admits that he is nothing of himself but at the same time recognizes his qualities and most of all knows how to make them bear fruit. St. Francis de Sales based his guidance of souls on our awareness of our nothingness, but he was careful to insist that we have to be mindful of all the good that is in us by grace; this consideration, he taught, "is the foundation of generosity of soul."[5]

Prayer

O Lord, give me a generous heart, capable of undertaking great things for You.

— Fr. Gabriel, DI, p. 839

Or else:

Teach me, O my God, always to go straight ahead, to fight with courage, and to parry the blows of the devil who is trying to frighten me.

— Fr. Gabriel, DI, p. 841

Thoughts

- A right humility ... dilates, instead of troubling or depressing the soul, making it more capable of serving God.

  — St. Teresa of Avila, WP ch. 39, p. 241

- You are nothing of yourself... You are nothing, but God is with you.

  — Curé of Ars, TD2, May 29

Resolutions

1. To consider attentively the graces we have received from God in order to encourage ourselves to employ our talents. To identify those talents and beg God that we may use them for the good.
2. To struggle with perseverance against negative feelings that restrain our generosity.
3. To set aside time for people who would appreciate our lending an attentive ear.

---

[5] *Works of St. Francis de Sales*, VI, p. 755.

THE FRUITS OF HUMILITY

Thursday of the 10th Week after Pentecost

God speaks to us:

Mary said, "...My spirit rejoices in God my Savior; because He has regarded the lowliness of His handmaid."

St. Luke 1:46-48

Meditation

Holy Scripture abounds in passages bearing witness that God gives His grace to the humble. The humility of sinners has always disarmed the anger of God: Mary Magdalene found the forgiveness of her sins at the feet of Jesus; the publican was justified by his humble prayer. To know in what high esteem God holds humility, we have only to look at the perfect model of all virtues, the God-man. Yes, our Lord humbled Himself from the manger to the cross and He purchased our salvation at the price of the vilest humiliations for Himself. Let us also look at the Blessed Virgin: she attracted the Word to become incarnate within her because of her humility, as she sings in her *Magnificat*. Let us also consider all of the great divine works. Before entrusting high offices to His servants, God requires of them a witness of humility: Moses, Gideon, Jeremy, and John the Baptist are striking examples. How beautiful and instructive is the dialogue between God and Moses on Mount Horeb! "Who am I that I should go to Pharaoh, and should bring forth the children of Israel out of Egypt? ... They will say: The Lord hath not appeared to thee. ... I beseech Thee, Lord, I am not eloquent, not simply from yesterday and the day before nor since Thou hast spoken to Thy servant; for I have great impediment and slowness of tongue" (Ex. 3:11; 4:1 and 10). God is touched by the humility of Moses and dispenses him from speaking, but not from the mission of guiding the Hebrew people toward their freedom.

Let us learn from these examples to appreciate humility at its true value. If we wish to be great before God and draw His blessing down upon us, let us be small in our own eyes and not be afraid of appearing small in the eyes of others. Let us remain humble in our thoughts, knowing that, of ourselves, we are nothing; humble in our desires, knowing how to be satisfied with the place that is ours, without wanting to put ourselves above others—even knowing how to efface ourselves before others and accept from them with calm and patience the humiliations that forge our humility.

Lord Jesus, impressed by the delightful fruits of humility, I ardently desire to acquire this virtue. I know that it will help me preserve my faith, obey my superiors, keep chastity, and embrace mortification.

Prayer

O my great and good Creator, how much I owe to You! You came to take me in my nothingness, to make me what I am, by Your mercy!
— St. Francis de Sales, TD, October 11

Or else:

Deprive me, O Lord, of every remnant of confidence in myself.
— Fr. Gabriel, DI, p. 309

Thoughts

- For the greatest results God most often employs the weakest.
— St. Francis de Sales, TD, September 28
- A person who is knowledgeable and humble will offer his judgment simply, when it is asked, and then will let others speak.
— Curé of Ars, TD2, June 25

Resolutions

1 Not to make a decision without first having recourse to prayer.

2 To avoid trying to shine in conversations and not to be afraid of seeming less than we are.

3 To let others express their opinions without interrupting them, and not wanting at all cost to impose our own point of view.

THE MEANS OF ACQUIRING HUMILITY

Friday of the 10th Week after Pentecost

God speaks to us:

Who is as the Lord our God, who dwelleth on high: and looketh down on the low things in heaven and in earth?

Psalm 112: 5-6

Meditation

One of the means of acquiring humility is to consider the perfections of God. As we contemplate the grandeur, the majesty, the holiness of God, we become more aware of our littleness and we are immediately drawn to put ourselves in our proper place before Him. When we consider His infinite goodness, His infinite wisdom, His infinite mercy; when we compare His virtues to our own, how can we still take ourselves for someone extraordinary?

We imagine that we exist of ourselves, we think we are capable of doing good of ourselves, whereas the only thing we are able to do is manage the capital which we have received from God. What would we say of a statue that gloried in its beauty as though that beauty came from the statue itself and not from the artist who sculpted it? Yet we are acting the same way, when we wallow in self-satisfaction. Unfortunately, this mistaken feeling of being the source of our own qualities affects our behavior toward those around us. If we acknowledged our misery, we would be more inclined to indulgence with other people than to severity. Every time we condemn our neighbor in thought or in word, we are revealing outwardly that disordered attachment which we have to ourselves.

Let us remember the attitude of St. Francis of Assisi, who considered himself as a great sinner despite all his virtues. In his humility, he claimed, "If God had showered His mercy on any criminal as much as He has showered it on me, that man would be ten times better than I."⁶ So let us distrust the hasty judgments which we bring to bear on our neighbor, and which can be completely mistaken.

Lord Jesus, that I might acquire humility, help me to contemplate Your infinite wisdom and goodness. For my part, I promise to avoid drawing glory from my talents, knowing that they all come from You.

Prayer

Give me, O my God, a thorough knowledge of myself! Let me be really convinced that I am nothing and that You are everything.
— Fr. Gabriel, DI, p. 306

Or else:

Grant that I may know my nothingness, O Lord, for the more I recognize it with simplicity and humility of heart, the more You will take pleasure in being my All.
— Fr. Gabriel, DI, p. 306

Thoughts

- Let us begin by looking heavenward, and then looking into ourselves. Humility comes from seeing the infinite distance that separates Heaven from the abyss.
— Padre Pio, TD, August 17
- If we want to be just in the eyes of God, let us confess our injustice, humiliate ourselves, lower ourselves; let us acknowledge ourselves unworthy, and God will deign to shower His mercy upon us.
— Fr. Emmanuel, M, p. 259

Resolutions

1. To contemplate for ten minutes some of the perfections of God: His almighty power, His wisdom, His goodness, His mercy…, and to see by contrast the insignificance of our own virtues.
2. To accept wholeheartedly the humiliations that the day may bring.
3. To recite or sing a *Magnificat* to thank God for His graces.

---

[6] Thomas de Celano, *Life of St. Francis of Assisi*, p. 258.

PRAYER

Saturday of the 10th Week after Pentecost

God speaks to us:

Two men went up to the Temple to pray.
Gospel of Sunday: St. Luke 18:10

Meditation

Prayer manifests our dependence on God and is one of the most effective means to develop in us the virtue of humility. Last Sunday's Gospel presented us with two men who were going to the Temple to pray. While we pray is when Jesus most showers His mercy upon us. This is what we ask during the Collect of this same Sunday: "O God, who dost manifest Thine almighty power most chiefly in sparing and showing mercy, multiply upon us Thy mercy, that as we hasten towards Thy promises, Thou mayest make us partakers of heavenly treasures."

The texts from last Sunday were inviting us not to live like beings without reason. They can therefore help us to become aware of our relations with God, who is both our Creator and our Savior.

Prayer is one of the most effective means of nourishing our virtue of religion. And as St. Augustine says, "learning to pray well is learning to live well." And so the Church, whom our Lord gave as our guide to Heaven, has organized a service of prayer, a service which priests accomplish in the name of all faithful. The prayer *par excellence* is the Holy Sacrifice of the Mass, and around this redemptive sacrifice divine praise is maintained night and day by the Divine Office, which prepares for the sacrifice and continues it.

Among all prayers, the *Our Father* truly "is God's prayer," St. Cyprian tells us, for "His instruction comprises all our petitioning in one saving sentence."[7] This is a filial and collective prayer: the entire Catholic family

---

[7] St. Thomas Aquinas, *Catena Aurea* I, Part I, Commentary on St. Matthew, p. 235.

is brought together in the word *our*. Before looking to his own interests, the Christian soul is concerned with the glory of God: "Hallowed be Thy name, Thy kingdom come…"

Lord Jesus, thank You for having taught us the beautiful prayer of the *Pater Noster*.

Prayer

O Jesus, You who know so well how to contemplate Your Father, teach me to contemplate You! I am such a little child. I am here close to You. Without ceasing to contemplate Your Father, You can speak to me in the depths of my soul without language or words, and guide me as You wish.

— Charles de Foucauld, TD, January 22

Or else:

Give to us, my God, this bread of grace which is absolutely necessary to our life; give us this bread of angels which is Your body and Your blood; give us this bread, Your nourishment which consists in doing the will of Your Father.

— Charles de Foucauld, TD, February 8

Thoughts

- Prayer is a sweet friendship, an astonishing familiarity… It is a gentle conversation with our Father.

  — Curé of Ars, TD2, June 17

- A prayer that is very pleasing to God is to ask the Blessed Virgin to offer to the eternal Father His divine Son, all bleeding, all torn for the conversion of sinners.

  — Curé of Ars, TD1, September 15

Resolutions

1. To meditate for ten minutes on the seven petitions of the *Our Father*.
2. To respect our schedule in what concerns our spiritual life.
3. To turn quickly to God when we are tempted.

THE HEALING OF THE DEAF-MUTE

11th Sunday after Pentecost

God speaks to us:

His ears were at once opened, and the bond of his tongue was loosed, and he began to speak correctly.

Gospel of Sunday: St. Mark 7:35

Meditation

Today's Gospel recounts to us the healing of a deaf-mute. This episode occurred during the last year of our Lord's life. Two camps are already well defined: those who follow Jesus and those who reject Him; those who hear His word and those who disdain it; those who convert and those who harden their hearts. Despite everything, our Lord continues to try to draw the stray sheep to Himself. He never wearies. Everywhere He passes, He seeks to do good, and so He heals this deaf-mute.

Among the sick people healed by our Lord, some owe their salvation only to their own zeal. Not fatigue nor fear of compromising themselves in the eyes of others could stop them from reaching our Lord. At His approach, they were not afraid of importuning Him with their prayers. But other times, it is a father, a mother, or devoted friends who rendered the sick person the service of bringing them and presenting them to Jesus. This is what happened with the deaf-mute. His infirmity had prevented him from knowing the almighty power and the goodness of Jesus Christ. When the man was led to Jesus, his loved ones took upon themselves to ask the divine Savior to lay hands on him.

Before healing the sick man, our Lord begins by drawing him out of the crowd, showing us our own need to step away from the agitation of the world, to leave the noise of the world in order to hear the voice of God.

In the modern world, it is difficult to be recollected and to ponder the great questions which every man ought to ask himself one day or another: "Where did I come from? Where am I going? What is the meaning of life? Why am I here on earth?" If we want to answer these questions, it is good to step back and take a moment away from our usual activities, far from the agitation of the world, far from the noise of the world.

And so, if God is to act in our heart, we must, like this sick man, step aside from the frantic rhythm that characterizes nearly everyone's life today. It can be a good thing to run, certainly, but it must be in the right direction! Let us therefore take the time to stop, calm our thoughts, and open ourselves to the call of God.

Prayer

O Jesus, how worthy of love You are when You open our ears, closed by the hardness of our heart, and let them hear the sweet sound of Your voice!

— Friend of the Parish Clergy, VII, p. 501

Or else:

Heal me, O Lord, and I shall be healed; save Me, and I shall be saved.

— Jer. 17:14

Thoughts

- The deaf-mute of the Gospel could only be healed of his double infirmity by a kind of creation: God had to give him an ear able to hear.

  — Friend of the Parish Clergy, VII, p. 500

- By a second miracle, even more impressive than the first because it touches both the body and the soul, the deaf-mute understands a language which he could not have learned.

  — Friend of the Parish Clergy, VII, p. 500

Resolutions

1. To recite the Act of Faith (see page 263).
2. To take the time to prepare our Mass by reading the propers in the missal ahead of time.
3. To describe to the children one of the miracles at Lourdes.

THE RITUAL OF THE MIRACLE

Monday of the 11th Week after Pentecost

GOD SPEAKS TO US:

[Jesus] put His fingers into the man's ears, and spitting, He touched his tongue.

Gospel of Sunday: St. Mark 7:33

MEDITATION

Our Lord begins by placing the deaf-mute close to Him, then He goes through a whole ritual before healing him. *"He placed His fingers into the man's ears, and spitting, He touched his tongue.* And looking up to heaven, He sighed, and said to him, *'Ephpheta,'* that is, 'Be thou opened'" (Mk. 7:33-34). All this ritual may be a little surprising for us. How is it that the mere shadow of the Apostles was enough to heal the sick who drew near to them, and yet Jesus, who is God, performed all these mysterious rituals before working His miracle? Our Lord could very well have done without them, certainly, but He acted in this way for several reasons.

First, by taking His time, so to speak, in working this miracle, our Lord tries the faith of those who came to Him. Our Lord wants our faith, and that is why He does not act right away. We very often see this same attitude in different circumstances of His life. So, we should not be surprised ourselves if our first little prayer is not answered. Let us know how to be patient. Let us know how to wait. God does not always respond immediately to our first request, because He is God. He sees things differently than we do. In Heaven, in eternity, He perceives everything from much higher and so He sees events differently than we do. Let us therefore learn to walk at His pace as we try to do His will.

Moreover, our Lord uses His fingers, His hands, His words, His saliva to accomplish the miracle, to show us that His humanity is the channel which is meant to lead us to His divinity.

Our Lord took a human nature like our own so that it might be both a channel and a model for us, according to the plan of God. We cannot act as though the humanity of our Lord did not exist and go straight to His divinity. His humanity is the bridge which gives us access to the divinity. It was as man that our Lord suffered and died. Man had sinned, man had to do reparation.

Thus, our Lord uses His body to heal this man who was deaf and mute, and His divine power emanates from His words, His hands and His gestures.

Prayer

Lord Jesus, reach out Your divine hands toward me; touch me with Your fingers, and pour into me You adorable Spirit.

— Fr. Emmanuel, M, p. 262

Or else:

O sighs of Jesus, let my soul hear You!

— Fr. Emmanuel, M, p. 264

Thoughts

- The fingers of our Lord represent the operations of the Holy Ghost, who is called the finger of God.

  — Fr. Emmanuel, M, p. 262

- Our Lord sighed. A sigh is a sign of pain; our Lord suffers from what we suffer; the gentle tenderness of His compassion for us is beyond that of even the tenderest of mothers.

  — Fr. Emmanuel, M, p. 264

Resolutions

1 To reread this Sunday's Gospel attentively.
2 Not to lose patience when we see that our prayers are not answered as rapidly as we would wish.
3 To dust off our statues and crucifixes and other objects of piety.

LITURGICAL RITUALS

Tuesday of the 11th Week after Pentecost

GOD SPEAKS TO US:

Do this in remembrance of Me.

St. Luke 22:19

MEDITATION

In contrast to other miracles, our Lord used a whole ritual to heal the deaf-mute, putting His fingers in the man's ears and saliva on his tongue, raising His eyes to heaven, sighing deeply and saying: be opened! He did so because He foresaw that one day men would be bold enough to condemn outward worship and the rites of Holy Mother Church. And so, by anticipation our Lord willed to consecrate the venerable rites which the Church would use to communicate grace to souls. Thus, for example, at baptism, the priest takes saliva on his finger, applies it to the ears of the child and says again this word *Ephpheta*, which means: be opened. Following what Jesus did, the Church surrounds the sacraments with rites that explain the effects of the sacrament and give to the faithful the sense of mystery, the sense of the sacred.

God is transcendent, infinitely superior to us. For this reason, we must not be surprised at not understanding everything, not grasping everything about our holy religion.

Let us not forget that God is a "hidden God" (Is. 45:15) according to the expression of the prophet Isaias, and surely this is what our Lord wants to make us understand by using a mysterious rite in the healing of the deaf-mute.

This meditation can help us better understand why it is so important to remain faithful to the liturgy, which sanctified so many generations that came before us. In simplifying too abruptly the rites of the sacraments, we run the risk of losing little by little the sense of the sacred, the sense of mystery and therefore the sense of God. The Church has an expression, *Lex orandi, lex credendi*, "the law of prayer confirms the law of faith"[8]; in other words, "As we pray, so also do we believe." Therefore, if we change the manner of praying, we run the risk of gradually changing our way of believing. To avoid this danger, let us love the liturgy of the Church and let us try to study it in order to understand it better.

Lord Jesus, enlightened by Your example, I realize all the importance of a liturgy which conveys the sense of the sacred and the sense of mystery, to help us live and breathe already here below the heavenly realities which You have prepared for us in the next world.

Prayer

God be forever blessed for bringing us to baptism!
— Fr. Emmanuel, M, p. 267

Or else:

O God, You have given us the faith; deign to keep us in it always, Lord, so that we may aim straight for You who are our God, our hope and our eternal happiness.
— Fr. Emmanuel, M, p. 266

Thoughts

- The priest takes saliva and touches the ear and the nose of the child, saying… *Ephpheta*, be opened. Open your ears to hear the divine word; open your sense of smell to savor the sweet fragrance of grace and of eternal life.
— Fr. Emmanuel, M, p. 265

- The one to be baptized is anointed [with the oil of catechumens] on chest and back, as if to mark upon him that he will be all

---

[8] An expression of principle attributed to Pope St. Celestine I (5th century), "Pseudo-Celestine Chapters" in DZ 246 (139). "Let us examine these sacred words which were handed down from the Apostles throughout the world and which are uniformly used in every Catholic church, and thus find in the prayers of the liturgy confirmation for the law of our faith *[ut legem credendi lex statuat supplicandi]*." *The Church Teaches*, p. 224. See also *Sources of Catholic Dogma*, p. 56, "…that the law of supplication may support the law of believing."

Tuesday of the 11th Week after Pentecost

surrounded with the mercy of God, which will always go before him and follow him.

— Fr. Emmanuel, M, p. 266

Resolutions

1. To read the ceremonial of baptism.
2. To make well the sign of the cross before and after every prayer.
3. To look back in our catechism at the section on baptism or the Holy Sacrifice of the Mass.

DETRACTION

Wednesday of the 11th Week after Pentecost

God speaks to us:

If anyone thinks himself to be religious, not restraining his tongue but deceiving his own heart, that man's religion is vain.

Epistle of St. James 1:26

Meditation

In recounting the episode of the healing of the deaf-mute, last Sunday's Gospel highlights a certain contrast. On the one hand, Jesus gives speech back to the man who was mute, and on the other hand He commands the witnesses of this miracle to keep silent.

Our tongue is a key element of human communication and it is a source of enrichment and edification when we use it to speak well of others. Alas! too often, we speak only to say evil of those around us.

Detraction first strikes God in His children, whom He loves. The poisoned arrow of the detractor pierces the divine heart before reaching the heart of our neighbor. Isn't it St. Theresa of the Child Jesus who said that God far prefers to hear the praise of souls, masterpieces which He Himself created, rather than to hear them torn down and criticized? Detraction also wounds our neighbor, without a shot being fired, because every man is attached to his reputation. That reputation is exactly what detraction comes to destroy in the heart of others.

Detraction can be compared to an act of murder. St. Francis de Sales says that "by a single stroke of his tongue the slanderer usually commits three murders. He kills his own soul and the soul of anyone who hears him by an act of spiritual homicide and takes away the social life [that is, the reputation] of the man he slanders."[9]

---

[9] St. Francis de Sales, *Introduction to the Devout Life*, bk. III, ch. 29.

Yes, we can kill a person with our tongue. Thus, our Lord, in the Gospel of St. John, tells us that the devil was "a murderer from the beginning." (Jn. 8:44) It is obvious that the devil did not commit a crime with sword or dagger but with his words, by leading Adam and Eve to lose the life of grace, supernatural life.

In certain cases, therefore, detraction is truly a crime.

Lord Jesus, help me to avoid all slander in order to keep my peace of soul and maintain a union of hearts, foretaste of the union of the blessed in the eternity of Heaven.

Prayer

Mary, most worthy of love, obtain for me always to be charitable in my conversations; inspire me with horror for slander and slanderers.

— St. Alphonsus Liguori, HDD, p. 48

Or else:

Purify my heart and my lips, almighty God, who purified the lips of the prophet Isaias.

— Prayer before the Gospel

Thoughts

- Let us avoid the very shadow of slander; let us not speak evil of anyone, without true necessity.

  — St. Alphonsus Liguori, HDD, p. 47

- The poor person who finds himself on the tongue of detractors is like a grain of wheat under the millwheel, being broken, crushed, and destroyed.

  — Curé of Ars, TD2, August 2

Resolutions

1. Not to speak ill of our neighbor; to be wary of sarcasm and caricature.
2. To learn to recognize the qualities of those around us and draw them to light in conversation.
3. To recite a decade of our rosary for people whom we have made suffer over the course of our life.

THE SIN OF THE EARS

Thursday of the 11th Week after Pentecost

God speaks to us:

To no man render evil for evil.

St. Paul to the Romans 12:17

Meditation

Unfortunately, it is not rare that we take a certain pleasure in hearing slander. Yet let us not forget that those who listen to words of detraction are guilty of the same detraction, because obviously there would be no slander if there were no ears eager to hear it. Detraction, backbiting, and calumny all succeed because of the ears open to receive it.

Let us look at the philosophical view that Socrates took of the subject, pagan though he was, in the 5th century before Christ. One day, someone came to see the famous philosopher and the conversation began.

"Listen, Socrates, I absolutely have to tell you how your friend behaved."

"Stop," interrupted the wise man. "Have you sifted three times what you are going to tell me?"

"Sifted three times?" the other answered, astonished.

"Yes, my good friend, sifted three times. Let us consider if what you must tell me can pass through all three sieves. The first is the sieve of truth. Have you checked whether what you are going to tell me is true?"

"No, I heard it said, and…"

"Fine, fine. But surely you ran it through the second sieve. The sieve of goodness. If what you have to tell me is not quite true, is it at least something good?"

"No, it is not something good—on the contrary…"

"Hmmm!" replied the wise man. "Let us try to pass it through the third sieve and see whether or not what you want to tell me is useful."

"Useful? Not exactly…"

Thursday of the 11th Week after Pentecost

"Well then," said Socrates, smiling, "if what you want to tell me is neither true, nor good, nor even useful, I prefer not to know it. As for you, I advise you to forget it."

What a lesson, coming from a pagan!

Lord Jesus, help me to close my ears, also, to words of ill will, uttered against my neighbor, that I may not fail in charity.

Prayer

Let us pray and beg the Lord, that over the course of this day, He may preserve us from all that could harm us. May our tongues be restrained.
— Hymn for Prime

Or else:

My God, I accept for love of You the battle against my bad nature.
— St. Alphonsus Liguori, HDD, p. 49

Thoughts

- If bad things are told us of our neighbor, let us try to excuse him; let us excuse at least his intention; better still, let us gently turn the conversation in another direction.
— St. Alphonsus Liguori, HDD, pp. 47-48.

- The first reaction of the man of good will is to refuse to believe in the truth of an evil report, until he has proof.
— Bishop Chevrot, p. 49

Resolutions

1. To avoid long conversations with people who tend to criticize.
2. To pray to our guardian angel before entering a conversation where we run the risk of speaking evil of another.
3. To take refuge in the Sacred Heart when we have suffered injustice from our neighbor, rather than speaking of it to those around us.

THE MORTIFICATION OF THE TONGUE

Friday of the 11th Week after Pentecost

God speaks to us:

Brethren, do not speak against one another.

St. James 4:11

Meditation

The *Imitation of Christ* contains an excellent prayer for avoiding detraction. I propose it to you as the beginning of your meditation today: "From such tales and from such indiscreet folk, protect me, O Lord! Do not let me fall into their power, nor behave in the same way myself… For what I do not tolerate in others, I must myself avoid at all costs. To remain silent about others makes for peace and goodwill, neither believing all that is said, nor repeating what one has heard… May we not allow ourselves to be carried to and fro by the windy blast of words, but rather pray that all our life, both public and private, may be ordered in conformity to Your Will."[10]

We beg God to protect us from slander, and at the same time we have to take realistic steps in combating the same fault in ourselves. Cardinal Mercier in his small work entitled *Christian Mortification* gathered advice on means of mortification from all the best spiritual authors. Here is what he says about the tongue: "Mortify that part of your body which naturally gives expression to your mind, namely, your tongue. Learn how to be silent."[11]

"Love to speak well of your brothers, especially those whom you are most inclined to envy… If anyone starts speaking with you in a way that damages the reputation of your neighbor, sometimes you can gently

---

[10] *Imitation of Christ*, III, ch. 45.
[11] *Christian Mortification*, p. 8.

correct the person who is speaking, but most often it is better gently to turn the conversation in another direction or indicate that you are not happy with the subject by a gesture of dissatisfaction or by intentionally not following what is said."[12]

Let us be generous in this battle and learn to be silent about others.

Lord Jesus, that I might not slip into words of calumny, I resolve to avoid those who tend to speak ill of others and to keep silent when my neighbor's reputation is at stake.

Prayer

Lord, place a guard before my mouth and a barrier around my lips. May my heart not turn to evil words which serve as a pretext to sin!

— Prayer for the incensing of the altar

Or else:

O Holy Ghost, ... deign to pour Yourself forth in our hearts, by a new effusion. May our mouth, our tongue, our mind, our senses, our strength, proclaim Your praise; may the fire of charity produce its flames in us, and may its ardor also enkindle our neighbor.

— Hymn of Terce

Thoughts

- There is a proverb: least said, soonest mended. Almost never do we regret having held our tongue and kept ourselves from saying too much.

  — Bishop Chevrot, VH, p. 32

- In conversation, I will be modest without insolence; free without austerity; gentle without affectation; flexible without contradiction, if reason does not demand that I contradict; cordial without dissimulation.

  — St. Francis de Sales, TD, July 9

---

[12] *Ibid.*, pp. 14-15.

Resolutions

1. To consider for ten minutes some of the graces we have received, in order to bless God for them.
2. To close a conversation before it degenerates into gossip.
3. To avoid cutting people off in conversation; to control our own emotions and be attentive to what our neighbor is feeling.

LISTENING TO GOD

Saturday of the 11th Week after Pentecost

God speaks to us:

Speak Lord, for Thy servant heareth.

I Kings 3:9

Meditation

The Epistle and the Gospel from last Sunday revealed to us the triumph of the grace of God: the triumph of grace in St. Paul and also in the miracle of the healing of the deaf-mute. For each one of us, baptism was the triumph of grace. And when we receive absolution in the sacrament of penance, once again we have the triumph of grace in our soul.

Like the witnesses of the healing of the deaf-mute, seized with wonder, we ought to proclaim that God "has done all things well" (Mk. 7:37). He went His way doing good. Blessed be His holy Name!

In order to welcome the graces of God, let us learn to listen. God speaks to souls by the inspirations of grace, by remorse of conscience, by the happy and sad events of our lives. He speaks in every page of Holy Scripture, both the Old and the New Testament. The whole mission of the Word of God on earth was to speak to men and to call them. God has called us to life, He has called us to the grace of faith, and He has called us to fulfill a particular task. Do we not have a tendency, unfortunately, to cover the voice of God by the voice of our telephones, our computers, and so on? The more we have our ear turned to God, the easier prayer will become for us. Let us make our own the prayer of the Psalmist: "Lord, Thou wilt open my lips: and my mouth shall declare Thy praise" (Ps. 50:17). It is the duty of every one of us to speak to God and to speak of God. When Jesus entered Jerusalem on Palm Sunday, the people greeted Him with the acclamation of Psalm 117: "Blessed be He that cometh in the name of the Lord" (Ps. 117:26). We pronounce the same exclamation with the priest at Mass, at the end of the *Sanctus*. Jesus is the keystone, that is, the stone which is indispensable for the cohesion and solidity of the building, whether the Church or civil society. St. Joan of Arc inscribed the Name of Jesus on the folds of her standard when she went to war for her country. Catholics live happily when they praise Him, and they die in peace when they utter this name which gives access to Paradise.

Lord Jesus, that grace may triumph in me, help me to be always listening for Your voice.

Prayer

Lord make me hear; make me hear Your voice, Your word, Your eternal truth.
— Fr. Emmanuel, M, p. 262

Or else:

Grant me the grace finally to make the firm resolution to stop neglecting Your inspirations, to stop yielding to temptation, to be loving, faithful, courageous, generous; to do at every moment what You expect of me.
— Charles de Foucauld, TD, June 22

Thoughts

- Write My words in your heart, [says Jesus to the faithful soul,] and meditate on them earnestly; they will aid you in temptation.
— *Imitation of Christ*, III, ch. 3
- God hears the prayer of saints because saints listen to the words of God.
— Fr. Calmel, 365 D, November 5

Resolutions

1. To take ten minutes during the day to recollect ourselves, visit a church, and read the texts of the day.
2. To limit our use of telephone and internet in order to foster the life of the family, whatever the cost to ourselves.
3. To slip a word of faith into the conversations we will have over the course of the day, as occasion makes fitting.

FROM JERUSALEM TO JERICHO

12th Sunday after Pentecost

God speaks to us:

A certain man was going down from Jerusalem to Jericho.
Gospel of Sunday: St. Luke 10:30

Meditation

The Fathers of the Church have revealed to us the spiritual meaning of the parable of the Good Samaritan, in all its details.

Our Lord speaks to us of a man who *went down from Jerusalem to Jericho*—from Jerusalem, at 2,500 feet above sea level, to Jericho, nestled in the valley of the Jordan.

This man represents Adam and the whole human race.

Jerusalem, which means "vision of peace," represents the heavenly Jerusalem, to which man lost access by his sin. Jericho, which means "moon," symbolizes change, corruption—ultimately, the state of fallen man, after original sin. Mankind *went down from Jerusalem to Jericho*.

Man, who had such a perfect nature, enriched over and above by grace and the gifts of immortality, impassibility,[13] integrity,[14] and knowledge, left Jerusalem to go down to Jericho.

This man "fell in with robbers" (Lk. 10:30), with brigands—that is, he fell into the power of the devil and his angels.

These robbers stripped him and covered him with wounds. They took from him the garment of innocence by making him lose the state of grace, and they covered him with wounds, weakening his nature and giving him an inclination to evil. They wounded him in all his faculties by ignorance, malice, weakness, and concupiscence.

Finally, these robbers "went their way, leaving him half-dead" (Lk. 10:30). Ever since original sin, man is there, lying on the ground, half-

---

[13] Impassibility: the quality of not being subject to suffering.
[14] Integrity: a gift allowing the passions to be subject to reason, and reason to God.

dead, incapable of reaching eternal life by himself, powerless to regain his health without the help of God. Such was the work of Satan, "a murderer from the beginning" (Jn. 8:44).

The descent from Jerusalem to Jericho therefore symbolizes the Fall.

O my Jesus, aware of my native misery, I beg for Your help. Lord Jesus, have pity on me!

Prayer

O Lord, the God of my salvation, I have cried in the day and in the night before Thee.

— Alleluia

Or else:

O Heavenly Father, … set me free from evil passions, and heal my heart from all disorderly affections; that, healed and cleansed in spirit, I may grow able to love, strong to endure, and steadfast to persevere.

— Imitation of Christ, III, ch. 5

Thoughts

- This man fell then among robbers… who, through the disobedience of the first man, stripped the race of mankind of the ornaments of virtue, and wounded him, that is, by ruining the gift of the power of free will.
  — St. Thomas Aquinas, *Catena Aurea*, III.i, commentary on St. Luke, p. 372

- How great is the frailty of man, ever prone to evil!
  — Imitation of Christ, I, ch. 22

Resolutions

1. To meditate for ten minutes on the Fall of man in order better to realize our misery.
2. To make a precise resolution for fighting against our predominant fault.
3. Not to be surprised at the defects of our neighbor and to put up with them patiently, knowing how to recognize his qualities.

THE GOOD SAMARITAN

Monday of the 12th Week after Pentecost

God speaks to us:

A certain Samaritan as he journeyed came upon him.
Gospel of Sunday: St. Luke 10:33

Meditation

A priest passed by without taking care of the wounded man; he preferred to step to the side. This priest symbolizes Aaron, and so the priesthood of the Old Testament. Priests offered sacrifices in the Old Testament, but these sacrifices were powerless to bring grace back to man. Then a Levite passed by, without taking pity any more than the first. This Levite is a figure of Moses, who was of the tribe of Levi and who received the Law from God. But the Mosaic Law was only capable of denouncing evil, not putting a stop to it. *A certain Samaritan as he journeyed came upon him.* This Samaritan represents our Lord. According to St. Jerome, the word *Samaritan* means *guardian*. Our Lord certainly is the guardian of our souls. He holds the remedies for giving health back to our souls and He helps us to persevere in good. Moreover, when the Jews said to Him, "Thou art a Samaritan, and hast a devil" (Lk. 8:48), Jesus denied that He was possessed by a devil, but did not deny that He was the guardian of the sick. This Samaritan was going down, as our Lord came down from Heaven to redeem us. And he *came upon him.* Jesus likewise came to us, and He took upon Himself all our miseries. "Seeing him, [he] was moved with compassion" (Lk. 10:33). And so our Lord also looks at us with eyes full of mercy.

"He went up to him and bound up his wounds, pouring on oil and wine" (Lk. 10:34). Oil relieves pain. It symbolizes mercy. Our Lord pours oil on the wounds of the sinner by giving him the virtue of hope, which gives him back the strength and courage to start again on his path. As for the wine, it is the symbol of the blood of our Lord. The priest at the altar changes the wine into blood. The wine is therefore very appropriate as a symbol for the blood of our Lord. When the Samaritan pours wine on the wounds of this man, he is showing us that it is by the blood of Jesus our Savior that the wounds of our soul can close and heal. The mercy of God and the Precious Blood of Jesus are the remedies to all our evils.

Merciful Jesus, Good Samaritan, have pity on the poor sinner that I am. Purify me by the virtue of Your divine blood.

Prayer

Blood of Christ, torrent of mercy, save us.
— Litany of the Precious Blood

Or else:

O almighty and merciful God, of whose gift it cometh that Thy faithful do unto Thee worthy and laudable service: grant us, we beseech Thee, that we may run without stumbling towards the attainment of Thy promises.
— Collect of Sunday

Thoughts

- Now when [our Lord] came He was made very near to us by His taking upon Himself our infirmities, He became a neighbor by bestowing compassion.
  — St. Thomas Aquinas, *Catena Aurea*, III.i, commentary on St. Luke, p. 374

- What! To be a Christian and see your brother suffering without weeping with him, without being sick with him! That is to be without charity; it is to be a mere painting of a Christian.
  — St. Vincent de Paul, TD2, February 4

Monday of the 12th Week after Pentecost

Resolutions

1 To thank God the Father for having sent His Son to redeem us, and also for the grace of strength received at our last confession.

2 To read in our catechism the section on Extreme Unction.

3 To call or write to a sick person, or to someone of our acquaintance who is suffering.

THE EXTENT OF CHARITY

Tuesday of the 12th Week after Pentecost

GOD SPEAKS TO US:

Thou shalt love thy neighbor as thyself.

Gospel of Sunday: St. Luke 10:27

MEDITATION

In the literal sense, the parable of the good Samaritan is meant to help us open our heart to the miseries of our neighbor. The same love of God should appear in my relations with God and in my relations with others.

This parable also helps us understand that the term *neighbor* does not extend merely to those who share our convictions, but extends to all men.

Jesus wants to keep us from falling into the snare of a selective charity, a charity limited only to the small number of our friends. "If you love those that love you, what reward shall you have? … Do not even the Gentiles do that?" (Mt. 5:46, 47). Catholic charity is universal, which means it extends to all men. If a man nourishes grave bitterness toward a single person, he loses charity and thereby the state of grace.

When we say that our charity must be universal, we do not mean that we should practice it in the same way toward all men, since we have limited strength and a limited budget. There is an order to be respected in the practice of charity. All the rest being equal, we should help first those who are united to us by ties of blood, religion and homeland.

We cannot fall into the trap of those who try to help those farthest from them to the detriment of those near.

Moreover, charity is not limited to the sharing of material goods. The corporal works of mercy should not make us forget the spiritual works of mercy. It is very good to help someone who is in material difficulty. But it is even better to help someone who does not know the meaning or the purpose of life and who wishes to be enlightened. Spiritual works of mercy are of greater price because our soul has much more value than our body. Our Lord Himself has told us, "What does it profit a man, if he gains the whole world, but suffer the loss of his own soul?" (Mt. 16:26).

Lord Jesus, we wish to imitate the good Samaritan by having compassion on the miseries of those around us.

Prayer

O Lord, make me understand that true charity allows of no exception, but embraces with sincere love our neighbor, whoever he may be.
— Fr. Gabriel, DI, p. 757

Or else:

Lord, make it so I draw near to You all those who draw near to me.
— St. Francis de Sales, TD, July 8

Thoughts

- Let us love men as Jesus loved them, wishing them as much good as He wished them, doing them all the good in our power, dedicating ourselves to their salvation, ready to give our blood for the salvation of each one of them.
— Charles de Foucauld, TD, April 19

- Charity is vast; it reaches even to the love of our enemies.
— St. Gregory the Great, TD, December 5

Resolutions

1 To recite the Act of Charity (see page 264).

2 To manifest our charity by doing well and quickly our regular chores and duties, for love of God.

3 To make the resolution not to brood over a disagreement or an offense that wounded us.

CHARITY: A VIRTUE THAT ACTS

Wednesday of the 12th Week after Pentecost

God speaks to us:

He bound up his wounds, pouring on oil and wine.
Gospel of Sunday: St. Luke 10:34

Meditation

Let us examine the Gospel of the good Samaritan under another angle. Our Lord is also showing us in this parable that when the life of a man is in danger, we have the duty to come to his assistance. And He shows us that our charity is only authentic if it translates into action. Charity is not content with just feeling kind toward our neighbor, or even with saying kind words. Charity expresses itself in action. Thus, charity does not stop at sterile compassion but puts everything in motion to bring our neighbor the help he needs.

Moreover, if we want to love our neighbor as we ought to love him, we must show courtesy toward him, and goodwill, and discretion.

We therefore must do everything we can to keep from harming our neighbor and displeasing him. To manage it, we have to take our neighbor's weakness into account. We sometimes say to ourselves, "My neighbor should not be so sensitive, so defensive, so nit-picky! He should not let himself be so upset over nothing." Maybe not! But in the meantime, we have to be realistic and take into account the way he is. As St. Bernard says, men are imperfect, and you are not allowed to act as though they were not.[15] They may be overly sensitive, but that is no reason to irritate them intentionally.

On the contrary, we must be gentle with the weaknesses of those around us. If we had to wait until all men were perfect and without

---

[15] St. Bernard, in Bourdaloue, *Complete Works*, II, p. 299.

weakness before we practiced charity toward them, it is obvious that the time for practicing this virtue would never come. So, it is often better in practice to put up with the defects of our neighbor, rather than try to correct them. It is better to accept reality than work stubbornly at making everyone around us perfect.

Lord Jesus, in order to increase my charity, I wish to work at reforming myself first instead of trying to make the people around me perfect. I realize that it is by correcting my defects, not by denouncing those of others, that I will merit the blessed eternity of Heaven.

Prayer

O Jesus, come from Heaven for the love of Your brothers, give me a charitable heart, so that I lend myself willingly to the good offices of charity.

— St. Alphonsus Liguori, HDD, p. 34

Or else:

Heart of Jesus, burning furnace of charity, have mercy on us.

— Litany of the Sacred Heart

Thoughts

- Not only must we take care to avoid all harshness and impatience, but we have to go out of our way to serve [others], even the most troublesome and difficult, with cordiality and great gentleness.
— St. Vincent de Paul, R, p. 9

- Let us have limitless delicacy in our charity. Let us not limit ourselves to great deeds but have a tender thoughtfulness that enters into detail and does those little nothings that spread such balm over hearts.
— Charles de Foucauld, TD, September 30

Resolutions

1. To open our eyes to see the good to be done around us.
2. To lend a hand spontaneously, without expecting recompense in return.
3. To be patient with people who have a difficult character.

RENOUNCING OUR OWN INTERESTS

Thursday of the 12th Week after Pentecost

God speaks to us:

Charity is not self-seeking.
1st Epistle of St. Paul to the Corinthians 13:5

Meditation

We would like to cling to our own interests and at the same time practice charity as God asks us to do, but according to St. Paul we cannot do both because they contradict each other: *charity is not self-seeking.*

The only solution if we want to love our neighbor according to the rules and order of charity is for us to learn how to renounce our own interest. And we can understand why. What is charity, after all? According to Holy Scripture, charity is the union of hearts and wills (Acts 4:32). How can we be united in heart with our neighbor if we remain turned in, twisted in on ourselves; if we live only for ourselves and we seek only our own advantage? We cannot.

Charity supposes forgetfulness of self. If we want to enter the interests of our neighbor, we first have to rid ourselves of our own interests. Only on this condition will we be really charitable. There is no other solution.

Renouncing our *self* is therefore indispensable if we are to satisfy the demands of charity, and that renunciation can go very far. Our Lord knows this perfectly, and so He sets the example to encourage us.

What interests did He not sacrifice for us? He sacrificed the interest of His goods, in living in the greatest poverty. He sacrificed the interest of His glory, in living in the greatest humility and accepting the worst humiliations. He sacrificed the interest of His freedom, taking "the form of a slave" (Phil. 2:7), as St. Paul says. He sacrificed the interest of His happiness, accepting to become a "man of sorrows" (Is. 53:3). He sacrificed the interest of His reputation and His life, in dying like a criminal. He sacrificed the interest of His holiness and His innocence, bearing Himself the weight of our sins.

Lord Jesus, strengthened by Your example, I wish to learn to renounce my claims, to keep from jealously guarding my own rights or being too anxious for my own honor. Help me to be generous toward my neighbor, to forget my own interests, to give without counting the cost, to fight without worrying about the wounds.

Prayer

Give me patience, Lord, even in this trial.
— *Imitation of Christ*, III, ch. 29

Or else:

Not my will, Lord, but Thine; not my good, my interest, my advantage, but Thine; not me, but Thee, nothing in view of myself, all in view of Thee.
— Charles de Foucauld, TD, April 27

Thoughts

- Do not seek your interest but that of others.
— St. Benedict, TD, May 30
- The Lord always preferred us over Himself. He wants us to have such a love for others that we always prefer them to ourselves.
— St. Francis de Sales, TD, May 21

Resolutions

1 To interest ourselves in our neighbor without considering our own interest.

2 To watch over the purity of intention of our actions; to make a morning examination of conscience on this point, thinking about what the day will bring.

3 To dominate our natural antipathy and do good to a person with whom we have little in common.

THE SPIRIT OF SACRIFICE

Friday of the 12th Week after Pentecost

God speaks to us:

In this we have come to know His love, that He laid down His life for us; and we likewise ought to lay down our life for the brethren.

1st Epistle of St. John 3:16

Meditation

Charity commands us to abandon our own interests for those of our neighbor, and there are cases when we should be ready to give even our very life for him. *In this we have come to know the love of God*, St. John tells us, *that He laid down His life for us; and we likewise ought to lay down our life for the brethren.* Thus, for example doctors must be ready to come to the aid of the sick during an epidemic. Soldiers must be ready to stand in the way of an unjust invader, at the risk of their own lives. And we could take many other examples.

So, we have to be ready in certain cases to renounce life itself. All the more should we be ready to renounce our reputation. Unfortunately, every day we see acts of anger and hatred and revenge, when a person's supposed honor is threatened! There we have another disorder opposed to charity.

We can look at another domain as well: the need to renounce our material goods in order to preserve charity. Jesus Himself commands it: "From him who takes away thy goods, ask no return" (Lk. 6:30). A very demanding statement, which may even appear superhuman! When we hear it, we automatically say to ourselves, "But am I not allowed to demand that what belongs to me in justice be given back to me, and to use normal means to protect my rights?" Yes, you are allowed to, but only if that justice is compatible with charity. Which is far from always being the case. For example, if someone lends us money and he does not have enough to pay it back, what good does it do to pursue him in justice, except to increase his debts and make him even more destitute? In those circumstances, renouncing our own right becomes a precept of mercy.

That is why our Lord, on another occasion, did not hesitate to say, "If anyone would go to law with thee and take thy tunic, let him take thy cloak as well" (Mt. 5:40).

Lord Jesus, today again I desire to perfect my virtue of charity. That I may do so, help me to foster in myself the spirit of sacrifice.

Prayer

Lord, make me an instrument of Your peace. Where there is hatred, let me sow love. Where there is offense, let me sow pardon. Where there is discord, let me sow union.

— St. Francis of Assisi

Or else:

Melt my heart, Lord, in the flame of Your charity.

— Fr. Gabriel, DI, p. 977

Thoughts

- The divine Master loved us enough to sacrifice for us all His interests as God-man.

   — Bourdaloue, CW, II, p. 291

- There is only one manner of giving oneself to God in self-denial and sacrifice: to give oneself entirely, without keeping anything for oneself.

   — Curé of Ars, TD2, February 5

Resolutions

1. To go without using some material good during the day (specify which), or forget a debt which is due to us (or both).
2. To lend a hand in something that costs us, but which would make another person happy.
3. To offer up a slight suffering (thirst, tiredness, some vexation) and wait a little bit before resolving it.

ON THE ROAD TO HEAVEN

Saturday of the 12th Week after Pentecost

God speaks to us:

Setting him on his own beast, [the Samaritan] brought him to an inn and took care of him.

Gospel of Sunday: St. Luke 10:34

Meditation

Once he had addressed the most urgent need, the Samaritan placed the wounded man on his own mount and brought him to the inn.

This mount of the Samaritan symbolizes the flesh of Jesus. The humanity of Jesus is indeed the necessary means for reaching His divinity. We must believe in the Incarnation of the Word of God; we must believe in God made man in order to be transformed into God.

God became man so that man might reach God. On this mount, the flesh of our Lord, we reach the inn which is the Church. Only united to the body of our Lord by baptism will we have access to the holy Church of God. The Church is this place of rest, this life-giving place where man can find all the resources he needs to return to health.

But the good Samaritan could not remain long on earth and had to return to Heaven, from whence He had come down. This is why it is written, "the next day he took out two denarii and gave them to the innkeeper" (Lk. 10:35). What is this "next day" if not the day of the Resurrection? And the two denarii represent the two precepts of charity, love of God and love of neighbor, which must be observed in order to remain in good health at the inn, that is, the Church.

Finally, the Samaritan says to the innkeeper, "Take care of him; and whatever more thou spendest, I, on my way back, will repay thee" (Lk. 10:35). The Samaritan, that is, our Lord, will come to settle all our expenses on the last day; He will come back at the end of the world to judge us and He will then render to each one according to his works.

Lord Jesus, with all my heart, I come to You with confidence to receive the care which You wish to bestow on me. Give me the heart of an apostle so that I might draw toward the inn, Your Church, the souls of those around me, in order that they, too, might benefit from the graces which You have poured upon me so generously by the channel of the sacraments of Penance and Holy Eucharist.

Prayer

O sweet hand of Jesus our Savior, please draw near to my soul; only touch it and it will be healed.

— Fr. Emmanuel, M, p. 273

Or else:

Ah! Lord my God, be blessed for all that You have done to give me the place which You have given me in Your Church. How much it has cost You, Lord; and how little it has cost me.

— Fr. Emmanuel, M, p. 274

Thoughts

- Jesus carried us to the inn, that is, to His Church. There He takes care of us, He shelters us, He guards us, He nourishes us, He heals us, and He puts us in a state to return to the Heavenly Jerusalem.
— Fr. Emmanuel, M, p. 274

- The Holy Church is an apothecary's shop, full of precious, health-giving medicines. These are the sacraments which our Savior and Master left us to heal us of our infirmities.
— St. Francis de Sales, TD, February 8

Resolutions

1. To spend ten minutes reflecting on the benefits which Jesus showers upon us with confession and communion.
2. To thank Jesus for the grace of our baptism which brought us into the Church.
3. To thank the priests, the Brothers and the Sisters who are "good Samaritans" for us every day.

OUR NATIVE MISERY

13th Sunday after Pentecost

God speaks to us:

For indeed, I was born in sin; guilt was with me already when my mother conceived me.

Psalm 50:6

Meditation

One day as He was going to Jerusalem, Jesus healed ten lepers. By this miracle, our Lord wishes in the first place to remind us of the bad blood we inherited from Adam, and then He wishes to stir up in us a hatred for sin.

Looking around us at the rise in delinquency, violence, hatred; seeing the tide of impurity sweeping over our poor world; realizing mankind's inability to prevent wars among nations, every one of us is brought before this truth of our Catholic faith: that man is not good by nature; man is damaged, he is wounded in his nature. This fact is not because of God but because of sin, original sin and our personal sins.

If he is not on the alert, man can forget the most basic truths about his nature and his destiny. Moreover, anyone who examines his conscience regularly quickly perceives that he more readily goes after his ease than after his duty. Finally, anyone who is honest with himself is very aware that his passions play tricks on him and tend to short-circuit his reason.

If we do not know how to recognize our weaknesses and our bad tendencies, we will necessarily find ourselves moving away from God. Truly, if we are not careful, we will fall little by little into sin, and then settle more deeply into it. The tragedy is that we are not always aware of this deviation, because we do not become bad all at once. Only little by little do we lose our energy, our strength of soul, our convictions, and we may still consider ourselves to be fervent whereas in fact we have already set off in a wrong direction and are starting to go off the path.

Our Lord, who knows our weakness better than we do, therefore wants to give us a hatred for sin and a remedy for escaping it.

Lord Jesus, help me to realize the malice and the ugliness of sin since You compare it to leprosy. Help me to avoid it whatever the cost, and to make reparation for the disorders of my past life.

Prayer

Consider my lowness and weakness, O Lord, for You know all things. Have mercy on me, and raise me from the mire, that I may not stick fast in it.

— *Imitation of Christ*, III, ch 20

Or else:

[My God,] strengthen me with heavenly courage, lest my old and wicked enemy of the flesh, not yet wholly subject to the spirit, prevail and gain the upper hand.

— *Imitation of Christ*, III, ch. 20

Thoughts

- Do not be surprised at your weaknesses. Instead, accept yourself as you are; blush at your infidelities toward God, and abandon yourself peacefully to Him, like a little child in the arms of his mother.

    — Padre Pio, TD, June 7

- My weakness is apparent to me, for evil fancies rush in on me more readily than they depart.

    — *Imitation of Christ*, III, ch. 20

Resolutions

1. To recite the *Confiteor* from the bottom of our heart (see page 263).

2. To decide finally to go on retreat or to renew the resolutions of our last retreat.

3. To perform acts of virtue contrary to our predominant fault and then notice the positive results, in order to encourage ourselves.

THE LEPROSY OF SIN

Monday of the 13th Week after Pentecost

GOD SPEAKS TO US:

[The lepers] lifted up their voice, crying, "Jesus, Master, have pity on us."

Gospel of Sunday: St. Luke 17:13

MEDITATION

Physical leprosy is the image of another, much more serious illness, another leprosy, much uglier and more repugnant: the spiritual leprosy due to sin. In fact, leprosy has three characteristics. First, the leper is eaten away, gnawed down by the infection, which disfigures him. The second characteristic of leprosy is how contagious it is. Finally, in the time of Jesus, lepers were excluded, banished from society if their sickness lasted. What leprosy does to the body, sin does to the soul.

Let us try to call up an image of what a leper looks like. Picture this body devoured by ulcers, this body starting to lose its human shape. Picture this face covered with wounds as painful as they are repulsive, and then let us realize that each time we commit sin, our soul becomes more ugly, more hideous than that body. By sin, we mean mortal sin, but we must not forget that deliberate venial sin leads us into mortal sin without our realizing it, if we are not careful.

Many of the old cathedrals of Europe have representations of devils and of hell. Each is always more horrible than the last. Do not go imagining that these carvings were designed to frighten little children or to hold Catholics in a state of terror; they were fashioned to help us understand the deformity which sin causes. When we meditate in front of these sculptures, we feel what an apt image leprosy can be for making us realize the disastrous effects of sin in our soul.

Monday of the 13th Week after Pentecost

The sinful soul becomes truly hideous. We answer: Not to our eyes. Indeed not, but God sees the deformity and that is why He holds sin in abomination. We know that man was created in the image and likeness of God. By sin, the soul loses that likeness; it starts to be in the image of the devil.

My God, preserve me from sin. Help me to make the decision once and for all to avoid it. Help me to strengthen my virtues, so that I never again commit a single mortal sin.

Prayer

O divine Savior, I, too, am a poor leper; receive me: "If Thou wilt, Thou canst make me clean!"

— Fr. Gabriel, DI, p. 157

Or else:

O Jesus Crucified, give me the grace to understand the great malice of sin.

— Fr. Gabriel, DI, p. 284

Thoughts

- This leper is you, if you are in a state of mortal sin. Through sin, you are condemned to death, to eternal death—you are condemned to hell.

  — St. Alphonsus Liguori, HDD, p. 198

- O souls redeemed by the blood of Jesus Christ, understand what you have become through sin, and have pity on yourselves!

  — St. Teresa of Avila, TD, June 13

Resolutions

1. To recite a decade of the rosary for the people far from God whom we will encounter today in the street, in the store, etc.

2. To meditate for ten minutes on the gravity of mortal sin, starting from the idea of the leper.

3. To support your teenagers by offering them an attentive ear, but without winking at their errors, so that they learn to make good use of their freedom.

CONFESSION: REMEDY FOR SIN

Tuesday of the 13th Week after Pentecost

God speaks to us:

When Jesus saw [the lepers], He said, "Go, show yourselves to the priests."

Gospel of Sunday: St. Luke 17:14

Meditation

Who among us, if he had leprosy, would not do everything he could to be healed? Who among us, learning that he has cancer, would not try at all cost to be free of it? Maybe we think our soul has less value than our body. Yet Jesus warned us, "What does it profit a man, if he gain the whole world, but suffer the loss of his own soul? Or what will a man give in exchange for his soul?" (Mt. 16:26) A single current of charity holds together all the saints in Heaven, the souls in purgatory and people on earth who are in a state of grace. Yet as soon as we commit a mortal sin, like the leper banished from society, we are immediately excluded from this communion of saints.

So let us listen to Jesus and take His words seriously. Let us seek today the remedy for the spiritual leprosy that is sin, in order to be healed. What is this remedy? The divine doctor revealed it to the lepers: *Go, show yourselves to the priests*. Our Lord does not prescribe chemotherapy for the soul or radiation; nor does He ask us to expiate our sins with a discipline until we draw blood or to feed on bread and water until our last breath. To bring us back to health, Jesus simply asks us to go show ourselves to the priest.

Let us always grow in love for the sacrament of penance, which takes souls off the path to hell and puts them back on the path to Heaven. Let us remember the devil's admission to the Curé of Ars:[16] "If there were

---

[16] Geneviève Esquier, *Men Who Believed in Heaven*, p. 314.

three like you on earth, my kingdom would be destroyed." And what was the principal occupation of the Curé of Ars, if not to hear confessions in order to absolve penitents? Let us not wait until we have committed grave sins before taking advantage of the graces of this sacrament. We do not wait until the illness is incurable before we make an appointment with the doctor. We go to him at the first signs of being sick.

Lord Jesus, I promise You to go quickly to the sacrament of penance each time the good of my soul requires it.

Prayer

O my God, how many times have I gone to confession without making a real effort at repentance! Lord, never more will I neglect to stir up my contrition.

— St. Alphonsus Liguori, HDD, p. 99

Or else:

O Jesus, I do not wish to seek in the confessional any other consolation than the joys of a conscience purified by the merits of Your blood.

— St. Alphonsus Liguori, HDD, p. 333

Thoughts

- Jesus Christ, the divine doctor, offers you a remedy like none other on earth, which most certainly wards off death, the inevitable condemnation which awaits you… This remedy is confession.
  — St. Alphonsus Liguori, HDD, p. 198
- His greatest pleasure is to forgive us. Let us therefore give this joy to this good Father: let us come back to Him and we will be happy.
  — Curé of Ars, TD2, February 26

Resolutions

1 To meditate for ten minutes on the benefits of the sacrament of penance and think what our life would have been without this remedy.

2 To move ourselves to contrition in order to make a better confession.

3 To take care over our examination of conscience by seeking out our sins and failings toward God, toward our neighbor and toward ourselves.

CONFESSION: SOURCE OF LIGHT

Wednesday of the 13th Week after Pentecost

God speaks to us:

Walk while you have the light, that darkness may not overtake you.

St. John 12:35

Meditation

People who live in sin are generally against the demands of religion. They find the "Catholic God" too severe, too harsh, too uncompromising, and they refuse to obey His Law when it runs contrary to their disordered passions. Therefore, it is often so difficult to bring people to God. The obstacle in them is not intellectual, but moral. Pascal in the 17th century already pointed this out. He said, "You would soon have faith, if you renounced pleasure."[17]

The first means of obtaining a loving, active, persevering faith is therefore to put order in our moral life. Once the moral obstacle has been lifted, if we want God to give us the immense grace of revealing Himself to us in the light of faith, then we need also to acquire humility. Pascal rightly affirmed, "To obtain [faith] from God, … we must kneel."[18]

Charles de Foucauld led a very superficial life in his youth. But little by little, with the help of grace, he began asking himself important questions about the meaning of life. Through his aunt he heard echoes of the magnificent apostolate of Fr. Huvelin, and one day he went to his confessional, in Paris, to meet him and ask him questions. "I have come to ask you a few questions about the faith," he announced, leaning down toward Fr. Huvelin yet without kneeling. "Go on your knees," the priest answered. Charles de Foucauld obeyed and did confess his sins then and there, and immediately he received enlightenment. All his doubts

---

[17] Blaise Pascal, *Pascal's Pensées*, section III, n. 240, p. 70.
[18] *Ibid.*, section IV, n. 250, p. 73.

vanished in an instant. Bossuet was right to say that "man is only great when he is on his knees." And so, for our faith to be profound, let us practice humility. This virtue will help us become aware of our state as a sinner and will give us the courage to have recourse to the sacrament of penance to find light and peace.

O Jesus, aware of my misery, I come to You. Enlighten me, heal me, guide me.

Prayer

O Jesus, who sweated blood for the expiation of my sins, give me the strength to accept in the confessional the sweat of humiliation.
— St. Alphonsus Liguori, HDD, p. 301

Or else:

O Mary, queen of sorrows, give me perfect contrition in all of my confessions.
— St. Alphonsus Liguori, HDD, p. 130

Thoughts

- There is no better medicine for the ills and wounds of the soul than frequent confession when it is made with a humble, sincere, and contrite heart.
— Fr. Gabriel, DI, p. 205

- Jesus awaits us in this Sacrament of His merciful love, not only to cleanse our soul in His precious Blood, but also to strengthen it in this salutary bath.
— Fr. Gabriel, DI, p. 205

Resolutions

1. To try to practice humility in order to make the admission of our sins easier in confession.
2. To choose a specific effort to make in order to lead a life in conformity with the will of God, so as not to fall into blindness.
3. To gather the most convincing arguments on the benefits of confession, so we are prepared to enlighten a sinner.

THE PRIEST IN THE CONFESSIONAL

Thursday of the 13th Week after Pentecost

GOD SPEAKS TO US:

Whose sins you shall forgive, they are forgiven them; and whose sins you shall retain, they are retained.

St. John 20:23

MEDITATION

To those who claim we should approach God directly, without any intermediary, our Lord answers, "Go, show yourselves to the priests" (Lk. 17:14). The priest exercises the role of mediator between God and man, notably in the sacrament of penance. It is not easy to go to confession. We can tend to shrink from the admission of our sins. There is a story in the life of St. Antoninus that he was once waiting for a penitent when he heard loud noises outside his confessional. He stepped out and saw the devil. "What are you doing here?" the saint asked. "I am restoring to that man, before his confession, the shame I took from him when he was committing sin."[19]

To dominate our apprehension, let us meditate on the reflections of Fr. Claude de la Colombière: "I am less surprised by those who fear confession because they do not wish to correct themselves of their sins, than by those who dread confession because they fear revealing their sins… The more the confessor knows you, the more esteem he has for you; the more difficult it is [for you to reveal your sins], the more he must admire

---

[19] Adapted from the account of St. Alphonsus Liguori in *Instructions on the Commandments and Sacraments*, Part II, ch. 5, p. 143. "St. Antoninus relates, that a holy solitary once saw the devil standing beside a certain person who wished to go to confession. The solitary asked the fiend what he was doing there. The enemy said in reply: 'I now restore to these penitents what I before took away from them; I took away from them shame while they were committing sin; I now restore it that they may have a horror of confession.'"

Thursday of the 13th Week after Pentecost

the confidence you have in him... The graver the sin and the better the confessor knows you, the more merit [for you] and, consequently, the more esteem the confessor must have for you, if he is reasonable, if he has sentiments in conformity with those of God and the angels who see your humility with joy and admiration. What extravagance, if the confessor were to condemn you in his heart while God absolves you and showers you with His graces! ... Maybe you have done nothing so heroic in all your life as this admission of your sin."[20]

And the holy Jesuit concluded that the priest, far from bringing to bear a negative judgment on the penitent who humbly admits his particularly grave sins, can only bless God in hearing this confession, seeing the courage of the penitent and considering the power of divine grace to change hearts.

O my Jesus, strengthened by these considerations, give me the courage always to make complete and sincere confessions.

Prayer

Holy Mother Mary, obtain for me the grace always to make good confessions.

— St. Alphonsus Liguori, HDD, p. 257

Or else:

My God, I will never enter the holy tribunal without being resolved to confess my sins as though I were about to die; I will never come out of the confessional with anxiety still in my heart. If I feel any hesitation, I will pray.

— St. Alphonsus Liguori, HDD, p. 278

---

[20] Claude de la Colombière, *Spiritual Writings*, pp. 332-333.

Thoughts

- When we go to confession, we have to understand what we are going to do. We could say we are going to unnail our Lord from the Cross.
  — Curé of Ars, TD2, March 17

- Let us go often to confession: it is wisdom; it is salvation.
  — St. Alphonsus Liguori, HDD, p. 226

Resolutions

1. To pray to God for the grace not to hide, or brush over, or minimize any sin in confession, and to pray that the confessor might receive light from God.

2. Before going to confession, to remind ourselves that the priest is only an instrument of God and that it is to God that we are speaking.

3. To set the date for a general confession, if we are aware of having made bad confessions in the past.

THE FAITH OF THE LEPER

Friday of the 13th Week after Pentecost

GOD SPEAKS TO US:

Jesus said to [the leper whom He had just cured], "Arise, go thy way, for thy faith has saved thee."

Gospel of Sunday: St. Luke 17:19

MEDITATION

In the Collect of last Sunday, we asked for an increase of the three theological virtues. We asked notably for the virtue of faith: "Almighty and everlasting God, give to us an increase of faith, hope and charity." To stay in the spirit of the liturgy, let us consider today this virtue of faith. St. Thomas says that faith has to do with invisible realities: *Fides, de non visis*.[21] Indeed, its object is God in His intimate life, the principal mysteries of eternal life and the means to reach it, the law of suffering as means of redemption of sin. Faith therefore concerns mysterious realities. Truths of faith to which we must adhere were revealed to us by the prophets of the Old Testament, but the essential revelation was by Jesus Christ. St. John states it clearly: "No one has at any time seen God. The only-begotten Son, who is in the bosom of the Father, He has revealed Him" (Jn. 1:18). Our Lord is God and He knows much better than we do what happens in the life beyond, which is why, when He speaks, we must believe Him.

Difficulty in believing comes from our skeptical and rationalistic spirit. Man in postmodern society tends easily to sift the truths of the faith through the filter of his reason and retain only those which seem to him in agreement with his own manner of seeing the world: "A triumphant God, that suits me; a suffering God… now that is more difficult to accept. A merciful God, I completely agree; a just God, who

---

[21] *Summa Theologica*, Ia-IIæ, q. 66, a. 6.

punishes those who break His Law and condemns them to an eternal hell… that bothers me, so I do not believe it."

In this way, the man of today constructs a religion of his own, rejecting the truths which run contrary to his manner of picturing things and contrary to his disordered passions. We surely do not fall into such an extreme, thanks be to God, but the fact of spending a great deal of time with non-Catholics can end up weakening us, as well.

Lord Jesus, I thank You for having given me the faith. I promise You to nourish my faith by prayer and to defend it when circumstances allow.

Prayer

Lord, I believe, but give me a firmer faith. Mary, my mother, enlighten me.

— St. Alphonsus Liguori, HDD, p. 324

Or else:

My God, give me that faith, that strong and lively faith which makes us act in all things according to the truths of the faith, which makes us live by faith, which makes us order all of life, all thought, all words and actions on the faith, that is, on love and hope, on truth, on perfection—on You, my God.

— Charles de Foucauld, TD, August 4

Thoughts

- How happy we are to believe! How beautiful and pure and lofty is the truth! And how simply human life unfolds, illumined by the light of the faith.

   — Charles de Foucauld, TD, August 12

- If we want to have strong faith, let us be as humble and simple as children.

   — Fr. Gabriel, DI, p. 915

Resolutions

1 To read and meditate on the collect of last Sunday.

2 To read a book of Catholic doctrine so that we will be able to defend our religious convictions.

3 To look back at our summer vacation and draw a few conclusions for vacation times in the future. For example: having more of a schedule.

THE DUTY OF GRATITUDE

Saturday of the 13th Week after Pentecost

God speaks to us:

One of [the lepers], seeing that he was made clean, returned, with a loud voice glorifying God, and he fell on his face at His feet, giving thanks; and he was a Samaritan.

Gospel of Sunday: St. Luke 17:15-16

Meditation

In last Sunday's Gospel, Heaven, by the Son of God made man, heard the prayer of the lepers. Yet only one of them returned to thank our Lord.

Is it not beautiful to see this Samaritan bowed to the ground in thanksgiving before our Lord? This gratitude is the expression of his faith, that faith which made him ask for his healing, along with his companions in misery: "Jesus, Master, have pity on us" (Lk. 17:13). And our Lord congratulates him on his faith, which only kept increasing. It was contained in his call for healing, it was strengthened in the obedience which led him to the priest, and it finally blossomed completely in his grateful return to Jesus. This sick man is truly healed, and his soul is entirely filled with light and joy.

St. Thomas Aquinas distinguishes three degrees in thanksgiving: to recognize the benefit granted, to give thanks for this benefit, and to give in return. The leper glorified God with a loud voice. He thanks Him and goes away filled with happiness, ready to live a better life as a sign of his gratitude. How many times have we ourselves benefitted from the mercy of God! How many times has our Lord saved us, purified us, healed us! Surely it was for the sake of causing in us a conversion from evil to good or from good to better. And this conversion should find expression in a more generous love toward Him, in a greater fidelity to His laws, a more zealous practice of Christian virtue.

Today, therefore, let us ask ourselves: "What have we done with our duty of gratitude?" To help us make progress in this domain, we conclude by offering for your meditation these words from an evening prayer: "What thanks can I render You, my God, for all the goods which I have received from You? You thought of me from all eternity; You drew me from nothingness, You gave Your life to redeem me, and every day You still shower me with an infinity of favors. Alas, my Lord, what can I do in gratitude for so much goodness? Join with me, blessed spirits, in praising the God of mercies, who never ceases to do good to the most unworthy and ungrateful of creatures."

Prayer

What shall I render to the Lord for all that He hath rendered unto me? I will take the chalice of salvation and call upon the name of the Lord.

— Prayer after the communion of the priest

Or else:

In Thee, O Lord, have I hoped: I said, Thou art my God, my times are in Thy hands.

— Offertory of last Sunday's Mass

Thoughts

- It is not rare to receive goods from the hand of God. He is so good that He gives to everyone. But it is not so common to see men thank God for the goods they have received from Him.
  — Fr. Emmanuel, M, p. 278

- Let us apply ourselves to saying well these tiny words: *Deo gratias.* Those words are all we need in order to become saints: *Deo gratias.*
  — Fr. Emmanuel, M, p. 279

Resolutions

1 To recite a *Magnificat* in thanksgiving for the benefits received over the course of our life, especially the grace of being Catholic.

2 To acquire the reflex of thanking spontaneously all those to whom we owe some benefit, and to say at the same time, interiorly: *Deo gratias.*

3 To rectify an attitude or some detail of organization which a person close to us has asked us several times to do.

THE THOUGHTS OF GOD

14th Sunday after Pentecost

God speaks to us:

My thoughts are not your thoughts, nor your ways My ways.

Isaias 55:8

Meditation

The thoughts of God are another name for His designs, which are always infallibly accomplished. This reality ought to be enough to reassure us, but it can also lead us to want to understand God's attitude toward us, especially when it runs contrary to our manner of seeing things. Why does this or that trial come into my life? Why do others seem to be more highly favored than I? Is this series of difficulties going to end soon? These are all questions that come spontaneously to our mind.

To prevent this kind of thinking from troubling our soul, it is good to remember what God Himself told us more than once in Holy Scripture: *"My thoughts are not your thoughts, nor your ways My ways.* For as the Heavens are exalted above the earth, so are My ways exalted above your ways, and my thoughts above your thoughts" (Is. 55:8-9).

For this reason, St. Paul, who had the sense of God, said to the Romans, "O man, who art thou to reply to God? Does the object molded say to him who molded it: Why hast thou made me thus? Or is not the potter master of his clay, to make from the same mass one vessel for honorable, another for ignoble use?" (Rom. 9:20-21).

This lesson from Holy Scripture ought to be a great help to us in our trials.

In order to keep our soul at peace in the ups and downs of daily life, let us learn to draw strength from our faith. God wants us to live by faith. Believing means turning our eyes toward God with a gaze of confidence in painful times as in joyful times, and accepting not to see everything clearly. Vision will be the reward of our faith, but it will not come until we have reached Heaven.

14th Sunday after Pentecost

Lord Jesus, in order to live in peace, I accept serenely to be what I am, and I promise You to make real efforts to welcome all the trials of life with the same serenity.

Prayer

O infinite Wisdom, O eternal, infinite God, ... just as it is impossible for You not to be God, so it is impossible for Your creature to understand You fully. He who wishes to attain to the sublime state of union with You, O Lord, must have great faith.

— Fr. Gabriel, DI, p. 701

Or else:

Teach me to believe, O Lord, even in darkness and obscurity; teach me to believe by relying only on Your word.

— Fr. Gabriel, DI, p. 701

Thoughts

- No thought is of God which brings anxiety and agitation to our soul, for God is the Prince of Peace.
  — St. Francis de Sales, TD, February 4
- Blessed is that simplicity which rejects obscure inquiry and advances along the sure and open road of God's Commandments.
  — *Imitation of Christ*, IV, ch. 18

Resolutions

1. To recite and meditate on the Act of Faith (see page 263).
2. To accept with serenity all events that run contrary to our desires.
3. To resist making comparisons between ourselves and those who seem more highly favored.

THE THOUGHTS OF THE HEART OF JESUS

Monday of the 14th Week after Pentecost

God speaks to us:

The thoughts of the heart [of Jesus] are from generation to generation, to deliver souls from death and to feed them in famine.

Psalm 32:11, 19

Meditation

The Introit of the Mass of the Sacred Heart speaks of the thoughts of God, and more specifically the thoughts of His heart.

What are the thoughts of the heart of Jesus? *The thoughts of the heart [of Jesus] are from generation to generation, to deliver souls from death and to feed them in famine.*

All the events of our life are ordered toward our salvation. God created us for Heaven and He allows trials to appear throughout our life in order to lead us there. These trials are measured out to us both to test our fidelity and to allow us to merit Heaven.

God would only have to show us for one instant the joys of Heaven or the sufferings of purgatory and we would accept all our trials immediately and wholeheartedly.

Let us therefore try to offer the sufferings that we endure, in reparation for our sins and to shorten our purgatory.

The Sacred Heart wants to deliver us from eternal death, and He wants to nourish our souls in time of famine.

That nourishment is most of all the Holy Eucharist. The Eucharist is here below the great treasure that makes sweet this land of exile and communicates divine life to us. It is the bread of immortality. Our Lord told us, "If anyone eat of this bread he shall live forever." (Jn. 6:51)

It is not given to us to know perfectly all the thoughts of God, yet we know that God is a God of peace, that He wants our true good, namely,

Monday of the 14th Week after Pentecost

our eternal salvation, and that the trials inherent to the present life are as many stair-steps bringing us higher toward Heaven.

We have been given a sublime means of reaching Heaven: receiving God Himself into our souls in holy communion.

Let us ask the Blessed Virgin for the same submission which she herself offered to the mysterious designs of God, in the joyful periods of her life but also in the periods of sorrow.

Most Blessed Virgin Mary, help me to find I the Holy Eucharist the spiritual strength that I need in order to live a holy life here on earth and deserve to join you one day in the blessed eternity of Heaven.

Prayer

O Jesus, deign to take me into Your Sacred Heart. Grant that it may be the sanctuary where I may be recollected, sheltered, and find my rest.

— Fr. Gabriel, DI, p. 623

Or else:

O Jesus, envelop me in the flame of Your charity and make me cling so closely to You that I can never be separated from You!

— Fr. Gabriel, DI, p. 628

Thoughts

- Our hearts were given to us only for Him who gave His own heart totally.

  — St. Francis de Sales, TD, February 2

- We will give Him our hearts; that is the only gift He cherishes. But our hearts just as they are, so that He might make them such as they ought to be, such as He wills them to be.

  — Pauline Jaricot, TD, September 19

Resolutions

1 To recite the Litany of the Sacred Heart (see page 267).

2 To make a spiritual communion.

3 To make a visit to the Blessed Sacrament as soon as the opportunity arises.

THE EXAMPLE OF THE PATRIARCH JOSEPH

Tuesday of the 14th Week after Pentecost

GOD SPEAKS TO US:

[Joseph] nourished them, and all his father's house, allowing food to every one.

Genesis 47:12

MEDITATION

Events apparently the most opposed to our good nonetheless serve the accomplishment of the divine plan. Let us take as an example the story of Joseph, as it is presented in the Old Testament.

Joseph has a series of dreams in which he sees his brothers bowed to earth before him. Out of jealousy, his brothers cast him into a cistern and then sell him to Ishmaelite merchants traveling to Egypt. Joseph finally ends up in the household of Potiphar, commander of King Pharaoh's army. There he falls victim to the calumny of his master's wife, furious that her disordered attraction to Joseph met only resistance. The filthy calumny that Potiphar's wife invented against Joseph finally leads to his imprisonment.

We know the end of the story: Joseph can interpret the dreams of Pharaoh's chief steward and his chief baker, and then the dreams of Pharaoh himself, and at last finds himself raised to the post of governor of all Egypt. When a great famine comes upon the region, Joseph can provide grain to his brothers, come to Egypt begging food for their survival.

So, we see that in the beginning of his life Joseph was threatened with death by his brothers because of the dreams prophesying that he would dominate over his family. His brothers were enraged and tried to be rid of him, which led to his being sold as a slave by his own family and ultimately, through this series of events, being raised to the level of vice-Pharaoh and governor of Egypt, thereby accomplishing that very prophecy of domination.

Thus, it is that whatever obstacles man places to thwart the plan of God, this plan always comes about, though seldom according to our own preferences. Indeed, the cross is the gift that God gives His friends. And so let us not be discouraged at the sight of human failings, because God triumphs through failure. This lesson today should give us peace of soul.

Lord Jesus, too often I want things to happen according to my views. Help me to widen my field of vision and make flexible my will, to submit myself constantly to Your divine plan.

Prayer

O Mary, give me the heavenly instinct to turn always toward God and toward you at the first shadow of temptation.
— St. Alphonsus Liguori, HDD, p. 141

Or else:

Lord, I believe in Your love for me! How could I still doubt it?
— Fr. Gabriel, DI, p. 87

Thoughts

- God is not a tyrant who crushes us, but a Father, who tests us because He loves us.
— Fr. Gabriel, DI, p. 176

- Through trials God is drawing to Himself souls that are dear to Him.
— Padre Pio, TD, December 13

Resolutions

1 To recite the Litany of Humility (see page 271) asking God for the grace to accept with serenity the difficulties and failures of life.

2 To continue to believe in God when the trials of life threaten to make us doubt, and to manifest our confidence by reciting acts of faith and hope.

3 In family conflicts, to honor the law of forgiveness.

THE TRIBULATIONS OF THE HOLY FAMILY

Wednesday of the 14th Week after Pentecost

God speaks to us:

She laid Him in a manger, because there was no room for them in the inn.

St. Luke 2:7

Meditation

An example drawn from the life of the Holy Family shows how the most unsettling events turn to the accomplishment of the divine plan. Let us consider the time when the most Blessed Virgin was expecting our Lord. She has come to her ninth month. Do you imagine St. Joseph was not striving to his utmost to ensure a warm welcome to the Infant God? And all his preparations are swept aside by the pride of Caesar Augustus, who decided to conduct a census of the whole world.

How is he to handle this unexpected situation? Joseph has family in Bethlehem and hopes to find a door open to receive them. But no, here is a new trial! From house to house, the answer is the same: We would have loved to welcome you, but it is impossible! There is no room. What a mystery! No room for the Holy Family! No room for God made man, for the Creator of the universe! Yet, far from letting his mind turn to bitterness, Joseph leads his family away from the village and finds a grotto that served as a shelter for farm animals. There would our Lady bring the Infant God into the world. From a human point of view, misfortune had rained down upon the Holy Family.

We have looked at these trials from a human standing, but now let us consider them in the light of Providence. In this new light, we see that God used the pride of Caesar Augustus for the accomplishment of His own plan. God knows how attached man is to the goods of this world, and He willed that His Son be born not in a palace, not even in a comfortable house, but in a poor stable. On the surface, the Roman emperor did spoil the projects of St. Joseph, but in reality, the workings of both the emperor and St. Joseph allowed the fulfillment of the plan of God. The prophet Micheas had foretold it: "And thou, Bethlehem, of the land of Juda, art by no means least among the princes of Juda; for from thee shall come forth a leader who shall rule My people Israel." (Mt. 2:6) With the perspective of time, we discover all the wisdom of the plan of God. It is a great lesson for us to see Jesus born in a poor stable.

Yes, Lord Jesus, by being born in such poverty, You teach me how detached I must be from the goods of this world.

Prayer

Help me, O Lord, to understand the meaning of that total detachment which is the indispensable condition for perfect union with You.

— Fr. Gabriel, DI, p. 227

Or else:

May Thy holy mysteries, O Lord Jesus, impart to us divine fervor: wherein we may taste the sweetness of Thy most loving Heart, and learn to despise what is earthly and love what is heavenly.

— Postcommunion for the Feast of the Sacred Heart

Thoughts

- It is in our most pressing needs that our confidence in God should shine out brightest.

    — St. Vincent de Paul, TD1, August 1

- Let us firmly believe that everything happens for our greater good.

    — St. Teresa of Avila, TD, September 21

Resolutions

1 To recite the third joyful mystery.

2 To accept wholeheartedly the discomforts of circumstance: a broken heater, a lost article of clothing, a missed appointment, a badly cooked meal.

3 To come to the assistance of someone who is in need by giving our time or our money.

THE MEANING OF OUR TRIALS

Thursday of the 14th Week after Pentecost

God speaks to us:

If anyone wishes to come after Me, let him deny himself, and take up his cross, and follow Me.

St. Matthew 16:24

Meditation

God wants our happiness. And yet, at certain times, we are very tempted to say: If God wants my happiness, why do so many trials come my way? Why do so many sinners enjoy perfect tranquility here below, whereas I am drowning in difficulties?

Jesus has given us the answer: "Amen, amen, I say to you, that you shall weep and lament, but the world shall rejoice" (Jn. 16:20). And St. Paul writes, "We sent Timothy, our brother and a servant of God in the Gospel of Christ, to strengthen and comfort you in your faith, lest any should be shaken by these tribulations. For you yourselves know that we are appointed thereunto" (I Thess. 3:2-3).

To the question: Why do so many just men have to suffer? Jesus answers, "Did not the Christ have to suffer these things before entering into His glory?" (Lk. 24:26). What is true of Him is true also of His Mystical Body. We therefore have to suffer what is lacking to Christ's Passion, for the sake of His body which is the Church.

Again, Holy Scripture says, "Son, when thou comest to the service of God, prepare thy soul for temptation" (Ecclus. 2:1). But God is faithful. He always measures His grace to our trials, so that we are never tempted beyond our strength (I Cor. 10:13). May we therefore take courage to carry our cross after Jesus! *If anyone wishes to come after Me, let him deny himself, take up his cross, and follow Me.* Let us not ask to receive during our exile that which God reserves for us in the heavenly homeland.

Thursday of the 14th Week after Pentecost

To help us accept our trials, let us look to God who lives in peace in Heaven. Let us remember that He wishes to communicate His peace to us. Our Lord said before His Passion, "Peace I leave with you, My peace I give to you" (Jn. 14:27). Yet the peace that our Lord offers us is not the peace of the world, which is a superficial peace, a peace of mere appearance, often an illusory, fragile peace, a pure fiction. The peace which our Lord offers us is a profound, lasting peace, which penetrates to the deepest regions of the soul, not merely to its surface.

O sweet Jesus, Prince of Peace, pray to the Father for us.

Prayer

It is in You, O Lord God, that I place my whole hope and trust. On You I lay all my trouble and distress.

— *Imitation of Christ*, III, ch. 59

Or else:

May Your creating gaze, O God, carve an infinite abyss within me and may Your infinite love come flooding in to accomplish Your will.

— Pauline Jaricot, TD, August 11

Thoughts

- God loves us, and all external events, all interior trials, are only means that God uses to lead us toward sanctification.
  — Charles de Foucauld, TD, January 11

- If God allows you to suffer from the harshness of life, remain calm and be patient. Your love for God will then be freely given, which is the way of saints.
  — Padre Pio, TD, October 5

Resolutions

1 To meditate for ten minutes on the happiness and peace of Heaven in order better to accept the vexations of this life.

2 To bear the cross of today and not make it heavier by ruminating over the past or worrying about the future.

3 To offer our sufferings for the expiation of our sins and for the salvation of a soul in difficulty.

TRUST IN PROVIDENCE

Friday of the 14th Week after Pentecost

God speaks to us:

Look at the birds of the air: they do not sow or reap… yet your heavenly Father feeds them.

Gospel of Sunday: St. Matthew 6:26

Meditation

God is Providence and we must trust in Him, but our reliance cannot be presumptuous. Certain people tend to be too nonchalant and let life wash over them, taking Providence as an excuse not to reflect and resolve their difficulties. "God will provide," they claim. Their behavior seems to reflect a beautiful spirit of faith, but it may also reveal a lack of understanding of the plan of God. Our heavenly Father never claimed that He would bake and deliver our daily bread. On the contrary, He asked us to earn it by the sweat of our brow.

The saying goes, "Help yourself and Heaven will help you." Heaven will help you, but let us not forget to do what depends on us to bring about our projects.

On the other hand, we sometimes encounter people who are too prudent by nature and tend to calculate everything in order to be sure of attaining their objectives.

These anxious temperaments consent only with great difficulty to face an uncertain future. Again, this attitude may not be entirely wrong, but it can betray a real a lack of trust in Providence. The Church does not want us to fall into this trap and for this reason last Sunday She held up for our meditation the passage in the Gospel where our Lord asks us not to be anxious over our material and temporal needs. He invites us to look at the birds of the air and the flowers of the field, and concludes by saying, "If God so clothes the grass of the field, which flourishes today but tomorrow is thrown into the oven, how much more you, O you of little faith!" (Mt. 6:30)

God is Providence: this is the truth which we must bear always in mind, to overcome our anxieties.

Oh yes, my God, I know that You are our Father and that You do not abandon those who place their confidence in You. I therefore promise You to do everything I can to push away sterile anxieties, without failing to work diligently toward the accomplishment of my life plans.

Prayer

O my God, You order and dispose everything according to Your own exalted purposes; teach me to trust fully in Your divine Providence.
— Fr. Gabriel, DI, p. 693

Or else:

O Lord, at the remembrance of Your immense goodness, all creatures break forth in praise and acclaim Your liberality.
— Fr. Gabriel, DI, p. 695

Thoughts

- Although things may not proceed according to our own views and thoughts, let us not doubt that Providence is leading all things toward our greater good.
— St. Vincent de Paul, TD2, September 20

- Given the weakness of our nature, it is extremely necessary for us that we have great confidence, that we not become discouraged, and that we tell ourselves that our efforts will ultimately triumph.
— St. Teresa of Avila, TD, February 10

Resolutions

1 To meditate on the fourth sorrowful mystery, asking for the grace of abandonment to divine Providence.

2 To schedule our time well so that our life might be as fruitful as possible.

3 In all of our vexations and trials, to take refuge immediately in the heart of Jesus, lifting our minds with ejaculatory prayers.

RECOURSE TO GOD

Saturday of the 14th Week after Pentecost

God speaks to us:

Better is one day in Thy courts above thousands.
Introit of Sunday: Psalm 83:11

Meditation

Last Sunday's liturgy invited us to live close to God. Let us reread the Introit. The Psalmist cries out, *Better is one day in Thy courts above thousands* far from You. "How lovely are Thy tabernacles, O Lord; my soul longeth and fainteth for the courts of the Lord" (Ps. 83:2). The place of predilection of the faithful soul is the church. The church is the place *par excellence* where our soul loves to take refuge, for there we can savor the presence of Jesus Christ in the Blessed Sacrament.

It is sometimes difficult and complicated for the faithful to spend time near Jesus in a church, but it is always possible for them to live near Him, present in their soul by His grace. Confidence is the first effect that flows from this intimacy with God. When our soul lives in the presence of our good God, we grow in confidence and abandonment to Providence, as Jesus reminds us in last Sunday's Gospel. He invites us not to be anxious about what we will eat or drink, nor about how we are going to be clothed, but to seek first the kingdom of God and His justice. Let us make no mistake. His words do not mean that we should be careless or imprudent in our way of managing our goods, but that we must reorder our preoccupations and give the first place to seeking to please God.

In the silence of prayer, our soul discovers little by little what God expects of us. We can imitate the peasant of Ars who devoted a long time every morning to prayer before the Blessed Sacrament, before going off to his work. When the Curé of Ars asked him what he was doing in front of the tabernacle, the man answered, "I look at the good God, and He looks at me."[22] The prayer of this good man consisted simply in contemplating our Lord present in the tabernacle, meeting His gaze and letting himself be loved by Christ.

Lord Jesus, help me to live in Your sweet company in order to accomplish Your will always and to merit one day to reach the eternal happiness of Heaven.

Prayer

O Spirit of prayer, O divine light, who make us certain of obtaining the goods that we ask, form in me that cry of a child who calls on his mother for help.

— Pauline Jaricot, TD, August 24

Or else:

O my Savior! How our soul needs Your help! We can do nothing without You. Enlighten us, that we may see that all our happiness depends on our perseverance and our avoiding bad companions.

— St. Teresa of Avila, TD, April 14

Thoughts

- Prayer is our best weapon: it is the key that opens the heart of God.
  — Padre Pio, TD, February 4

- You know very well how to express yourself when you speak to creatures; why can you not find the words when you are in a conversation with God?
  — St. Teresa of Avila, TD, April 24

Resolutions

1 To meditate for ten minutes on the presence of the Trinity in the depths of our soul and to beg for the grace of God.

---

[22] Fr. Trochu, *The Curé d'Ars*, part II, ch. 8, p. 197.

2 To recite a decade of the rosary in a church, and to take the time to look at the statues and the stained-glass windows, invoking the saints that they represent.

3 To act with purity of intention, that is, with the desire to please God and do His will.

THE RESURRECTION OF THE WIDOW'S SON

15th Sunday after Pentecost

God speaks to us:

[Jesus] went up and touched the stretcher; and the bearers stood still. And He said, "Young man, I say to thee, arise." And he who was dead, sat up, and began to speak.

Gospel: St. Luke 7:14-15

Meditation

This Sunday's Gospel presents to us one of the greatest miracles of Jesus, one of the three times He raised someone from the dead: the raising of the son of the widow of Naim. We are seized with emotion at this encounter of life and death. Life and death are in a constant conflict on this earth, a combat in which death is the stronger, and behold Jesus, in His almighty goodness, calls back from the tomb the young man of Naim.

"What is this tomb for you?" St. Ambrose asks. "This tomb is your bad habits. Your tomb is the lack of faith… Christ draws you from this sepulcher."[23]

St. Augustine also meditated on this miracle: "For you, a dead person is truly dead: you can strike him and shake him but you can never awaken him. For Jesus Christ, on the contrary, this young man was only sleeping. No one awakens a man asleep in bed as easily as Jesus draws this man from the tomb."[24]

Our Lord proclaimed, "I am the life!" (Jn. 14:6). Jesus possesses life in fullness and so life is His to give. It is He who can take life way and He who can give it back. He can also establish our life in Him forever. How good it is to contemplate the incarnate Word, source of eternal life!

---

[23] St. Ambrose of Milan, *Commentary on the Gospel of St. Luke*, p. 215.
[24] St. Augustine, *Complete Works*, XVII, 9, Sermon 98, p. 98.

As for us, let us ponder that the Holy Eucharist places within us the body of Jesus risen, like a seed of eternal life. Our Lord announced it very clearly: "he who eats this bread shall live forever" (Jn. 6:59). When the good God calls to Himself those who are dear to us, let us be consoled in remembering that our Lord desires to communicate to them eternal life, a life that is not fleeting and painful, but a life that is all glorious.

Lord Jesus, help me to live in holiness, so that on the last day I might find again those whom I love, shining with brightness, all radiant and illumined with the light of God, our God who is Light and Life.

Prayer

O Jesus, make me worthy to share in the joy of Your Resurrection.
— Fr. Gabriel, DI, p. 405

Or else:

Lord Jesus, good and gentle Jesus, who deigned to die for our sins and to rise for our justification, I beg You, by Your glorious Resurrection, to bring me out of the sepulcher of my vices and sins.
— Fr. Gabriel, DI, p. 407

Thoughts

- In His tenderness, the Lord says, "I do not will the death of the sinner, but that he be converted and live!"
— St. Benedict, TD, March 10

- Generally speaking, we do not have enough of a spirit of faith, and so we rarely think about the next life.
— Curé of Ars, TD1, October 17

Resolutions

1. To recite a decade of our rosary for the deliverance from purgatory of the soul of a family member.
2. To make a fervent communion.
3. To manage to arrive early enough at Mass to prepare ourselves and read the Gospel of the day.

THE SORROWING MOTHER

Monday of the 15th Week after Pentecost

God speaks to us:

With expectation I have waited for the Lord, and He had regard to me; and He heard my prayer.

Offertory of Sunday: Psalm 39:2

Meditation

Last Sunday's Gospel already occurred during Lent. The Church during that holy season was trying to touch the heart of sinners and give them hope, in order to bring them back to life.

The Church is fully aware of the state of human nature, and today She weeps again, Dom Guéranger tells us, "from the relapses of so many of those ungrateful children of Hers, to whom She had given a second birth, and at the cost of such pain and tears!"[25] St. John Chrysostom speaks also of the sorrow of our Mother the Church, in Her tenderness, at seeing so many souls return to the sin that means their death, so soon after uniting themselves with the mysteries of the Passion and Resurrection.[26]

Unfortunately, still today we see Catholics fall back into sin after their conversion, so that the words of Dom Guéranger are always true: "And if we compare these times of ours with the period when sainted pastors made Her words respected over all the world, is there a single Christian still faithful to the Church, who does not feel impelled by such contrast to be more and more devoted to a *mother* so abandoned as She is now?" And he concludes, "It is the duty of us Christians, who by God's mercy have been preserved from the general decay, to share in the anguish of our *mother*, the Church; we should humbly but fervently co-operate with

---

[25] Dom Guéranger, *The Liturgical Year, Vol. 11: Time after Pentecost, bk. 2*, p. 351.
[26] St. John Chrysostom, *Complete Works*, VII, pp. 535-536.

Her in all her zealous endeavors to reclaim our fallen brethren."[27] Let us therefore unite ourselves to the prayer of the Church to beg for the conversion of poor sinners. Let us think of all those monks and nuns who offer themselves as victims of reparation for the salvation of souls, and let us learn to associate ourselves with their prayers and their sacrifices. May the thought of the glory of God and the salvation of souls be our constant preoccupation, as well.

Lord Jesus, seeing around me so many souls who live far from You and do not know You, I can only join myself to the sorrows of Holy Church. To make up to You for so much indifference, I wish today to console You by being an example for those around me.

Prayer

O Jesus, teach me to pray, suffer, and work with You for the salvation of souls.

— Fr. Gabriel, DI, p. 944

Or else:

Let Thy continual pity, O Lord, cleanse and defend Thy Church: and because it cannot continue in safety without Thee, may it ever be governed by Thy goodness.

— Collect of Sunday Mass

Thoughts

- What joy we offer Jesus by bringing souls back to Him!
  — St. Alphonsus Liguori, HDD, p. 301

- When we think that the salvation of other souls may depend on our generosity, our fidelity to grace, or our immolation, then we can refuse nothing to our Lord, and we find the strength to accept even what is most bitter and painful.
  — Fr. Gabriel, DI, p. 942

---

[27] Dom Guéranger, *ibid.*, pp. 351-2, 353.

Monday of the 15th Week after Pentecost

Resolutions

1. To recite a decade of the rosary to beg for the conversion of a sinner.
2. To strive to be an example in our family and within our entourage, whether at work, in college, or in school.
3. Not to lose patience when something mechanical breaks down.

THE THOUGHT OF DEATH

Tuesday of the 15th Week after Pentecost

God speaks to us:

Remember thy last end, and thou shalt never sin.

Ecclesiasticus 7:40

Meditation

We have to learn to die to ourselves every day. We ought to do now in spirit what we will have to do in fact at the hour of our death, which requires that we detach ourselves from all those people or things to which we are too attached.

One of the means of this detachment is to look with clear eyes on the last ends, on death, and on our own death. Yes, one of the thoughts which we must keep always in our memory so as to live on earth in a holy way, is the thought of death. If we are asked to think of our death, it is not because it is the one truth on which the Catholic religion is built, but because a Catholic is a realist, one who loves the truth and who has the courage, with the help of God, to look at this truth head on, with all that it implies. In this Sunday's Gospel, Jesus Himself invited us to think of death. Yes, the account of this woman weeping over the loss of her only son is an invitation to us to consider this mystery of death.

Many things over the course of our life bring us before the thought of death: when we are stricken by a mortal illness, when we have barely escaped death in a car accident, when death touches someone near us, or else the liturgical cycle places the mystery of death before our eyes, on Ash Wednesday or during the month of November.

We must admit that nearly always we think of death with a certain apprehension, a certain fear and perhaps even a certain anguish. If we want to draw near the mystery of death with more calm, more serenity, more peace, we have to understand the advice which our Lord gives to the woman in today's Gospel. What is the meaning of the words that our Lord addresses to this poor widow: "Weep not" (Lk. 7:13)? They do not mean that we should have no emotion at the death of one near to us, but they invite us to order, to moderate, to temper the fear which we all have in the face of death, especially in the face of our own death.

Prayer

O good Jesus, ... at the hour of my death, call me and bid me come to Thee, that with Thy saints I may praise Thee, forever and ever. Amen.
— Prayer *Soul of Christ*

Or else:

O my Father, for the love of Jesus Christ, save me. I consent to lose everything, so long as You Yourself I do not lose.
— St. Alphonsus Liguori, HDD, p. 289

Thoughts

- Our Creator willed that the day of our death be a mystery to us, so that, never knowing when it will be, we may always think it to be near; and He willed that we be all the more fervent in our labors that we are uncertain of the day He will call us.
— St. Gregory the Great, TD, November 2

- In which direction will our soul go? In the direction we gave it on earth.
— Curé of Ars, TD2, November 14

Resolutions

1. To recite a decade of the rosary for the person near us who will be first to die.

2. To meditate for ten minutes on the blessed eternity of Heaven, in order to temper our fear of death.

3. To think of what we would have most difficulty leaving if we were to die today, and to make a concrete resolution to detach ourselves from it.

A SALUTARY MEDITATION

Wednesday of the 15th Week after Pentecost

God speaks to us:

O that they would be wise and would understand, and would provide for their last end.

Deuteronomy 32:29

Meditation

In order to accept death with more serenity, the great means once again is to detach ourselves from all disordered affection for creatures or for ourselves. All of these attachments, which one day or another we will have to break, are the main obstacle to our union with God. The man with no disordered attachment here below has no reason to fear death. We must tend always toward that state. Let us ask for the grace to be delivered from all empty, sterile, paralyzing fear of death. May the meditation on death, on the four last things, inspire us not with paralyzing fear but with sentiments of regret for our past sins as well as great desires of holiness, spiritual progress, perfection. As long as we are here on earth, our Lord is for us a Savior. In knowing Him as our Savior, let us take courage to acknowledge before Him all our weakness and to beg Him to have pity on those for whom He has shed His blood. Thus, will the thought of death become salutary for our soul.

From a practical, concrete point of view, the Church offers us certain prayers to help us purify our souls. These are the penitential psalms. These psalms contain words of profound regret, confidence and holy desire. If we recite these psalms from the depths of our heart, it will certainly bring peace to our souls and develop the sentiments that God wants us to have.

For these sentiments to be sincere, it might be a good idea for us to make a general confession of our life, when we have the opportunity, especially if we have the impression that in the past we have made incomplete confessions, or if we are already advanced in age. A general confession is a way to plunge ourselves into humility, pacify our souls and draw down on ourselves the blessings of God.

Lord Jesus, make it so that little by little the thought of death and meditation on the last things do not make me downcast but inspire me instead to take refuge in Your divine heart and in the sorrowful and immaculate heart of Your holy mother. Help me therefore to break all disordered attachments to creatures and to purify my soul often in the sacrament of penance.

Prayer

Tell me, Lord, what I must do to bring peace to my soul, and give me the strength to carry it out.

— St. Alphonsus Liguori, HDD, p. 119

Or else:

O Mary, recommend me to Your Son.

— St. Alphonsus Liguori, HDD, p. 104

Thoughts

- Apply yourself so to live now, that at the hour of death, you may be glad and unafraid.

  — *Imitation of Christ*, I, ch. 23

- Act at every moment as though that moment were the last of your life. What would we do, if we knew this hour to be our last? We would do what is most perfect... And why not do so already?

  — Charles de Foucauld, TD, January 4

Resolutions

1. To make an act of preparation for death, that is, to meditate for ten minutes on our own death and ask God for the grace to live in such a way that we no longer dread that moment.
2. To recite one of the Penitential Psalms (see page 273).
3. To take care over our examination of conscience and ask God for a profound contrition for our sins.

THE PARTICULAR JUDGMENT

Thursday of the 15th Week after Pentecost

God speaks to us:

God is a just judge, strong and patient: is He angry every day?
Psalm 7:12

Meditation

God is our Creator and our final end. We were created by Him and for Him: once the soul is separated from the body, God is all things. At the hour of death, the soul escapes the body and appears before Jesus to be judged by Him. This judgment should be our principal reason for fearing death. But our fear must not be excessive.

St. Augustine tells us that we should have the same sentiments, the same affections toward death as we have toward God. The holy Doctor explains, "God is both *lovable* and *terrible*: lovable, because He is a God of goodness; terrible, because He is a God of justice—'the God of revenge,' Scripture calls Him (Ps. 93:1)."[28]

Terrible, God does wish to be feared; *lovable*, He wishes to be loved. Death, also, has these two aspects: dreaded and desired. It is to be dreaded, because it could be the beginning of eternal sorrow; it is to be desired, because in the plan of God, death is meant to give us eternal joy. We therefore have to fear death and love it at the same time: fear it, mingling love into our fear, and love it, mingling fear into our love. Yet, just as God wills to be loved more than He is feared, so also we ought to love death more than we fear it. St. Augustine again helps us understand: "God would not be honored as He wishes, were we to fear Him more than

---

[28] Quoted by Bourdaloue, in *Complete Works*, II, p. 334.

we love Him; so also may we say that our sentiments are not perfectly Christian, if we fear death more than we hope in it."[29]

Prayer

My God, in the evening of life You will judge me according to my love. Help me to grow in love each day.
— Fr. Gabriel, DI, p. 1066

Or else:

Deign, O Lord, to grant me the experience of true love before You take me from this life, for it will be a great thing at the hour of my death to realize that I shall be judged by One whom I have loved above all things.
— Fr. Gabriel, DI, p. 1068

Thoughts

- That man has the perfection of love who strives after justice for the sake of love: he will not fear the approach of the Judge, nor dread eternal suffering.
    — St. Gregory the Great, TD, March 1

- Consider the abundance of divine goodness and return with tears to this merciful Judge. Gazing on His justice, do not make light of your sins; gazing on His goodness, do not yield to despair.
    — St. Gregory the Great, TD, March 16

Resolutions

1 To recite the fourth glorious mystery, asking for the grace of a happy death, particularly the grace that our death not be sudden and unexpected.

2 To recite the *Salve Regina*, begging the intercession of Mary at the moment of our great passage into eternity (see page 283).

3 To meditate on the Particular Judgment in order to regret profoundly whatever in our life has most wounded the divine heart of Jesus.

---

[29] *Ibid.*

CHRISTIAN HOPE

Friday of the 15th Week after Pentecost

God speaks to us:

With expectation have I waited for the Lord, and He had regard to me.
Offertory of Sunday: Psalm 39:2

Meditation

Death was first a chastisement. But today it can be a remedy for sin.

Let us remember the story of St. Francis Borgia. The sight of a cadaver is what led him to change his life. Let us remember also the life of St. Louis-Marie Grignion de Montfort. When he was a student in Paris, he spent many nights of vigil over the dead. He was led to reflect on the meaning of life, and these nights of watching are what gave him such tireless zeal for the salvation of souls.

Let us therefore not hesitate to think often of our death, for great graces are attached to this meditation.

A powerful means of coming little by little to see death in a more positive light than we naturally would, is to contemplate our Lord dying on the cross. Meditation on the death of Jesus ought to temper our fear of death. Our Lord loved death and gave to us His death to love; no more ought we to consider death only as a chastisement, but we have to see it as a passage leading to life, the true life, the life for which we were created. If we accept our death in union with the death of Jesus, we can turn our death into a beautiful testimony of love.

Knowing that our Lord, true God and true man, Innocence Itself, did not hesitate to undergo the torments of death in order to redeem us; and remembering how many times we ourselves have deserved that death on account of our sins: these thoughts should help us to accept our death in a spirit of reparation and in union with our Lord. The thought of Jesus' death can therefore soften the rigor of our own death.

Friday of the 15th Week after Pentecost

This life is so short; let us have always before our eyes the eternal recompense that our Lord has prepared for those who love Him. This consideration will help us cling to the will of God, not only in times of prosperity but also in times of adversity.

Lord Jesus, help me to face the reality of death and my last end, so that my life might be ever more fruitful in good works. Help me also to grow in the beautiful virtue of hope.

Prayer

O Lord, my God, You have the words of life! All mortals would find in them their heart's desire, if only they would seek.
— St. Teresa of Avila, TD, April 6

Or else:

O Mary, Mother of Good Hope, teach me the way of complete confidence in God.
— Fr. Gabriel, DI, p. 515

Thoughts

- Jesus took death upon Himself so that we would not be afraid of death; He showed us His resurrection so that we would believe our own possible.
— St. Gregory the Great, TD, April 20

- Daily direct your prayers and longings to Heaven, that at your death your soul may merit to pass joyfully into the presence of God.
— *Imitation of Christ*, III, ch. 23

Resolutions

1. To recite an Act of Confidence in God (see page 265).
2. To meditate for ten minutes on the Passion and death of our Lord on the cross.
3. To spend time listening to a person suffering from discouragement, and give him new confidence.

THE RESURRECTION OF THE BODY

Saturday of the 15th Week after Pentecost

God speaks to us:

The thoughts of His Heart are from generation to generation: …to save their souls from death, and feed them in famine.

Psalm 32:11, 19

Meditation

Many of the psalms refer to the resurrection of the body. "My flesh hath flourished again." (Ps. 27:7) These words concern us personally. It is a cry of hope for each one of us. St. Thomas Aquinas, commenting on this passage, tells us, "Man's youth is compared to a flower, for just as a flower announces the fruit, so the youth of a man announces the life to come. Thus, our flesh is said to flourish again, when in old age we become young."[30] "Only at the resurrection of the body will we be once again in the flower of youth, of health, of joy, and of beauty," Fr. Péronne explains. "Here below, this strength and vigor would be dangerous for us."[31]

The Psalmist writes also, "For Thee my soul hath thirsted; for Thee my flesh, O how many ways." (Ps. 62:2) St. Augustine comments on this passage, saying, "May this truth not seem to you incredible. If God made us when we did not exist, will it be hard for Him to make us again, after we have once been? May this truth therefore not seem to you incredible, on the pretext that you see the dead rot and turn to dust and ashes. Or if a dead man is burned, or dogs devour him, do you believe that this will be an obstacle to his resurrection?"[32]

Let us listen to St. John Chrysostom: "If you doubt the resurrection of

---

[30] Fr. Patrick Troadec, *The Four Last Things Seen Through the Psalms*, p. 94.
[31] *Ibid.*
[32] *Ibid.*, pp. 88–89.

the body, here is a striking proof for you: how can this body [of Enoch, who did not die and who is to appear at the end of time,] endure so long a time? ... Have you forgotten that God created man by drawing him out of nothingness? It will be much easier for Him to draw us back to life."[33]

Help me, Lord Jesus, to respect my body so that it may be glorified one day along with my soul in the blessed eternity of Heaven.

Prayer

Bless the Lord, O my soul: and let all that is within me bless His holy name... who satisfieth thy desire with good things: [at the resurrection,] thy youth shall be renewed like the eagle's.

— Psalm 102:1, 5

Or else:

I believe in the Holy Ghost, the holy Catholic Church, the communion of saints, the forgiveness of sins, the resurrection of the body, and life everlasting. Amen.

— *Credo*

Thoughts

- Winter will pass, and soon will come that springtime without end, all the more beautiful for this raging of the storms.

  — Padre Pio, TD, April 30

- God gives us graces so abundantly that all we have to do to get to Heaven is want it... Everything comes down to cooperating with grace.

  — Curé of Ars, TD2, April 19

Resolutions

1. Slowly to recite the *Credo*.
2. To turn our eyes from all impure pictures and our ears from all improper language.
3. To honor the Holy Trinity present in our soul, by a manner of dressing that is in harmony with our identity as a child of God.

---

[33] *Ibid.*, p. 90.

THE VIRTUE OF RELIGION

16th Sunday after Pentecost

God speaks to us:

Thou shalt love the Lord thy God with thy whole heart, and with thy whole soul, and with thy whole mind. This is the greatest and the first commandment.

St. Matthew 22:37-38

Meditation

Of the ten commandments, the first three concern God and the last seven concern our neighbor, to show the primacy of our duties toward God. If we practice charity toward our neighbor but forget our duties toward God, we are missing the essential. Indeed, love of neighbor flows from love of God. Fraternal charity should be founded on love of God and therefore presupposes the fulfillment of the first three commandments.

Our first duty toward God is the practice of the virtue of religion, that is, the adoration of God.

Man is a creature of God, and it seems natural that the first free act of a child would be to turn toward God, his Creator, to render Him homage and thank Him. Like Jesus upon entering this world, every man should say after Him, "Behold, I come to do Thy will, O God" (Heb. 10:9). That should be the first movement of the soul when it awakens to self-awareness. Man is by nature constantly bound to God. He ought therefore to practice the virtue of religion, above all through adoration—adoration within and without. Adoration as an interior disposition of the soul expresses itself through submission, an oblation of ourselves to God, our beginning and our end.

If already on this natural level the virtue of religion is a duty, even more so is it a duty on the supernatural level. From creature of God, man has been raised to the level of a son. It is obvious that he needs to foster this new bond of dependence, by living according to the new life begun at baptism. *Noblesse oblige!* The baptized soul is called to imitate Jesus, who is Son by nature, and like Jesus to offer himself totally and completely for the glory of his Father and the salvation of souls.

O Jesus, aware of my state as creature and of my dignity as child of God, I adore You and I love You. Help me to live a life always worthy of my nature and my destiny.

Prayer

Help me, O God, by Your grace, to render You all the homage of which I am capable.

— Fr. Gabriel, DI, p. 816

Or else:

O God, our Father, infuse into my soul the true spirit of piety and devotion.

— Fr. Gabriel, DI, p. 819

Thoughts

- The law of adoration, written in the book of nature and in the depths of our reason, was inscribed on the stone tablets of Moses and in the Gospel of Jesus Christ.
  — H.E. Bishop Pierre Marceillac, PL, 1918
- I forgot my own indignity and dared all things, asked all things, expected all things, convinced that God can refuse us nothing when we speak to Him through the wounds of Jesus.
  — Pauline Jaricot, TD, March 7

Resolutions

1. To recite three times the prayer, "My God, I believe, I adore, I hope and I love You. I ask pardon for all those who do not believe, do not adore, do not hope..."
2. To meditate for ten minutes on our duties toward God, in order to live more fully our dependence upon Him.
3. To offer a sacrifice for the salvation of an unbeliever.

THE SANCTIFICATION OF SUNDAY

Monday of the 16th Week after Pentecost

God speaks to us:

The Lord blessed the seventh day, and sanctified it.

Exodus 20:11

Meditation

In order to help us practice the virtue of religion, our good God chose a special day for Himself, a particular day of the week.

Already in the Old Testament, God had reserved to Himself the seventh day, or sabbath day, Saturday, on which He was to be honored in a particular way. Think back to the promulgation of the Decalogue, the ten commandments, on Mount Sinai. God said to Moses, "Remember that thou keep holy the sabbath day. Six days shalt thou labor, and shalt do all thy works. But on the seventh day is the sabbath of the Lord thy God: thou shalt do no work on it, thou nor thy son, nor thy daughter, nor thy manservant, nor thy maidservant, nor thy beast, nor the stranger that is within thy gates. For in six days the Lord made heaven and earth, and the sea, and all the things that are in them, and rested on the seventh day: therefore, *the Lord blessed the seventh day, and sanctified it*" (Ex. 20:8-11). The sabbath was a day set aside exclusively for God.

Our Lord told us very clearly that He had not come to abolish the Law but to fulfill it. Accordingly, He reserved to Himself Sunday to replace the sabbath. The *Catechism of the Council of Trent* gives us the reasons: "The Church of God has thought it well to transfer the celebration and observance of the Sabbath to Sunday. For, as on that day light first shone on the world, so by the Resurrection of our Redeemer on the same day, by whom was thrown open to us the gate to eternal life, we were called out of darkness into light; and hence the Apostles would have it called the Lord's Day."[34]

May this Sunday's Gospel, which speaks of respect of the Sabbath, remind us how important it is, and even how essential, to sanctify the day of the Lord. May our Lady obtain for us the grace to be absolutely convinced of it, in a time when this duty is too often neglected.

Help me, Lord Jesus, to sanctify Sunday by dedicating this day to developing my union with You.

Prayer

My God, I want Sunday to become again, for me and all my household, what it should be for everyone: the day of the Lord.

— St. Alphonsus Liguori, HDD, p. 324

Or else:

Live in us, Lord Jesus, and make us live of You and through You.

— Fr. Emmanuel, M, p. 289

Thoughts

- After having spent the whole week scarcely thinking of God, it is only justice that we spend Sunday praying and thanking God... The profanation of Sunday leads to indifference.

  — Curé of Ars, TD2, September 10

- Sanctify Sunday by refraining from all forbidden work, by assisting piously at the Holy Sacrifice of the Mass, and by dedicating this day to practices of devotion that will truly make it the Lord's day.

  — H.E. Bishop Cosme Jorcin, PL, 1926

Resolutions

1 To recite a decade of the rosary in reparation for the profanation of Sunday.

2 To read in our catechism the section about the precepts of the Church.

3 To make a point of stepping into the office in the morning in a good mood.

---

[34] *Catechism of the Council of Trent*, part III, ch. 3, p. 402.

ATTENDANCE AT MASS

Tuesday of the 16th Week after Pentecost

GOD SPEAKS TO US:

I will go unto the altar of God, unto God who giveth joy to my youth.
Psalm 42:4

MEDITATION

The Church, who is a mother, has determined that the sanctification of the Lord's Day should happen primarily through attendance at holy Mass. The first duty of man is to adore God. Yet for his oblation to be accepted by God, he must go through our Lord. Our Lord is the bridge, the pontiff, the intermediary, the mediator between God and us. Consequently, priest and faithful must be united to Him if their offering is to be agreeable to God. This union is symbolized by the drop of water mixed into the wine at the Offertory. When the priest, at the altar, pours a drop of water into the chalice, this drop represents the faithful, who are called to be purified by contact with the blood of Jesus, symbolized by the wine. Thus, priest and faithful are united to the grace of our Lord. By this union, Jesus brings us with Him into His oblation. It is marvelous.

We understand why the Church asks us to come to Mass every Sunday. There we practice the virtue of religion in the most beautiful way possible—the most sublime, the most perfect way possible. There is no more beautiful prayer here on earth than to offer oneself with our Lord on the altar. Let us not forget that the sacrifice of the Mass and the sacrifice of the Cross are identical. The priest is the same: our Lord Jesus Christ; the victim is the same: again, our Lord Jesus Christ; only the manner of offering is different: henceforth the sacrifice is unbloody. The Secret prayer of the ninth Sunday after Pentecost describes the marvelous effects of the Mass in these words: "As often as the memorial of this Victim is celebrated, the work of our Redemption is wrought." Therefore, there

Tuesday of the 16th Week after Pentecost

is nothing more beautiful for a Catholic than to unite himself to this burning furnace of love which is the sacrifice of Jesus, and then to live as a victim of love himself, in the image of the divine Master and His holy mother. Let us therefore resolve today to do all that is in our power to attend Sunday Mass every week.

Our Lady, grant me the grace to attend Mass in a spirit of oblation, as you yourself did on Good Friday, at the foot of the cross, on Calvary.

Prayer

O Jesus, immolated at every moment of the day on our altars, let me share in Your Sacrifice.

— Fr. Gabriel, DI, p. 481

Or else:

[Deign, O Jesus, divine victim of the altar,] to penetrate the minds of the faithful with the most radiant lights, and to move their hearts, so that they might receive through holy Mass the fruits of the tree of the cross: the abundant and infinitely precious graces of the redemptive immolation.

— H.E. Bishop Maurice Clément, PL, 1934

Thoughts

- [The sacrifice of the Mass] is the highest adoration, the greatest thanksgiving, the most effective expiation, the most powerful supplication.
  — H.E. Bishop Olivier de Durfort de Civrac de Lorge, PL, 1932

- In order to draw from the holy sacrifice [of the Mass] the most abundant fruits for your souls, you must unite yourselves to it in an effective way and offer it with the priest, for it is also your sacrifice.
  — H.E. Bishop Olivier de Durfort de Civrac de Lorge, PL, 1932

Resolutions

1. For ten minutes to unite ourselves to the Masses being celebrated around the world and to beg for the blessings of the divine Victim.

2. To attend Mass every Sunday and, if possible, at least once during the week.

3. To read in our catechism the section on the Mass, or to open our missal to read the Epistle and Gospel of the day.

SANCTIFICATION OF THE FAMILY
THROUGH MASS

Wednesday of the 16th Week after Pentecost

God speaks to us:

One of the soldiers opened His side with a lance, and immediately there came out blood and water.

St. John 19:34

Meditation

God willed to create woman by drawing from the side of Adam, during his sleep, what was necessary for her creation.

What happened then happened again at the birth of the Church, mystical Spouse of our Lord. As the new Adam slept the sleep of death, His heart was pierced, and from this heart was born the Church, His mystical Spouse. The birth of woman is the symbol of the birth of the Church from the side Jesus pierced by the lance. Water and blood flowed from His side opened by the blow of the lance: water, symbol of baptism; and blood, symbol of the Holy Eucharist and of the other sacraments. Thus, the grace of marriage is in relation to the sacrifice of our Lord Jesus Christ. It is this relation which makes it so imperative that Christian spouses come to Mass regularly. There they can renew or increase the grace received at their marriage.

By attending the renewal of the sacrifice of Jesus, Catholic spouses feel stronger to face the difficulties and trials inherent to their state of life, for they have the power to associate those difficulties with the redemptive sacrifice.

Moreover, the fecundity of the Church is also an image of the fecundity of Christian marriages. Drawing strength and courage from the sacrifice of our Lord, Christian spouses accept generously to bring into the world and to raise in a Christian manner the children that God gives them. The contemplation of the sacrifice of our Lord is a constant encouragement to increase in family virtues. We see how the Mass is truly the foundation stone of the Christian family.

It is certain that if all families were faithful to sanctifying their Sunday by attendance at the holy sacrifice of the Mass, we would not have to weep over so many divorces, so much disunity, so much selfishness—all the reasons family and society are in such decline.

Lord Jesus, as I become more aware of the place of Mass in the sanctification of the family, I wish to attend with always more devotion and to offer for my sanctification whatever sufferings I must endure.

Prayer

Give me, O Lord, a better understanding of the value and meaning of Your Eucharistic Sacrifice.

— Fr. Gabriel, DI, p. 478

Or else:

Hallowed be Thy name! Hallowed in my heart and through all my works; hallowed in my family and in all the universe.

— Pauline Jaricot, TD, May 6

Thoughts

- Nothing guarantees more surely the holiness of the Christian home than frequent communion.
  — H.E. Bishop Jean Chesnelong, PL, 1921

- Every member of the faithful who comes forward alone to the holy table unites himself to the source of joy, but how much more so does a family whose members come all together to receive the heavenly nourishment!
  — H.E. Bishop Jean Chesnelong, PL, 1921

Resolutions

1 To make a spiritual communion if we cannot receive sacramentally, offering it for the members of our family.

2 To renew before God the commitment made on the day of your marriage, and all day long to look only at the qualities of your spouse and to bless God for them.

3 To read in our missal the propers of the wedding Mass.

SANCTIFICATION OF SOCIETY THROUGH THE MASS

Thursday of the 16th Week after Pentecost

God speaks to us:

Jesus answered [Pilate], "Thou sayest it; I am a king."

St. John 18:37

Meditation

Catholic societies long ago gravitated to the altar and lived around it as their center. Since the family is the basic unit of society, as Catholics become holy, so does society. Thus, Cardinal Pie did not hesitate to proclaim that, "Sunday is the keystone of the entire religious and social edifice. Every dogmatic truth, every moral law, every useful practice is somehow tied to the sanctification of Sunday."[35] Indeed, "a society… is a moral person dependent upon God as are the individuals who make it up. Consequently, society has duties which it fulfills by collective acts of adoration, thanksgiving, contrition, and petition."[36] Moreover, at the foot of the altar, there are neither rich nor poor, neither wise nor ignorant, neither great nor little; there are only children of a same Father, redeemed by the same blood of Christ, drawing grace and strength from the same sacraments.

History teaches that the first Christian nation, France, eldest daughter of the Church, as long as she remained faithful to her vocation and to her Christian traditions, sanctioned with her authority the Church law of Sunday rest. Beautiful fruits resulted from this fidelity. Charitable initiatives of past centuries, such as schools, hospitals, homes for the

---

[35] *Works of His Excellency the Bishop of Poitiers*, III, p. 348.
[36] H.E. Bishop Olivier de Durfort de Civrac de Lorge, *Pastoral Letter*, 1932.

aged, and houses of formation of the clergy were all works that arose in the atmosphere of the liturgy.

Unfortunately, the impious Revolution wanted to destroy what God had established. The goal of the revolutionaries was to make Sunday a day without God, and ultimately a day against God. Today, we find the same attacks on Sunday rest. As Catholics, we have to react and not let ourselves be carried along by this wave of anti-Christianity, in spite of ourselves. Let us beg our good God to have pity on us and let us do what is in our power to give Jesus back the place in civilization that He deserves.

Prayer

Heart of Jesus, save my homeland! Give us back respect for Your holy day.

— St. Alphonsus Liguori, TD, p. 159

Or else:

O eternal Father, permit me to offer You the heart of Jesus, Your beloved Son, as He offers Himself to You in the Holy Sacrifice of the altar.

— Fr. Gabriel, DI, p. 479

Thoughts

- Civilization is not something yet to be found, nor is the New City to be built on hazy notions; it has been in existence and still is: it is Christian civilization, it is the Catholic City. It has only to be set up and restored continually... *Omnia instaurare in Christo.*

    — St. Pius X, "Our Apostolic Mandate"

- Until the last day of the world that Mass will be celebrated which presents to the Father the perfect sacrifice, treasure of all grace, reparation of all offense, consolation of all distress.

    — Fr. Calmel, 365 D, February 3

Thursday of the 16th Week after Pentecost

Resolutions

1. To pray to Jesus that He be restored to His rightful place in civilization, offering Him a decade of the rosary for this intention.
2. Not to criticize our superior and not to complain about our colleagues.
3. To uphold those schools that are truly Catholic and that dare to teach the doctrine of the Church as the center of education.

SERVILE WORKS

Friday of the 16th Week after Pentecost

God speaks to us:

The seventh day is the day of the Sabbath... Thou shalt not do any work therein, thou nor thy son nor thy daughter, nor thy manservant nor thy maidservant.

Deuteronomy 5:14

Meditation

Last Sunday's Gospel spoke of respect for the Sabbath. This is a good opportunity for us to remember what is entailed by the precept of the third commandment: "Keep holy the Lord's Day." Certainly, we are not to exaggerate and keep Sunday with the strictness of the Pharisees, but neither should we exaggerate in the other direction, as though there were no boundaries. The Pharisees thought everything was forbidden, but how many today suppose everything is permitted! The third commandment forbids us to accomplish servile works on Sunday, that is, works which demand physical strength, contrary to the rest prescribed by the Law of God. Manual works are therefore forbidden, like gardening or building projects around the house. Theologians specify that it would be gravely sinful for a person to do such work for more than two or three hours. We therefore must be organized in order to do this kind of work on another day. Let us remember the message of our Lady at La Salette. She said that the two things that displeased her divine Son the most were the blasphemies of peasants and people working on Sunday. "'Six days I have given you to labor, the seventh I have kept for Myself; and they will not give it to Me.' It is this which makes the arm of my Son so heavy."[37]

---

[37] Br. Paul-Marie, *The Apparition and the Secret of La Salette*, p. 12.

Friday of the 16th Week after Pentecost

In the same time period, the Curé of Ars was fighting to convince his parishioners to rest on Sunday.

Servile work is forbidden, but reading and study are permitted, as well as games that are in accord with the sanctification of Sunday. Works that serve the community are also permitted, such as restaurant work, transportation, and works related to health and safety.

The profanation of Sunday opens the door to the ruin of society... The prophet Ezechiel, speaking in the name of the Lord our God, deplored, "they had violated My Sabbaths, and their eyes had been after the idols of their fathers" (Ez. 20:24). And ourselves today: have we forgotten that nations are reborn at the foot of the altar?

Lord Jesus, teach me not to neglect the sanctification of the Lord's Day.

Prayer

O Lord, reveal to me the beauty of Your [law], teach me to love it ardently and trustfully.

— Fr. Gabriel, DI, p. 687

Or else:

May Your will be my will, my passion, my honor! Grant that I may seek it, find it, and accomplish it.

— Fr. Gabriel, DI, p. 821

Thoughts

- That we might belong to Him more completely and live in greater intimacy with Him, God wills that on this day, on Sunday, we set aside those daily cares and labors that absorb us too entirely.
— H.E. Bishop Alphonse Gaudron, PL, 1949

- Between God and us, it is not merely a question of commandments; it is essentially a question of love. God loves us; He has given us so many proofs of that love! What is our response?
— H.E. Bishop Alphonse Gaudron, PL, 1949

Resolutions

1. To ask forgiveness, by an act of contrition, for all the times that we have worked on Sunday, whether by thoughtlessness or by neglect of duty on other days.
2. To meditate for ten minutes on the Passion of our Lord and His death on the cross.
3. To use our Sunday to visit a sick friend or an elderly person or to call someone who is lonely.

SUNDAY REST

Saturday of the 16th Week after Pentecost

GOD SPEAKS TO US:

Observe the day of the Sabbath, to sanctify it, as the Lord thy God hath commanded thee.

Deuteronomy 5:12

MEDITATION

Why did God make this precept? Why is there an obligation to rest on Sunday? Above all, in order to allow our souls to rise up to God, and also to give us a chance to relax physically and strengthen the bonds among family members. If a man worked seven days out of seven, he would be exhausted physically and common life would be nearly impossible.

Let us remember the parable of the sower. The sower had sown seed in his field and noticed that some of the seed did not come to fruition because of the thorns that were growing all around and stifling the young seedling. Our Lord explains that the thorns are the cares of this world, that overwork which takes the soul and hinders it from rendering its duties to God. It is therefore a very good thing that God has given us this Sunday rest to keep us from overwork and to foster union in our families!

Let us therefore remember that the first goal of the restrictions imposed by the third commandment is to take away this obstacle to the flourishing of the divine life in our soul.

We can see the importance of Sunday rest and attendance at Mass in order to sanctify this day of the Lord. All of Sunday belongs to God, and so it is also a very good idea to attend vespers if we have the possibility, or at least say our rosary and take the time to learn more about the truths of religion. Let us remember what the Curé of Ars said: "I often think that most of the Christians who are in Hell lost their souls because of a lack of religious instruction."[38] And so let us make Sunday a day truly consecrated to God.

If we sanctify the Lord's day as true Christians, God will shower His blessings on us during our life on earth, and He will give us the eternal rest and happiness of Heaven.

Lord Jesus, encouraged by Your promises, I resolve from now on to be more faithful to the precept of Sunday rest.

Prayer

Glory be to God on high, and on earth peace to men of good will. We praise Thee; we bless Thee; we adore Thee; we glorify Thee. We give Thee thanks for Thy great glory.

— *Gloria* of Mass

Or else:

O Lord, save Thy people, and bless Thine inheritance. Govern them, and lift them up for ever.

— *Te Deum*

Thoughts

- The law of rest on Sunday is God's right, and it is also the right of the laborer; it is the sacred patrimony of his body and soul.
  — H.E. Bishop Jules de Carsalade du Pont, PL, 1902
- In ordaining one day of the week as a day of rest for man, God's first intention was to ensure him the necessary freedom to look to his soul and accomplish his religious duties.
  — H.E. Bishop Cosme Jorcin, PL, 1926

Resolutions

1. To reread last Sunday's Gospel.
2. To invite someone to Mass next Sunday so that he might fulfill this religious duty.
3. To avoid shopping or selling on Sunday, to help it better remain a day of rest.

---

[38] J. Frossard, *Select Thoughts of the Curé of Ars*, p. 18.

JESUS CHRIST, SON OF GOD

17th Sunday after Pentecost

God speaks to us:

What do you think of the Christ?

St. Matthew 22:42

Meditation

This Sunday's Gospel recounts that, "while the Pharisees were gathered together, Jesus questioned them, saying, *"What do you think of the Christ?"* (Mt. 22:41-42) When we read the Gospel attentively, we realize that Jesus had only one desire, one concern, throughout His entire public life, and that was to show the Jews, and to all men, that He was the awaited Messiah, the Word incarnate, the living image of the Father.

It is this good news that the whole Gospel announces. We see it very well in the conversation with the Samaritan woman, as our Lord draws her little by little to rise from earthly considerations to spiritual considerations, until finally she is able to say, "I know that Messias is coming, and when he comes he will tell us all things." And Jesus answers her, "I who speak with thee am He" (Jn. 4:25-26).

With Nicodemus, it is the same thing. We find this same progression, this same spiritual lifting up toward the proclamation of the divinity of our Lord: "No one has ascended into heaven except … the Son of Man who is in Heaven" (Jn. 3:13).

Today's Gospel brings us the same idea: *What do you think of the Christ?*

We know the answer to this question.

We know that Christ is the Word of God, the second Person of the Holy Trinity, who took a human nature to redeem us from sin and lead us to eternal life. Yet even though we know our Lord, maybe we sometimes forget to reproduce in ourselves certain aspects of His life, certain particular traits of His existence.

Let us try to reflect on what our Lord should be for us and in us. We know that He should be our model, our reference, our ideal. "It is now no longer I that live, but Christ lives in me" (Gal. 2:20). Christian life consists in living the life of our Lord, modeling ourselves on Him. The imitation of Jesus Christ is therefore a duty for every one of the faithful. If we examine ourselves on this point, what do we find?

Lord Jesus, I see very well that I have a hard time reproducing Your virtues in my life. Yet You are my model. Help me to imitate You in my daily life.

Prayer

O gentle Jesus, gentleness itself, O Lamb of God, who bear and take away the sins of the world, have pity on us.

— Fr. Emmanuel, M, p. 417

Or else:

O Lord, in simplicity of heart I offer myself to You this day, to be Your servant for ever: I do this as an act of homage to You, and as an act of perpetual praise.

— *Imitation of Christ*, IV, ch. 9

Thoughts

- Let the life of Jesus Christ be our first consideration.
  — *Imitation of Christ*, I, ch. 1
- We must strive to be penetrated by the spirit of Jesus Christ by reading over and over His words and His examples, meditating on them again and again, always.
  — Charles de Foucauld, TD, April 16

Resolutions

1. To read attentively the Gospel of this Mass.
2. To reproduce today one virtue of Jesus, the one we lack the most.
3. To bear witness in favor of Jesus Christ at the next opportunity, and even to create an occasion.

THE LOVE OF GOD FOR US

Monday of the 17th Week after Pentecost

God speaks to us:

Not that we have loved God, but that He has first loved us.

1st Epistle of St. John 4:10

Meditation

St. John, the Apostle who penetrated the most deeply into the heart of our Lord, reminds us in his first Epistle that the fundamental reason why we ought to love God is that He first loved us. What is true of God the Father is also true of Jesus, the incarnate Son of God. When our Lord came to this earth, we were His enemies, since original sin had broken the bond that united us to Him. We were ugly and disfigured by sin. And so our Lord loved His enemies in order to turn them into His friends. He loved us in order to make us beautiful. St. Augustine asks himself, "How shall we become lovely? By loving Him who is always lovely. As the love increases in thee, so the loveliness increases: for love is itself the beauty of the soul."[39] Most sublime, is that to give us this beauty, Jesus took our ugliness on Himself: "No majesty, no beauty, as we gaze upon Him" (Is. 53:2). Our Lord as God is beauty itself, yet He lost that brilliance in taking on our condition of slaves. Since our Lord loved the wicked so as to make them good, and He loved the sick so as to make them healthy, we should love Him in return with all our heart and love all men, even our enemies.

We must realize that at our birth we were enemies of God, since the stain of original sin closed us off from His love. St. Paul understood this very well when he wrote to the Romans, "If when we were enemies we were reconciled to God by the death of His Son, much more, having

---

[39] St. Augustine, Homily IX:9 on the First Epistle of St. John, in *Nicene and Post-Nicene Fathers, First Series,* vol. VII, p. 518.

been reconciled, shall we be saved by His life" (Rom. 5:10). To doubt our Lord's love for our soul is to doubt our Lord Himself, "for God is love" (I Jn. 4:8).

Lord Jesus, whatever my difficulties and my trials, help me to remember everything that You endured for my salvation, so that I may never again doubt Your love for me.

Prayer

My God, Thou hast created me for Thyself; grant that I may return to Thee and unite myself to Thee by love.

— Fr. Gabriel, DI, p. 1008

Or else:

O my Savior, You refused me neither Your blood nor Your life, and could I refuse You something You might ask of Me? No, my Jesus! You gave Yourself entirely to me, and I give myself entirely and without reserve.

— St. Alphonsus Liguori, HDD, p. 238

Thoughts

- Let us often tell ourselves the double story of the graces which God has given to us personally since our birth, and of our own infidelities; in those two tales we will find the most certain and the most moving proof of God's love for us, especially for those of us who have lived far from Him.

  — Charles de Foucauld, TD, June 18

- The love of God for us worries us more than any other love, since it is the most serious love of all, and the strongest.

  — H.E. Bishop André Fauvel, PL, 1957

Resolutions

1. To recite the act of charity and then meditate on it for ten minutes.
2. To read in our missal the account of the Passion of Jesus (Holy Week).
3. To recite or sing a *Magnificat* in thanksgiving for the graces received over the past weeks (see page 272).

CHARITY AND FRIENDSHIP

Tuesday of the 17th Week after Pentecost

God speaks to us:
No longer do I call you servants... but I have called you friends.

St. John 15:15

Meditation

Before describing charity as a virtue, St. Thomas Aquinas in his *Summa Theologica* defines it as a friendship. St. Ambrose in the fourth century spoke in the same way. For these two holy doctors of the Church, charity, the most beautiful fruit of a soul in the state of grace, is a friendship. In other words, every soul in the state of grace is a friend of God. What a marvelous thing, when you think about it!

St. Thomas takes the writings of Aristotle and applies to charity all the characteristics that the philosopher attributes to friendship. Charity, like any friendship, is first a love of benevolence, which means, a love by which I seek the good of the one I love and not a selfish satisfaction. Thus, charity leads me to desire God's happiness, and leads God to desire my happiness.

In the love of friendship, not only do we will and do good toward someone, but we will and do good toward someone who also loves us and shows himself to be our friend. In other words, there is reciprocity. St. Paul was in great wonder before this truth, and cried out, "the Son of God loved me and gave Himself up for me" (Gal. 2:20). He does not say that Christ loved men but rather, "He loved *me*." Convinced of this truth, St. Paul had only one desire: to answer love for love. Knowing that we are loved by God is the secret of happiness, the nourishment of our interior life, the motive force of our spiritual progress.

Finally, St. Thomas points out a third aspect of friendship. For a friendship to be possible between two beings, there must not only be love of benevolence and reciprocity, but a certain resemblance. The love of friendship assumes that we can have certain things in common, that we can share the same joys and the same sufferings and delight in the same happiness. For this sharing to exist, there must be a certain resemblance between two friends; we even have the saying, "Birds of a feather flock together." By nature, there is an abyss between God and us, and so God deigned to come down to our level in order to raise us up to Him, communicating to us through grace a participation in His divine life.

Lord Jesus, from this moment on, I desire to foster this friendship which You have granted me the joy to share, by Your grace.

Prayer

Lord, I come to You very simply, with total confidence, like a friend of my heart.

— Elizabeth of the Trinity, Diary, January 26, 1900

Or else:

Ah! dear friend of my heart, unite this poor soul of mine to Your singular goodness!

— Fr. Gabriel, DI, p. 1010

Thoughts

- Seek the friendship of God and you will have found your happiness... Souls who follow this interior path will know peace and sweetness.

  — Curé of Ars, TD2, July 14

- Oh, what happiness it is to make our life a heart-to-heart, an exchange of love, when we know how to find the Master in the depths of our soul. Then we are never alone anymore.

  — Elizabeth of the Trinity, L 161

Resolutions

1. To recite the *Our Father* slowly, in order to realize more fully the degree of intimacy which exists between God and ourselves.

2. To pause for a few minutes and think more deeply about the three characteristics of friendship presented in this meditation.

3. To nourish our friendship with God over the course of this day by repeating often, "Lord Jesus, I love You. Help me to love You more."

INTIMACY WITH GOD

Wednesday of the 17th Week after Pentecost

God speaks to us:

I live in the faith of the Son of God, who loved me and gave Himself up for me.

Epistle of St. Paul to the Galatians 2:20

Meditation

If we fear God more than we love Him, we will tend to flee moments of silence, shorten our thanksgiving, and avoid any silent prayer. On the contrary, if we love God more than we fear Him, we will love conversing with Him, drawing near to Him, and sharing with Him our joys and our sufferings, our desires and our fears. This relationship is what God wants of us. Do we really believe it? Is this truth really a part of us?

To believe in this truth, we need the faith. We need to have faith that a certain intimacy with God is possible in this life. We need to desire this intimacy and have the courage to break with anything that could hinder it. Any disordered attachment to a person or to oneself is an obstacle to this intimacy. It takes courage to eliminate from our life any willful attachment to the pleasures of the world, or to dangerous companions, or to some failing which we do not want to correct. When we find this courage, life quickly becomes much more beautiful, more fulfilling, more delightful. Alas, if we do not know how to love God in practice, in our life of every day, it is the sign that our faith is very weak.

Yes, we need to be honest: if we are so little concerned with the love of God for us, the reason is that the truths of religion have not yet penetrated deeply into our life. It is therefore good for us to put ourselves face to face with the great truths of our holy religion. In order to warm this virtue of charity in our heart, let us remember what God has done and what He still does for each one of us. If we do reflect generously, then little by little we will learn to see things as He sees them, to love what He loves, to detest what He detests. We will continually place our life more in harmony with His.

O our Lady, Queen of all the saints, help me to understand that God is present right now in my soul, and to do everything possible to dwell with Him in gentle confidence.

Prayer

Lord, give me light and strength to root out of my heart all that hinders me from being united to You.

— Fr. Gabriel, DI, p. 1011

Or else:

O Jesus, I wish to die, to decrease, to deny myself daily more and more, in order that You may grow and be exalted in me.

— Fr. Gabriel, DI, p. 1013

Thoughts

- This union of God with His little creature is such a beautiful thing!... In this intimate union, God and the soul are like two pieces of wax melted together.

  — Curé of Ars, TD2, June 23

- Holiness is charity, but charity in the *real*; charity to the point of heroism.

  — Fr. Calmel, 365 D, March 14

Resolutions

1. To spend ten minutes in the company of the Holy Trinity present in our soul.

2. To pinpoint the main obstacle in us to union with God and then make concrete decisions for removing them.

3. To call on our spirit of faith in order to keep our conversation around the dinner table edifying, especially when children are present or when we are among friends.

HOLINESS AND CHARITY

Thursday of the 17th Week after Pentecost

God speaks to us:

[God] chose us in Him before the foundation of the world, that we should be holy and without blemish in His sight.

Epistle of St. Paul to the Ephesians

Meditation

Every saint seems to us to be so different from all the others. They lived in different eras and had very different kinds of lives. Some are honored as martyrs, others as virgins, still others as confessors or doctors. Some lived in the world, others drew out of society and went into the desert. Some died young, others lived to extreme old age. They are each one very different, yet they have one thing in common, one thing which was the motive force of their life, their soul, all their behavior. That one thing in common is charity. The word *charity* is synonymous with *holiness*.

Ever since original sin, we all have deep inside of us a wellspring of selfishness and disordered love of ourselves. All of our disorders, all of our weaknesses, all of our miseries flow from this evil fount. The remedy to this evil is none other than charity. Whereas the selfish man brings everything back to himself, the saint refers everything back to God. And this openness to God, this preference, this choice for God which the soul makes, is an effect of charity.

And so, if we want to be saints, let us ask God often in our prayers to communicate His charity to us. We are children of God since our baptism. Our soul was made beautiful, ennobled, transformed to welcome the three divine Persons, Father, Son and Holy Ghost. From that time, two men live in us, a good one and a bad one. As long as we stay in the state of grace, there is more good in us than evil. It is true, alas, that we are more riddled with misery than we imagine, for we have deep flaws and failings that we do not suspect. Yet we are also much more worthy of love than we imagine, since God is within us, if we are in the state of grace. We therefore must not live constantly in fear, in crisis, in anxiety. God is a God of peace, and the foundation of that peace is charity, the love of God which dwells in us by grace.

Prayer

I draw near to [You], Jesus, the "fountain of life and holiness," with an ardent desire to drink from this inexhaustible fount.

— Fr. Gabriel, DI, p. 8

Or else:

O my sweet Savior, it was not only for certain privileged souls, but also for me, that You willed to merit the fullness of the life of grace which is sanctity.

— Fr. Gabriel, DI, p. 10

Thoughts

- If God is love, and if there is no authentic love outside of God, and if genuine love can flow only from a person who is in God, then we see how vain and detestable is any false, disordered love.
  — H.E. Bishop Marcel Dubois, PL, 1957
- Living in God who enfolds me and enfolds all being, I live in Love: Love is so close to me. When I act, my action also must be enfolded in this Love.
  — H.E. Bishop Marcel Dubois, PL, 1957

Resolutions

1 To meditate for ten minutes on the life of our favorite saint and then to call upon him several times over the course of the day.

2 To seek after sanctity in being very thorough in our work, for the love of God.

3 In difficulties, to fly to God right away so as not to fall into the trap of discouragement.

NO CHARITY WITHOUT SELF-SACRIFICE

Friday of the 17th Week after Pentecost

God speaks to us:

Fill up my joy by thinking alike, having the same charity, with one soul and one mind... each one looking not to his own interests but to those of others.

Epistle of St. Paul to the Philippians 2:2 and 4

Meditation

Because of the sequels left by original sin, man naturally tends to focus on himself, to seek his own ease and his comfort, without thinking of God and his neighbor.

For this reason, even though the commandment of charity may seem very natural, it requires a great spirit of renouncement and sacrifice, because it runs contrary to the disordered tendencies of our nature. Since we have a wellspring of selfishness inside us and charity is in radical opposition to that selfishness, we have to learn gradually to remove all disorder from our manner of loving.

Charity and self-seeking are incompatible, because living for self, turning everything to self, is incompatible with referring everything to God. Jesus told us very clearly that "no man can serve two masters" (Mt. 6:24).

What hinders the grace of God from coming to fruition within us, if not our self-seeking? When we seek ourselves, we fold in on ourselves and can no longer love. Love is ecstatic by definition; it goes outward toward the one loved.

For this reason, our Lord did not hesitate to say, "If anyone wishes to come after Me, let him deny himself" (Mt. 16:24). Certainly, our Lord was not wanting to impose total poverty on everyone, but He does ask everyone to be detached from the goods of this world. May those who have goods be as though they did not have them, as St. Paul says (I Col. 7:30).

Theologians explain that there are stages to pass through, in this conquest of charity. Spiritual authors speak of the purgative way as the first step, which consists above all in keeping away from sin. The second consists in seeking above all to do good, and the third aims primarily at reaching intimate union with God.

Lord Jesus, that I may accomplish Your will always, help me to renounce disordered love in myself.

Prayer

Show me, O Lord, the narrow path that leads to true life, to union with You.

— Fr. Gabriel, DI, p. 230

Or else:

With Your help, O Jesus, I want to fight more strongly against sin and try to overcome all my evil tendencies, inclinations and habits.

— Fr. Gabriel, DI, p. 154

Thoughts

- Love Christ, love Him with all your strength, and for the love of Christ, fall in love with sacrifice. There is no bargain price for true love; it is very demanding.

  — Padre Pio, TD, October 11

- We approach the infinite perfection of God only in the measure in which we take upon ourselves the work of complete self-denial.

  — Fr. Gabriel, DI, p. 153

Resolutions

1. To recite the sorrowful mysteries in reparation for all our disordered attachment to creatures.

2. To consider in what domain we need to work on self-denial: conversation, friendship, relaxation (excessive use of electronic devices…) and to take concrete action in consequence.

3. To avoid sources of fragmentation and distraction (radio, computer, cell phone) in order to unite ourselves more intimately with God.

PURITY OF INTENTION

Saturday of the 17th Week after Pentecost

GOD SPEAKS TO US:
If thy eye be sound, thy whole body will be full of light.
St. Matthew 6:22

MEDITATION

Our external actions reveal the state of our soul, and most important of all are the internal motives that pushes us toward this act rather than this other. We need to have an upright intention, a pure intention in each one of our actions. We can go to Mass out of routine or out of obligation, or else simply to see a particular person. We can also go to Mass out of love of God. Externally, the actions are the same, but in the eyes of God they are each very different. The same external act will be meritorious for some, not for others, depending on the purity of their intention. It is the same for our duty of state. We can set to work out of obligation, out of pleasure or out of love of God. The same action is meritorious for some and not for others. In this light, the most everyday actions, like running the vacuum, cleaning our office or our bedroom, mowing the lawn, all take on a new dimension. We can look at the life of St. Theresa of the Child Jesus. She did nothing extraordinary and yet she put her whole heart in her most humble tasks and so became a great saint, "the greatest saint of modern times."[40]

This is a great encouragement for us. It is not given to everyone to be able to fast or give alms, but everyone has a heart to love with. When actions are good or indifferent in themselves, the only thing that matters is our own uprightness and purity of intention.

---

[40] Statement of St. Pius X, quoted by Fr. Bernard Bro, O.P., *Saint Thérèse of Lisieux*, p. 15.

"Purity of intentions consists in doing all our actions, even the slightest, with the sole aim of pleasing God. This purity of intention is what gives all the merit to our works, because an action is good or bad in the eyes of God depending on whether we perform it with a good or a bad intention. There can be no better intention than pleasing God."[41]

Prayer

My God, from now on, this will be the cry of my heart: all for You, and only for You! Blessed Virgin, obtain for me to be faithful to this motto.
— St. Alphonsus Liguori, HDD, p. 143

Or else:

O Savior, You know what my heart is trying to say. It speaks to You, fountain of mercy; You see its desires—ah! they tend toward You only, they long for You only, they want You only.
— St. Vincent de Paul, TD2, January 30

Thoughts

- It is not the greatness of an action that gives it merit, but the purity of intention with which we perform it.
— Curé of Ars, TD2, September 7
- As we perform a good action toward our neighbor, we still have to be aware of the intention of that work: are we perhaps seeking the reward of their immediate gratitude?
— St. Gregory the Great, TD, April 13

Resolutions

1. To take special care with our prayer in the morning, in order to make our day a real offering to God and be zealous in fulfilling our slightest duties.
2. To foresee in the morning what the difficulties of the day are likely to be, so as to maintain our purity of intention through to the evening.
3. To offer for a special intention whatever is unpleasant in our work.

---

[41] St. Alphonsus Liguori, *Holiness Day by Day*, p. 143.

SPIRITUAL PARALYSIS

18th Sunday after Pentecost

God speaks to us:

And behold, they brought to [Jesus] a paralytic lying on a pallet.
Gospel: St. Matthew 9:2

Meditation

The Church offers today for our meditation one of the most striking miracles accomplished by our Lord, the healing of the paralytic of Capharnaum. At the beginning of His ministry, our Lord mainly preached in Galilee and He lived most of the time in Capharnaum, since the inhabitants of Nazareth refused to hear His preaching.

So it happened that one day when He was preaching in a house packed with people, four men let down from the roof through the ceiling a paralytic, who is suddenly there at the feet of our Lord. Obviously, this appearance interrupts our Lord's preaching. Our Lord's simple reaction is to say to the paralytic, "Take courage, son; thy sins are forgiven thee."

As always, the Pharisees, blinded by their pride, far from accepting these words of our Lord, murmur interiorly that He blasphemes, since God alone has the power to forgive sins. Instead of recognizing the divinity of our Lord, divinity manifested by all the miracles He has already accomplished, they paint Him as a liar and a blasphemer.

Though they never speak a single word, our Lord can see what they are thinking and feeling; He uncovers their malice and tries to enlighten them by asking, "Which is easier to say, 'Thy sins are forgiven thee,' or to say, 'Arise, take up thy pallet and go to thy house.'?" (Mt. 9:6). And immediately the sick man stands up, takes the stretcher under his arm and leaves the house—by the door this time—and goes back to his own house.

In this way, Jesus uses the healing of a man's body to prove the action He has performed on his soul. The physical paralysis from which this man suffered was in fact an apt image of the paralysis affecting his soul.

Sin paralyzes; it closes the soul in on itself and keeps it from advancing. The soul that lives in this way is a slave of sin and can no longer move freely. Today, let us realize more fully the gravity of sin, which hinders us from taking the smallest step toward God.

O Jesus, divine Savior, deign to free me from my sins!

Prayer

Make the flood of Your mercies, the abundance of Your graces flow into us, Lord; return to us the innocence that we have lost, and give us peace.

— Fr. Emmanuel, M, p. 417

Or else:

Good St. Joseph, obtain for me repentance and forgiveness.

— St. Alphonsus Liguori, HDD, p. 70

Thoughts

- Poor sinners: when I think that there are people who die without having tasted even for an hour the happiness of loving God!
  — Curé of Ars, TD2, October 23

- Tell your heart: "We tripped a little and stumbled; let us set off again brightly, watchful over ourselves." And every time you fall, do the same thing.
  — St. Francis de Sales, TD, February 14

Resolutions

1. To meditate for a few minutes on the gravity of mortal sin.
2. To recite one of the sorrowful mysteries of the rosary in begging pardon for our sins.
3. To say a prayer for the conversion of a member of our family and end with the words, "Our Lady of Holy Hope, convert us!"

JESUS, DOCTOR OF SOULS

Monday of the 18th Week after Pentecost

God speaks to us:

When the crowds saw [the healing of the paralytic], they were struck with fear, and glorified God who had given such power to men.

Gospel of Sunday: St. Matthew 9:8

Meditation

Jesus came on earth to heal humanity wounded by sin. The miracle of the healing of the paralytic shows us the greatness, the power and the goodness of our Lord. "Take courage, My son; thy sins are forgiven thee" (Mt. 9:2). Jesus first looks to the moral health of the unhappy man. The miracle of spiritual healing comes before that of bodily healing. Our Lord wants to make us understand that the one great evil is sin! Indeed, sin alone touches man in his vital core, because it puts the soul in a state of rupture with God. By His Incarnation, Jesus came into the world. His gaze is always upon us, following us. He knows perfectly what we are, what we think, what we do. He reads hearts. And so let us meet that gaze, to discern what He expects of us. Let us pause for a few moments to see where we are in our Christian life.

Is our faith increasing or decreasing? Is it under-nourished? Do we pray with regularity, and with confidence? Are we more and more courageous in the practice of our duty of state? Are we intent on doing good to others?

To some extent, are we like that paralytic before our Lord, held down by the chains of sin?

Our eyes may not know how to see events with the eyes of the faith, and we are probably a little cowardly, at least sometimes, in our duty to bear witness to that faith before a world that is dying because it has forgotten God.

Moreover, how much do we appreciate the sacrament of penance?

Do we realize the benefits of frequent confession? The great Pope Pius XII summed up those benefits in these words: "By [frequent confession] genuine self-knowledge is increased, Christian humility grows, bad habits are corrected, spiritual neglect and tepidity are resisted, the conscience is purified, the will strengthened… and grace is increased."[42] To us, also, does Jesus speak the words, "Arise and walk," through the priest who gives us absolution.

O Jesus, doctor of souls, help me not to neglect my examination of conscience and to have frequent recourse to the sacrament of penance.

Prayer

Heart of Jesus, atonement for our sins, have mercy on us.
— Litany of the Sacred Heart

Or else:

Lamb of God, who takes away the sins of the world, give us peace.
— *Agnus Dei* of Mass

Thoughts

- We will live well when we start making an examination of conscience every night.
  — Curé of Ars, TD2, September 4

- The light to know our sins and their wickedness, the repentance to detest them, the firm intent to renounce them, the sincerity to acknowledge them, the spirit of penance to atone for them: all of these are graces which can only come from God.
  — St. Alphonsus Liguori, HDD, p. 36-37

Resolutions

1 To take special care with our daily examination of conscience, starting today.

2 To reread last Sunday's Gospel.

3 With great intent, to place ourselves in the presence of God before praying.

---

[42] Encyclical *Mystici Corporis*, §88. Translation from the Vatican website.

THE SACRAMENT OF PENANCE

Tuesday of the 18th Week after Pentecost

God speaks to us:

The Son of Man has power to forgive sins.
Gospel of Sunday: St. Matthew 9:6

Meditation

The first requirement for healing a sick person is to identify his illness. The efficacy of the remedies chosen to combat the evil depends on the quality of the diagnosis. For this reason, Jesus created the sacrament of penance. Experience shows that those who go to confession regularly know themselves better than those who only go to confession rarely. The more we space out our confessions, the more we tend to see our sins as only relative and not so bad. On the contrary, the more frequently we go to confession, the easier it is for us to make a serious examination of conscience. The sacrament of penance is therefore an effective means for us to know ourselves better.

If we are to make progress, we must also sincerely regret what in our life displeases God. Let us avoid anything that smacks of routine, whether in our confessions or in our acts of piety. The essence of confession is not in the simple statement of our sins but in contrition. This regret is not always something we feel. It is in our will above all, and not in our senses. It leads us to will to detach ourselves from sin. This regret is what gives us horror for sin and a desire to progress. When we regret a sin, we necessarily tend to make efforts to avoid committing it again, but if we do not regret a sin, we will fall back into it on the first occasion. Regret for our sins appears in our firm purpose of amendment, that is, in the determined resolution to make real efforts to turn away from evil.

If we do not take effective means for not falling back into sin, our regret is not truly sincere. What is this firm purpose? What is that disposition of the soul which should be ours every time we come out of the confessional? The fundamental orientation that we need to have is the desire to accomplish the will of God at every moment. Sin is what is opposed to the will of God; virtue is what is in conformity with the will of God.

Lord Jesus, give me the grace always to correspond to Your divine will, for there is the secret of holiness.

Prayer

O holy Infant Jesus, who wept in the arms of Mary, remind me to call upon Your mother before confessing my sins, in order to obtain sorrow for my sins.
— St. Alphonsus Liguori, HDD, p. 37

Or else:

O Jesus, You who are ever seeking the prodigal son, despise not my contrite and humble heart, but purify it in Your precious Blood.
— Fr. Gabriel, DI, p. 204

Thoughts

- Contrition is the balm of the soul… Let us quickly heal our soul first.
  — Curé of Ars, TD2, March 1
- Let us always pray with careful recollection before every confession, to ask God to help us.
  — St. Alphonsus Liguori, HDD, p. 37

Resolutions

1 To stir up greater contrition in our soul by remembering that our sins offend God.

2 To set a no-later-than date from one confession to the next, and already decide when we will go to confession in the immediate future.

3 To make a specific resolution for avoiding the sin into which we fall most often.

OUR SPIRITUAL HEALING

Wednesday of the 18th Week after Pentecost

GOD SPEAKS TO US:
And he arose, and went away to his house.
Gospel of Sunday: St. Matthew 9:7

MEDITATION

Through the healing of the paralytic, our Lord showed us how much He desires our healing, how much He wishes to see us healthy—and healthy spiritually, above all. Here as always there is a connection between the physical form given back to the paralytic and his spiritual health.

In taking care of the paralytic, Jesus desires to heal him fully, to heal him once and for all. The cure would have been useless if it were passing and only lasted briefly. But our Lord does nothing by halves. Likewise, when He heals us in the sacrament of penance, Jesus wills our full, total, definitive healing.

Unfortunately, our spiritual health is often compromised by our continually falling back into sin. In the spiritual life, "if you are not moving forward, you are moving backward." As long as we are on this earth, we are *in via*, we are on the road, we have not yet reached our goal, we are not yet in the homeland, we are not yet in Heaven. We therefore need to be always moving forward. We must not imagine this progress as something we feel happening: grace is not in the domain of the senses. Yet, year by year, we ought to be noticing a certain progress. Alas! the experience of souls shows us that this is far from always being the case.

Many souls have episodes of fervor and then let go a little, become lukewarm and finally neglect and lose in part the gifts received from God. If we want to live always fervently, if we want to grow in the love of God and neighbor, we must open our soul to the action of grace. It is above all by living near our Lord that we will manage to be always breaking away from sin and the occasions of sin, more and more. The closer we live to God, the more we appreciate His company and the more we discover in ourselves whatever displeases Him, whatever pains Him, whatever is opposed to His love.

Lord Jesus, starting today, I wish to live more constantly in Your sweet company, by praying with greater regularity and frequently receiving the sacraments. To these supernatural means I will join natural means, for example striving to flee near occasions of sin.

Prayer

O Mary, obtain for me to weep over my sins with Jesus.
— St. Alphonsus Liguori, HDD, p. 42

Or else:

Lord, do whatever You wish; only keep me from offending You and from letting my virtues fade, if in Your goodness You have granted me any virtue.
— St. Teresa of Avila, TD, March 23

Thoughts

- There is only one means of avoiding sin, and that is to love. There is only one means of keeping from opposing God, and that is to be united to Him.
— Fr. Calmel, 365 D, March 2

- In my opinion, we would grow in virtue much more in contemplating the divine perfections than in keeping the eyes of our soul firmly fixed on this vile clay from which we draw our origin.
— St. Teresa of Avila, TD, December 7

Resolutions

1. To meditate for ten minutes on one of the perfections of God: His goodness, His power, His mercy.

2. To flee the near occasions of sin: this or that person or entertainment or reading; avoiding a particular use of the internet…

3. To pray with little phrases and liftings-up of the soul to tell the good God how much we love Him and how much we want to love Him: "Lord Jesus, I love You. Help me always to love You more."

THE FAITH OF THE PARALYTIC

Thursday of the 18th Week after Pentecost

God speaks to us:

Jesus, seeing their faith, said to the paralytic, "Take courage, son; thy sins are forgiven thee."

Gospel of Sunday: St. Matthew 9:2

Meditation

In last Sunday's Gospel, St. Matthew emphasizes the virtue of faith. Faith in Jesus is what animates the paralytic as well as those transporting him: *Jesus, seeing their faith...* The Evangelist wanted to teach us in this way that no disposition of the soul touches the heart of our Lord as much as faith does. Faith is a homage that we render to God in justice. Its proper expression is adoration, and it presupposes humility and confidence in the almighty power and the goodness of God. These qualities are all present in the soul of the paralytic and his companions.

This scene invites us to define the nature of faith, which is a virtue that God infuses into our soul. Its seat is in the intellect, but it also calls upon the will, because the truths which it presents to us are not self-evident. This virtue of faith disposes us to give our assent to the truths revealed by God and taught by His Church. The Apostle St. Paul specifies that the faith embraces all the invisible realities that make up the treasure of our hopes (Heb. 11:1). We received faith at our baptism, and we set it into motion with those first lessons of catechism received on our mother's knee, or perhaps a little after.

So as not to be discouraged by those around us who do not have the faith, let us remember that faith is the most certain of all knowledge. Miracles, prophecies and the witness of history are the three great proofs of the veracity of the Catholic religion, guarantees of its divine origin.

It is our duty not to diminish our faith by fear of displeasing the world.

St. Paul tells us that faith is a shield (Eph. 6:16). If our shield has holes in it, the arrows of the enemy will pierce through and strike us. St. John describes the faith as an instrument of triumph (I Jn. 5:4). But if our weapons are defective, they will no longer carry off the victory.

The faith which should animate us and which we have to spread is the faith in all its integrity, that of the doctors, the confessors and the martyrs—a living and active faith.

Prayer

O Jesus, I come to You like [the Apostle] Thomas; grant that I may not be unbelieving, but faithful.

— Fr. Gabriel, DI, p. 424

Or else:

My God! Make the faith live again in our midst, through the invocation of Mary and the meditation of the mysteries of Jesus.

— Pauline Jaricot, TD, May 12

Thoughts

- In our sad age of dead faith and triumphant impiety, the best means of preserving ourselves from this evil is to strengthen ourselves by the nourishment of the Eucharistic.

  — Padre Pio, TD, June 27

- If a man does not unlock in the light of faith, and with the hand of love the gate of heaven by means of this key, he never will enter there.

  — St. Catherine of Siena, D, p. 286

Resolutions

1. To recite and meditate on the Act of Faith, considering the three signs of its certainty: prophecies, miracles and the events of history.

2. To make an act of faith in God whenever some difficulty arises, and quickly to offer that difficulty to Him, in a spirit of reparation for our sins.

3. In temptations against faith, simply repeat again and again, with our hand on our heart like St. Vincent de Paul, "Lord, I believe; help my unbelief."

ARISE AND WALK

Friday of the 18th Week after Pentecost

God speaks to us:

Which is easier, to say, 'Thy sins are forgiven thee,' or to say, 'Arise and walk?'

Gospel of Sunday: St. Matthew 9:5

Meditation

When we return to God's friendship after a good confession, we receive special graces not to fall into those sins again. Someone who stays faithful to God after a good confession clearly shows the good disposition of his soul as he was going to confession. On the contrary, a person who falls just as often, confession after confession, casts doubt on whether or not he is really confessing with the right disposition.

What is the sign of a sincere regret for our sins? The mark of true penance, that is, of true repentances for our sins, is a determined and absolute will not to fall again, the definite will to renounce those sins once and for all—what we call firm purpose of amendment. If this will in us is truly uppermost and genuine, we are going see the effects. St. Bernard recognized that nothing is stronger than our will when it is undivided, in agreement with itself. So, if our resolution has no effect, it is the sign, the indication, the mark of a mediocre will, a soft will, a will without determination.

It can be good for us to stop and assess where we are in this regard. We know perfectly well, from our daily life, that when we absolutely want something that is possible for us, we put all our strength, all our energy, all our cleverness into obtaining it, and we generally succeed. For example, when our honor is at stake, we throw everything into defending ourselves and we generally do manage to clear our name. If we know that a given person is slandering us behind our back, we do not hesitate to find him and ask him to take back what he has said. Or else, when we have just recovered from an illness and we are afraid of a relapse, we are ready for any sacrifice to avoid it. We do not hesitate to follow the most rigid diet if we know that our life is at stake.

So, in the moral domain, if we do almost nothing to pull ourselves out of a state of sin, it means our repentance is not powerful or complete.

O my Jesus, help me to be firmer in my resolutions so as not to fall so often into the same sins.

Prayer

My God, do not let us fall.
— Fr. Emmanuel, M, p. 259

Or else:

O Mary, make me faithful to God until death.
— St. Alphonsus Liguori, HDD, p. 53

Thoughts

- God takes pleasure in seeing you take your little steps...
— St. Francis de Sales, TD, October 8

- Go straight to God, without taking detours. In this life we have to put one foot in front of the other, following in the steps of Jesus Christ, without slacking, without stopping, without looking to right or to left, ahead or behind… We have to walk and keep on walking.
— Pauline Jaricot, TD, February 24

Resolutions

1. To reflect seriously on the steps to be taken so as not to fall back into a specific sin.
2. To make an examination of foresight, to keep from falling into sin.
3. Over the course of the day to practice the virtue contrary to our predominant fault.

ACTS AND FRUITS OF PENANCE

Saturday of the 18th Week after Pentecost

God speaks to us:

Go thy way, and from now on sin no more.

St. John 8:11

Meditation

A person who continually falls back into sin may have had graces and desires of repentance, but certainly he did not have the acts and the fruits of repentance. The acts of repentance are effective and actual renouncement of sin, and the fruits of repentance are all the forms of satisfaction that we offer to God for our sins. A sinner who constantly falls back into the same sin may have received graces of repentance, for example on a retreat when he became aware of the gravity of his sins and wept over his current state. This sorrow in his soul was the mark of a special grace from God, but more was needed to destroy all his will to sin. At that moment of a grace of repentance, the sinner was a little like Esau when he realized that he had lost his birthright. He was profoundly unhappy but did not go on to change his behavior.

For our conversion to be effective, for it to be deep and lasting, it is not enough that we weep for a moment over our sins; we must express our repentance in our daily life, by a change of behavior. When our Lord touches our soul, let us know how to welcome His graces by sincere repentance, and let us prove the depth of this repentance not only by desire but by acts and fruits of repentance. Certainly, we cannot change completely overnight, because oftentimes we are prisoners of our bad tendencies; but it is important that we ask ourselves, "Do I really want to become good, yes or no?"

If yes, do I take the right means to do so? It is true that I cannot destroy all my defects with a wave of the hand, but it is very important that I focus my efforts in a particular direction. Otherwise, not only will I not progress, I will gradually lose all fervor, and as the years go by it will be less and less easy for me to pray and make sacrifices and perform acts of piety. I will be satisfied with a minimum, without ever putting my whole heart in what I do. So, it is up to me now to take all the means which God has placed before me.

Prayer

Heart of Jesus, wounded for love of us, make me worthy to make reparation for all the wounds our sins have inflicted upon You.
— Fr. Gabriel, DI, p. 617

Or else:

Ah! my God, do not allow me to fall back into that blindness. I now detest all those cursed satisfactions, and I love You above all things. Virgin most prudent, heal my folly.
— St. Alphonsus Liguori, HDD, p. 55

Thoughts

- To do penance is to suffer in expiation of the sins we have committed. Voluntary penance is to impose mortifications on ourselves as expiation; providential penance is to accept in a spirit of expiation all of the vexations that Providence sends our way.
— St. Alphonsus Liguori, HDD, p. 268
- Courage, my brother; do penance and change your life. Do not wait for time to go by. Give yourself to God; start loving Him really.
— St. Alphonsus Liguori, HDD, p. 156

Resolutions

1. To make a sacrifice in a spirit of repentance.
2. To plan ahead and schedule to attend a retreat at least every two years, in order to keep up our fervor; to decide on a no-later-than date for our next retreat.
3. Not to complain about the disagreeable events of the day but to accept them generously, in a spirit of reparation for our sins.

THE FIRST ESPOUSALS

19th Sunday after Pentecost

God speaks to us:

[Moses] took the blood and sprinkled it upon the people, and he said: "This is the blood of the covenant which the Lord hath made with you [on the condition that you keep] all these words."

Exodus 24:8

Meditation

As we look upon the whole of creation, we can only admire the unity of the divine plan. The hope granted to our first parents was confirmed by the patriarchs, developed in the chosen people, deepened with the prophets, and took on a new dimension with the Wisdom books.

The great stages of Revelation underline how rich and definite is the eternal plan: the victory over the serpent, the covenant with Noah (Gen. 9:8-17), with Abraham (Gen. 17:10-14), and then with Moses (Ex. 19:3-6). To Noah God gave the sign of the rainbow; to Abraham, that of circumcision; to Moses, God gave the Law. In addition, bloody sacrifices mark these key dates in the Covenant. This Covenant—which is both individual and collective—creates a framework in which man is called to live, the way a spouse lives with her husband.

Thus did God gradually reveal the great mystery of His plan of salvation, which brings man back into His love and into the great mystery of God's nature, the mystery of His Name: *He Who Is*, is *Love*; God, Being itself, is Love itself. This name of *Love* is just as mysterious, just as impenetrable, as the first name: "He Who Is" (Ex. 3:14). What a mystery, in which God *emerges* from His blessed solitude and shows His face in the mirror of a covenant, an alliance, by which He binds Himself, and loves, and gives Himself, and forgives…

What a mystery, this love of God, whose only reason is love itself, which receives nothing in comparison to what it gives, is never discouraged and never wearies, endures intact the cruelest betrayals, and perseveres, unchangeable in its force and fullness, until this unbelievable tenacity at last attains what it desired.

Yet this mystery of divine love too often encounters the refusal of the creature. From God, man received the freedom to respond positively to His plan of love, but alas! this means he has the possibility of refusing to correspond to this plan. Man can enclose himself in his selfishness and die in sin.

My God, help me not to waver and hesitate before Your repeated advances, but once and for all to answer love for love.

Prayer

O Lord of heaven and earth! the joys which You bestow on souls who give themselves entirely to You! What endearments, what sweet words are these...

— Fr. Gabriel, DI, p. 1074

Or else:

O my Lord, my Mercy and my Good! What more do I want in this life than to be so near You that there is no division between You and me?

— Fr. Gabriel, DI, p. 1074

Thoughts

- It is love that attracts, that draws God to His creatures.
  — Elizabeth of the Trinity, *Heaven in Faith*, §9[43]

- "To be a Spouse," is to have our eyes in His eyes, our heart entirely taken, completely penetrated, outside of itself and lost in Jesus, our soul full of His soul, full of His prayer, all our being captivated and given.
  — Elizabeth of the Trinity, Personal Notes, 13[44]

---

[43] In *Elizabeth of the Trinity: The Complete Works*, vol. 1, p. 97.
[44] In *Elizabeth of the Trinity: The Complete Works*, p. 905.

19th Sunday after Pentecost

Resolutions

1 To meditate for ten minutes on the mercy of God, remembering His repeated advances and invitations in the Old Testament (see today's meditation).
2 To read Exodus chapter 24 in our Bible.
3 To offer someone our help, spontaneously, for love of God.

THE WEDDING-FEAST OF THE SON

Monday of the 19th Week after Pentecost

God speaks to us:

All of you drink of this; for this is My blood of the new covenant, which is being shed for many unto the forgiveness of sins.

St. Matthew 26:27-28

Meditation

The Covenant between God and the chosen people foretells a new Covenant. The prophets Jeremias (Jer. 30-31) and Ezechiel (Ez. 36:24-29) rejoiced in this future renewal, while Jesus, a new Moses, far superior to the first, made it a reality. The new Covenant is sealed in His precious blood. St. Paul explains this fact to the Hebrews (Heb. 3 and 9). The sacrifice of Jesus establishes definitively this union between God and redeemed humanity. In reality, God never broke His Covenant, but renewed it by a threefold change: a change as regards those involved in the covenant, since the new alliance no longer ties God to Israel, but Christ to the Church; a change as regards the observances of the covenant, both moral and in the forms of worship, since the old morality and forms of worship yield to those of the Gospel; a change with regard to the spirit of the covenant, since the Holy Ghost Himself inscribes the new Covenant in the hearts of men, making this alliance one of interior holiness, above all. St. John the Baptist defined himself as the friend of the Bridegroom, who is our Lord, when he said, "He who has the bride is the bridegroom; but the friend of the bridegroom, who stands and hears him, rejoices exceedingly at the voice of the bridegroom. This my joy, therefore, is made full" (Jn. 3:29).

Moreover, Jesus Himself in the Gospel of St. Matthew used this same image of a marriage to describe the relations of God with Israel (Mt. 9:14-15). When the disciples of the Precursor came to Jesus and asked Him,

"Why do we and the Pharisees often fast, whereas Thy disciples do not fast?" our Lord answers, "Can the wedding guests mourn as long as the bridegroom is with them? But the days will come when the bridegroom shall be taken away from them, and then they will fast." Here, Jesus is showing very clearly that He is Himself the Bridegroom. Our Lord is the Bridegroom, because He unites in Himself a human nature with the divine nature, and because He came in order to seal the New Alliance in His blood, from which will be born the Church, His mystical Bride.

Prayer

O most beautiful Spouse of my soul, I offer You my will which seeks You above all else, to love You with an eternal ardor, and be united to You forever.

— Fr. Gabriel, DI, p. 1071

Or else:

May I be all Yours, Lord, and You all mine.

— Fr. Gabriel, DI, p. 1072

Thoughts

- How did God the Father celebrate the wedding feast of His Son? By uniting our nature to His Son through the Incarnation, and uniting His Church to Him, through baptism and the other sacraments.
  — Fr. Emmanuel, M, p. 313

- The Son of God, great as He is, chose a poor little bride for Himself, a bride ugly and deformed by sin. But He healed her and united Himself to her—united indissolubly by His Incarnation.
  — Fr. Emmanuel, M, p. 313

Resolutions

1 To take ten minutes out of the day to consider today's meditation, thinking in particular about the joy of John the Baptist, which is meant to be our joy, as well.

2 To renew today the promises of our baptism (in our missal).

3 Always to keep our thoughts, our choice of words and our conversation worthy of the divine Bridegroom of our soul.

THE SPOUSE

Tuesday of the 19th Week after Pentecost

God speaks to us:

She comes, the daughter of the king, all fair to see, her robe of golden cloth.

Psalm 44:14

Meditation

The bride of God is Israel; the bride of God in Christ is the Church, the new Israel, and it is also our Lady, ideal image of the Church, the Queen at the side of the King.

By the Covenant, God bound Himself to the chosen people by oath. By His own will, He is the God of this people, and they are the people of God. In the history of the chosen people, God willed to reveal Himself as God, as the particular God of Israel, and as the Bridegroom of Israel. Thus, this chosen people received the names of "servant of Yahweh," "firstborn son," "flock of the Lord," and "favorite vineyard."

Beginning with the prophet Osee, the chosen people received the name of *bride*! "Judge your mother," God cries out through the voice of the prophet; "judge her: because she is not My wife, and I am not her husband." (Os. 2:2) This bride is called by many names, all rich in meaning: "the virgin of Israel" (Jer. 31:4 and 21), and "the daughter of Sion" (Lam. 1:6; Is. 1:8), "the daughter of Jerusalem" (Lam. 2:13), "the virgin" (Is. 7:14), "the queen" (Ps. 44:10).

Thus, God presents Israel to us in the image of a woman, a virgin and a mother.

In the silence of prayer, let us try to discern this divine love, as God contemplates this woman who is Israel and tells her, "Thou hast wounded My heart, My sister, My spouse, thou hast wounded My heart with one glance of an eye." (Cant. 4:9) This woman is a virgin: "My sister,

My spouse is a garden enclosed, a garden enclosed, a fountain sealed up." (Cant. 4:12) And this virgin is a mother. She conceives and bears Emmanuel, by a miracle of virginity, as a sign of the divine power, for the Messianic kingdom. (Is. 7:14)

Thus St. John in his Apocalypse, indicating the role of Mary in the battle against the Enemy, combines in a single brief image the woman of Genesis, the woman of the prophecy of Isaiah, the woman of Cana, the woman of Calvary, and shows us the great sign in the heavens, that which St. Paul called the great mystery, the sign which is none other than the woman clothed in the sun and giving birth to her Son and to the members of His Mystical Body (Apoc. 12).

Our Lady, Ark of the Covenant, pray for us.

Prayer

Ah, [Mary,] unite me to my God, and unite me so that I can never be separated from His love.

— St. Alphonsus Liguori, GM, p. 185

Or else:

Oh Mother of Mercy… do help me and save me.

— St. Alphonsus Liguori, GM, p. 199

Thoughts

- God has the name of Master so that we might fear Him, of Father so that we might honor Him, and of Bridegroom so that we might love Him.

  — St. Gregory the Great, TD, January 19

- To be a "bride of Christ"… is to have all rights over His heart… It is a heart-to-heart for our whole life long… It is to live with… always with….

  — Elizabeth of the Trinity, Personal Notes 13

Resolutions

1. To meditate for at least ten minutes on the *fiat* of Mary on the day of the Annunciation.
2. To recite a decade of the rosary for women who are unable to have children and for mothers who have a handicapped child, so that they might always have the strength to accept their trial.
3. To acquire the habit of ejaculatory prayer, to beg for the intercession of the Blessed Virgin in every circumstance, saying for example, "O Mary, my good mother, protect me."

THE ATTITUDE OF THOSE INVITED TO THE FEAST

Wednesday of the 19th Week after Pentecost

God speaks to us:

[The King] sent his servants to call them that were invited to the marriage, and they would not come.

Gospel of Sunday: St. Matthew 22:3

Meditation

Those invited to the marriage are the Jews. They received the invitation from the prophets over the course of the Old Testament. Yet, in their blindness, those who had been invited refused to come. They did not listen to the messages of the prophets; they refused to believe them. But God is infinitely patient and He never stopped trying to reach them, in spite of this first refusal. He never stopped repeating His call, sending the same message. "Again he sent other servants, saying, 'Tell them that were invited: Behold, I have prepared by dinner, my beeves and fatlings are killed, and all things are ready: come ye to the marriage'" (Mt. 22:4). Oh, marvel of stubbornness! "They neglected: and went their ways, one to his farm, and another to his merchandise" (Mt. 22:5). Indeed, after the death of the first servants, God sent new prophets, all the way to John the Baptist. Finally, He sent His own Son to call the Jews to the marriage feast. Jesus called to them when He said, "Come to Me, all you who labor and are burdened, and I will give you rest" (Mt. 11:28). Our Lord called them when He cried out, "If anyone thirst, let him come to Me and drink" (Jn. 7:37). He called them finally one last time from the cross itself, crying out, "I thirst" (Jn. 19:28).

Despite all God's advances, the Jews obstinately refused. They took no account of the invitation and "went their ways, one to his farm, and another to his merchandise." What do "farm" and "merchandise" mean here? They mean material occupations. St. Paul tells us, "The sensual man does not perceive the things of God" (I Cor. 2:14).

Those who were invited therefore deliberately refused the beautiful offer which was held out to them, to come to the marriage feast. But their madness did not stop there. Their attitude was even more reprehensible, more lamentable, more deplorable. They went so far as to put to death the servants of the king. "And the rest laid hands on his servants, and having treated them contumeliously, put them to death" (Mt. 22:6). They put to death the prophets, they crucified Christ, they killed the Apostles.

My God, never allow me to fall into blindness.

Prayer

Oh! may my soul be numbered with those who hear You, my God. You call to me; make it so I always answer You, so that I might be present at the marriage feast in time and in eternity.

— Fr. Emmanuel, M, p. 314

Or else:

By Your grace, my God, grant me to answer the vocation You have given me.

— Fr. Emmanuel, M, p. 315

Thoughts

- How many times did God through His prophets invite the Jews to the marriage of the Savior. But the Jews refused to come: they forgot all of God's warnings, and when the Bridegroom was in their midst, they did not recognize Him.

  — Fr. Emmanuel, M, p. 314

- O what a tremendous mystery! God calls, and there are souls that do not listen to Him; God calls, and there are souls who listen.

  — Fr. Emmanuel, M, p. 314

Wednesday of the 19th Week after Pentecost

Resolutions

1. To take fifteen minutes of silence over the course of the day to listen to God and to act in consequence: to set aside our cell phone and limit as much as possible our use of the internet.
2. To say a prayer for priestly and religious vocations.
3. To make the sign of the cross with attention and devotion, remembering the price of our salvation. To help the children (young and old) to make this sign of the cross seriously.

THE WEDDING GARMENT

Thursday of the 19th Week after Pentecost

God speaks to us:

The king went in to see the guests; and he saw there a man who had not on a wedding garment.

Gospel of Sunday: St. Matthew 22:11

Meditation

To be allowed into the marriage feast of the king's son, there is one condition. Our Lord affirms that we need to have a wedding garment if we are to participate. We are all invited to the feast, but we must have that garment in order to partake. Those who do not have this garment at the moment of their death will be cast "into the exterior darkness: there shall be weeping and gnashing of teeth" (Mt. 22:13). What is meant by this garment? Obviously, it must mean something which is not shared by good and bad alike, since it is precisely what the wicked are lacking. By process of elimination, let us consider what this garment can signify. Of all the gifts of God, which is the one not shared by good and bad alike? We owe to God the fact of being human and not mere animals, but that gift is common to wicked men and good men.

Every day, light shines from the heavens and rain falls to allow plants and trees to grow, but God showers these gifts on good and bad alike. Let us enter the hall of the marriage feast and look closely at each of the guests, that is, baptized Catholics. Baptism is a gift of God as well, but it too is given to the wicked and the good. Is the wedding garment the gift of faith? No, not that either: the faith is not the gift meant by the wedding garment. St. James tells us that even devils believe and tremble (Jas. 2:19). Devils have faith, but they do not have the wedding garment.

So what is this gift? St. Paul gives us the answer. In his Epistle to the Corinthians, he cries out, "If I distribute all my goods to feed the poor, and I deliver my body to be burned…" (I Cor. 13:1-3)—those are all riches described by St. Paul! Still, none of these gifts is the wedding garment.

O great St. Paul, what then is this gift? The Apostle defines it very clearly: "Yet [if I] do not have charity, it profits me nothing" (I Cor. 13:3). Charity then is the wedding garment, or else that synonym of the word *charity*, the state of grace.

Lord Jesus, deign to clothe me in the wedding garment so that I might serve You here below and merit to join You one day in Heaven.

Prayer

O Lord, grant that Your grace in me may not be void.
— Fr. Gabriel, DI, p. 731

Or else:

O Lord, grant that by charity I may really participate in Your life of love.
— Fr. Gabriel, DI, p. 725

Thoughts

- Think of the wedding hall that was the soul of [St.] Paul… How strongly he was united by love to Almighty God, since he considered that, for him, life was Christ alone, and death was a gain!
— St. Gregory the Great, TD, January 25

- At the death of each one of us, the King visits His guests and then He sees if each of us is wearing the wedding garment, that is to say, sanctifying grace, divine charity, in which our Lord clothed us at our baptism.
— Fr. Emmanuel, M, p. 318

Resolutions

1. To foster our interior life by frequently casting an inner gaze of love upon God in our soul.
2. To recite a decade of the rosary for catechumens and to beg for the grace of baptism for a pagan.
3. To remain in the state of grace at all costs, and so to turn to the Blessed Virgin for help at the least temptation.

HELL

Friday of the 19th Week after Pentecost

God speaks to us:

The king said to the waiters: "Bind his hands and feet, and cast him into the exterior darkness: there shall be weeping and gnashing of teeth."

Gospel of Sunday: St. Matthew 22:13

Meditation

Yesterday we saw that the wedding garment, in which we must be clothed if we are to participate in the wedding feast of the king's son, is sanctifying grace. The man who does not have this garment, who is separated from God by mortal sin, has no claim to enter the wedding feast, that is, the happiness of Heaven. *Bind his hands and feet, and cast him into the exterior darkness: there shall be weeping and gnashing of teeth.*

Thus, one of those invited to the feast is not allowed in, because he did not put on his wedding garment. What can this exclusion mean, if not exclusion from Paradise? Indeed, the parable begins with the words, "The Kingdom of Heaven is likened to a king, who made a marriage for his son" (Mt. 22:2). The happiness of Heaven is presented in the form of a meal. And the motive of the soul's exclusion is his failure to wear the proper garment. Not only is that guest kept out of the feast, but he must endure the pains of hell: *Bind his hands and feet, and cast him into the exterior darkness: there shall be weeping and gnashing of teeth.* Let us meditate for a few moments on this great truth of our faith which the Church placed before our eyes last Sunday. Since it is difficult to consider every aspect of the pains of hell in a single glance, let us think first about its eternity. We read in St. Matthew that God will tell the damned on the day of Judgment, "Depart from Me, accursed ones, into the everlasting fire which was prepared for the devil and his angels" (Mt. 25:41). Likewise, St. Paul affirms that those who do not obey the Gospel of our Lord Jesus Christ "will be punished with eternal ruin, away from the face of the Lord" (II Thess. 1:9). Hell is indeed eternal. In the 13th century, Pope Innocent IV wrote to the bishop of Tusculum, "If anyone dies unrepentant in the state of mortal sin, he will undoubtedly be tormented forever in the fires of an everlasting hell."[45]

Prayer

[The sinner] did not want the joys of the wedding feast; let him then weep eternally... My God, preserve me from such a sentence!
— Fr. Emmanuel, M, p. 318

Or else:

O Justice of my God, how dreadful you are! My God, how I love instead to take shelter in the bosom of Your mercy, and there to enjoy the marriage feast of the Savior whom You gave us!
— Fr. Emmanuel, M, p. 316

Thoughts

- If you can endure so little now, how could you endure the pains of hell?
  — *Imitation of Christ*, I, ch. 24

- My very dear brethren, since never-ending groaning in hell is to follow these present joys, then flee here on earth all vain rejoicing, if you fear to weep hereafter.
  — St. Gregory the Great, TD, January 18

Resolutions

1 To meditate for ten minutes on the eternity of hell, thinking of the torments that we fear the most.

2 To repeat several times over the course of the day the prayer of Fatima: "O my Jesus, forgive us our sins, save us from the fires of hell, and lead all souls to Heaven, especially those most in need of Thy mercy."

3 To offer the vexations and sufferings of our day for the conversion of a sinner.

---

[45] DZ 839 (457), in *The Church Teaches*, p. 348.

HEAVEN

Saturday of the 19th Week after Pentecost

God speaks to us:

The kingdom of Heaven is likened to a king, who made a marriage for his son.

Gospel of Sunday: St. Matthew 22:2

Meditation

The marriage of the king's son invites us to think about the happiness of Heaven. In Heaven, the just delight in all that is good without suffering any evil. To form a better idea of the happiness of Heaven, we can imagine a great artist. Imagine him truly a genius, without rival anywhere on earth. He has managed to develop his art to the point of perfection, and now, having all the time in the world, a massive fortune and all the materials he needs, he decides to bring into reality the dream of a lifetime, the masterpiece of all masterpieces. He sets to work; he engages all his talent, all of his energy, all of his abilities and his entire fortune to bring about this dream. Once he has finished, his painting is superb, but to the great surprise of all around him, the artist himself remains dissatisfied. He gives in to thoughts of discouragement. He sees the great distance there is between his dream and the reality he has produced. Face to face with the clear evidence of his own limitations, he is discouraged, downcast, demoralized. If the hand and the power of this artist had been equal to the desires and aspirations of his soul, the work of art in front of us would have been even more sublime, more beautiful, more majestic. Certainly, in that case, the artist would have been satisfied with his masterpiece; he would have attained his ideal.

Maybe we think this example gives us an idea of what Heaven must be: the ideal of happiness that a man imagines for himself. Yet, that is not what Heaven is, because whatever happiness you imagine, however magnificent and sublime it may be, what you are imagining still remains a human happiness. Heaven is not a human ideal; it is a divine ideal. As far as God is above man, so far God's ideal is above any that the most brilliant, piercing mind could ever conceive. God has a divine ideal, in proportion to His nature. And God is all-powerful, with no limits at all, so that He is entirely capable of attaining His ideal. Not only can He attain it, but He is able to make certain of His creatures participate in that same ideal. Such is precisely the plan of God.

O Jesus, I thank You for having prepared for me a place in Heaven, so that I might share in Your own happiness. Help me to become worthy of that happiness by a life which is pleasing to You.

Prayer

Through the intercession of Your saints, O Lord, may I tread the way of holiness courageously.

— Fr. Gabriel, DI, p. 1130

Or else:

O blessed, heavenly souls! Help us in our misery and intercede for us with the divine Mercy, so that we may be granted some part of your joy and you may share with us some of that clear knowledge which is now yours.

— Fr. Gabriel, DI, p. 1132

Thoughts

- My God, how beautiful is Heaven! ...The blessed drink their fill! Each one sees himself there, sees his name written in letters of love, letters that love alone can read and love alone has inscribed.

  — St. Francis de Sales, TD, November 3

- Paradise is all filled with penitent souls. No one enters Heaven without penance and without acknowledging himself to be a sinner.

  — St. Francis de Sales, TD, November 8

Resolutions

1 To recite a decade of our rosary to beg that a saint among our ancestors intercede on our behalf.

2 To contemplate for a few minutes the happiness of the saints in Heaven and to recall moments when we have been filled with spiritual joys.

3 To seek the virtue that will allow us to increase the most rapidly in charity and to consider how to put it into practice this very day.

THE EXISTENCE OF GUARDIAN ANGELS

20th Sunday after Pentecost

God speaks to us:

See that you do not despise one of these little ones; for I tell you, their angels in Heaven always behold the face of My Father in Heaven.

St. Matthew 18:10

Meditation

We are going to spend this week in the company of the angels. Jesus taught us clearly that little children have angels that protect them (Mt. 18:10). The Fathers of the Church repeated the same truth. For example, St. Basil tells us, "No one will deny that every believer has an angel that accompanies him, acting like a kind of pedagogue and shepherd and directing his life."[46] Already *The Shepherd of Hermas*, a work which reflects the common thought of the 2nd century AD, said that "every man has a guardian angel whose inspirations and advice he ought to follow in order to practice justice and keep from evil."[47] In later centuries, the teaching of the Church became even more precise. Honorius of Autun (†1151) wrote that, "each soul, at the moment it is united to the body, is confided to an angel, who always spurs it toward the good and reports all of its actions to God."[48]

Padre Pio was very severe with anyone who cast doubt on the existence of guardian angels, as we see in the following anecdote. A young seminarian, quite full of himself, had come to see Padre Pio, not out of veneration but merely from curiosity. He was convinced that the Capuchin priest was a false mystic. He began by going to confession to him, to test his talents as a confessor. But as he knelt to begin his confession, he suddenly forgot everything he was going to say. So, Padre Pio revealed to him not only the sins he had meant to confess, but other sins as well, from his

---

[46] St. Basil of Caesarea, *Against Eunomius*, bk. III, 1, p. 186.
[47] "Angels" in *Dictionary of Spirituality*, II, p. 586.
[48] *Elucidarium*, II, 31, in *Patrologia Latina*, vol. 172, 1154 B.

past life, and which he had never brought up in the confessional because he had not realized their gravity. Padre Pio said to him, "That is serious, very serious," and the pious religious suffered to the point of tears as he revealed these things to the seminarian himself. After the confession, the seminarian stayed to exchange a few words, and Padre Pio asked him, "Do you believe in your guardian angel?" The seminarian answered, "I have never seen him." And Padre Pio replied with two great slaps across the seminarian's face, telling him to turn around and look: "You see, there he is, right there!" The seminarian turned around. He did not see anything, but when he looked back into the face of Padre Pio, it was obvious that the religious was seeing the angel. "Your guardian angel is with you and he is protecting you," the Capuchin told him firmly. From that moment on, the young seminarian never again doubted the existence of his guardian angel.

Prayer

O my good guardian angel, you who have been witness to my infidelities and to my return, help me to bless the Lord; tell in my place the greatness of His mercy for those who turn back to Him with all their heart.

— Pauline Jaricot, TD, October 2

Or else:

Guardian angels, watch over us.

— Invocation to our guardian angels

Thoughts

- Each has [his] own beautiful angel beside [him] who sees the Face of God.

— Elizabeth of the Trinity, L 227

- May the angels of God cover you with their wings, and guard you over the whole path of your life.

— Elizabeth of the Trinity, TD, October 3

Resolutions

1 To call upon our guardian angel several times over the course of the day and in particular whenever we set out on any travel.

2 To think back to a circumstance in our life when we barely escaped some misfortune, and to bless God and His angels for our safety.

3 To be attentive and docile to good inspirations.

THE TRIAL OF THE ANGELS

Monday of the 20th Week after Pentecost

God speaks to us:

Thy heart was lifted up with thy beauty.

Ezechiel 28:17

Meditation

The angels are about to learn that God intends to become man and that they are to adore Him as God-Man. Even for an angel, such a thing is incomprehensible. Faced with what is unintelligible, Lucifer closes himself off from grace. He is shocked, indignant at this plan of God which is contrary to his own manner of seeing things. Near him, another Seraphim, Michael, is pondering also. Yet instead of wrestling in frustration with the mystery which God has revealed to him, Michael maintains within himself a great inner peace. He abandons himself entirely to the divine plan.

These two attitudes of Lucifer and Michael ripple throughout the nine choirs of angels, echoed high and low, each making his choice. There are those who give themselves over to the doubts of Lucifer, and those who submit humbly, after the example of Michael.

Lucifer is there, faced with a choice whose consequences he sees very clearly: either he submits and keeps the friendship of God, or he digs into his position and commits the irreparable. If he does so, he will separate himself from God forever.

It is very possible that Lucifer received the help of St. Michael and of other angels before he came to his final decision. Unfortunately, he chose to remain in his blindness. Instead of only seeing God and submitting his will, he looks at himself. As Ezechiel says, his "heart was lifted up" at the sight of his own beauty (Ez. 28:17). He no longer thinks in reference to God; he thinks in reference to himself. He has never seen God, but himself he sees. And he is dazzled at the sight, and takes pleasure in that false, deceptive impression. His heart swells with pride at his own beauty.

He begins to believe that all of his natural qualities are sufficient for his happiness and that he can live very well without God. He imagines that he can do without the supernatural beatitude which God is offering him, and seek a natural beatitude in himself and by his own strength. In a word, he despises the grace of God and claims he has no need for it. Lucifer has forgotten where his gifts and his being come from; he simply admires himself! And at last he renounces true happiness once and for all. His decision is made: *Non serviam*; "I will not serve, I will not adore what comes after me and is below me."

Lord Jesus, for nothing in the world do I want to imitate the revolt of Lucifer. I beg You, help me to stay faithful to You until death.

Prayer

Visit, we pray Thee, O Lord, this house, and drive far from it all snares of the enemy. Let Thy holy Angels dwell therein to keep us in peace, and may Thy blessing be always upon us. Through Jesus Christ, our Lord.

— Last prayer of Compline

Or else:

Angel of God, my powerful defender, pray for us.

— Prayer to our guardian angel

Thoughts

- I was watching Satan fall as lightning from Heaven.

  — Lk. 10:18

- How art thou fallen from heaven, O Lucifer, who didst rise in the morning? How art thou fallen to the earth, that didst wound the nations? And thou saidst in thy heart: I will ascend into Heaven, I will exalt my throne above the stars of God… I will be like the Most High.

  — Is. 14:12-14

RESOLUTIONS

1 To avoid all self-complacency as well as all complaining about what happens in our life.
2 To meditate for ten minutes on the fall of Lucifer and the other wicked angels and draw a parallel with times we ourselves have fallen.
3 To highlight the qualities of other people and try to fade into the background ourselves.

ST. MICHAEL THE ARCHANGEL

Tuesday of the 20th Week after Pentecost

God speaks to us:

And there was a battle in Heaven; Michael and his angels battled with the dragon, and the dragon fought and his angels. And they did not prevail.

Apocalypse 12:7-8

Meditation

When Lucifer had the boldness to wish to become like to God, a cry shook the heavens, a louder cry than the monstrous blasphemy of Lucifer: "Who dares to say he is the equal of God? Who is like God?" St. Michel, so gentle and merciful, dared to defend the honor of God, which had been insulted. He was followed by billions of angels.

Church history teaches us that Pope St. Sylvester consecrated a sanctuary to St. Michael on the Sabine hill, already in the first half of the fourth century. In the fifth century, during the pontificate of St. Leo the Great, the feast of St. Michael was celebrated in Rome. Several apparitions of St. Michael then took place in Italy: in 525, on Mount Gargano; in 590 in Rome to Pope St. Gregory the Great, in the place called ever since the Castel Sant'Angelo. And in France, on October 16, 708, there occurred the first of three apparitions of the archangel St. Michael to the bishop of Avranches, St. Aubert. On October 16, 709, this saint consecrated to the archangel the church which was to become in the fourteenth century the marvelous basilica of Mont Saint Michel. These events took place during the reign of Childebert III, grandson of the Merovingian Clovis II, which shows that already under the first dynasty of the kings of France, the Catholic faith shone brightly in the provinces of Armorica and Neustria. By allowing these apparitions, God was showing that He wishes man to imitate St. Michael in his praise and adoration of God.

In the opinion of St. Francis de Sales and of Pius IX, as well as many other pontiffs, "devotion to St. Michael is the great remedy against disdain for the rights of God, against rebellion, and against all skepticism, materialism and atheism."[49] These are precisely the evils of our world today. May concern for the honor God be a keynote of our lives; may we become souls of adoration, praise and prayer, in imitation of St. Michael. Let us pray more faithfully to the great archangel. His protection will strengthen us and allow us to conquer alongside him, by the blood of the Lamb. It will obtain the health of our souls and of our lives on earth, and it will be a pledge of eternal happiness in Heaven.

Prayer

Holy Archangel Michael, defend us in battle, that we may not perish in the dreadful judgment.

— *Alleluia* of the Mass of St. Michael

Or else:

O Most glorious prince Michael Archangel, be mindful of us, and here and everywhere entreat the Son of God for us.

— Antiphon of the *Magnificat* for the feast of St. Michael

Thoughts

- Today my whole heart sings the challenge of Michael, "Who is like God?"

  — Elizabeth of the Trinity, TD, September 29

- St. Michael, though a prince of the heavenly army, is the most zealous to render homage to God and always eager for the honor to speed, at His word, to the aid of one of His servants.

  — St. Augustine, CW, vol. V, p. 41

Resolutions

1 To read the prayer to St. Michael (see page 266).

---

[49] *The Guardian Angel*, July 1895, pp. 75-78. Review of the Archconfraternity of the Holy Guardian Angels, based near Lyon, France, published from 1891 to 2021.

Tuesday of the 20th Week after Pentecost

2 To read in our missal the propers of the Mass of St. Michael, September 29.

3 To pray to St. Michael especially in temptations that concern the excessive or improper use of internet, radio and telephone.

THE MISSION OF GUARDIAN ANGELS

Wednesday of the 20th Week after Pentecost

GOD SPEAKS TO US:

He hath given His angels charge over thee, to keep thee in all thy ways.
Psalm 90:11

MEDITATION

Our guardian angels protect, support and guide us.

They are our protectors, as we sing during compline. Psalm 90 praises the man who dwells in the aid of the Most High. God protects in a marvelous way anyone who lives in closeness to Him. He does not take obstacles away from that person, but He helps to overcome them. This psalm affirms very simply that God has commanded His angels to guard us in all our ways. They will carry us in their hands lest we dash our foot against a stone. The psalm uses this image to explain that the mission of the angels is to protect us from all dangers. In Psalm 33, the angel of the Lord camps around those who fear God. Those who have respect for God and love Him with all their heart will receive the grace to be protected by their guardian angel.

It is also the role of the angels to support us in a particular way in our trials. When Jesus was in agony in the Garden of Olives, an angel came to strengthen Him (Lk. 22:43). And so, in the difficult moments of our life, we ourselves can be certain of the support of our guardian angel.

Finally, angels are guides for us by the example of their virtues. We could speak of their purity or their goodness, but let us look instead at another virtue which is just as necessary in our life—namely, their reverence toward superiors. In creating the God-Man and our Lady, God placed above the angels these creatures of a lower nature. A man is a much lower being than an angelic spirit, because of his body. That God should lower Himself to the point of taking on a human nature is for an angel incomprehensible, inconceivable. From that moment on, the angels would no longer hold the first place in creation; this place would be held by Jesus and Mary. In learning this plan of God, Lucifer rebelled, but the good angels bowed their wills, thus giving to men a beautiful lesson of humility.

My good guardian angel, protect me, support me, guide me.

Prayer

O my dear angel, I beg you, go to where my Jesus is resting. Tell this divine Savior that I love Him, that I love Him with all my heart... This heart is too little to hold such a great King, but I wish to make it larger by love and faith.

— St. Louise de Marillac

Or else:

Burning Seraphim, light my soul afire; most wise Cherubim, teach me; ... most holy Angels, guard me, that I might serve, bless and glorify the most Holy Trinity now and forever. Amen.

— Invocation to the nine choirs of angels

Thoughts

- Behold I will send My angel, who shall go before thee, and keep thee in thy journey, and bring thee into the place that I have prepared.

  — Ex. 23:20

- Nothing is so gentle, so gracious and so capable as the angels. From the moment of our birth, they take care of us, to guard us during our pilgrimage.

  — St. Francis de Sales, TD, October 2

Resolutions

1. To recite the first joyful mystery, asking for the virtue of humility and submission to superiors.
2. To read Psalm 90 (see page 282), considering especially the beneficent work of angels.
3. To obey promptly and joyfully the example of the angels.

ANGELS IN THE OLD TESTAMENT

Thursday of the 20th Week after Pentecost

God speaks to us:

Jacob saw in his sleep a ladder standing upon the earth, and the top thereof touching Heaven: the angels also of God ascending and descending upon it.

Genesis 28:12

Meditation

Angels are our ambassadors before God, as the following event bears witness. When Tobias was napping at the foot of a tree, the droppings of a bird fell on his eyes and damaged them so much that he lost his sight. After this difficult trial, the Archangel Raphael was sent by God to support him and his entire family. There followed a long series of events, and Tobias finally recovered his sight. St. Raphael then revealed his identity, telling him, "When thou didst pray with tears, and didst bury the dead… I offered thy prayer to the Lord" (Tob. 12:12).

The prophet Elias also received the protection of angels. He had ordered the death of the prophets who adored idols. Queen Jezabel was furious and sought revenge. When Elias learned of her intentions, he fled into the desert, but after he had walked very far and was exhausted, he had a moment of such discouragement that he longed to die. And suddenly an angel appeared and gave him food, so that he might continue his path all the way to Mount Horeb, where God appeared to him (III Kings 19).

A third event taken from the Old Testament once again shows the role of angels (IV Kings 6). The prophet Eliseus, by a special gift of God, was able to discover in advance the designs of the king of Syria against the king of Israel. He warned the king of Israel of the plans of his enemies, foiling their projects. When the king of Syria learned what Eliseus had done, he wanted to have him killed. An immense troop of soldiers arrived in the town where Eliseus was staying, so that the servant of Eliseus fell into a panic. But the prophet calmly reassured him, saying, "Fear not: for there are more with us than with them" (IV Kings 6:16). And at that moment God allowed the servant to see a multitude of horses and chariots of fire surrounding the prophet. These chariots were the sign of the presence of angels who had come to support Eliseus in his combat. God then struck the Syrians blind, so that they were unable to seize the prophet.

These examples are a good illustration of how close the angels are to us and the power of their protection. Let us call upon them with confidence, in troubles and in tranquility.

Angels of God, you who are so close to us, protect us.

Prayer

O God, who hast constituted the services of Angels and of men in a wonderful order, mercifully grant, that they who ever stand before Thy face to do Thee service in Heaven, may also defend our life upon earth.
— Collect of the Mass of St. Michael

Or else:

Glorious prince, Raphael Archangel, be mindful of us; here and everywhere, pray always for us to the Son of God.
— Antiphon of the *Magnificat* for the feast of St. Raphael

Thoughts

- The angels who are charged to watch over us constantly present our actions to the Lord, day and night.
  — St. Benedict, TD, October 2

- Let us put ourselves on the level of our smallest brothers and we will be equal to the angels in Heaven.
  — St. Gregory the Great, TD, October 2

Resolutions

1 To invoke St. Raphael, patron of travelers, whenever we leave the house.
2 To thank our guardian angel for his help.
3 In difficult interactions with our neighbor, to pray to the guardian angel of that other person.

St. Michael in History

Friday of the 20th Week after Pentecost

God speaks to us:

And another angel came and stood before the altar, having a golden censer; and there was given to him much incense, that he might offer it with the prayers of all the saints upon the golden altar which is before the throne of God.

Apocalypse 8:3-4

Meditation

"St. Michael took up the defense of the honor of God against Lucifer, concerning the Incarnation of the Word, and St. John Chrysostom supposes that St. Michael was also one of the first to offer Christ homage on the day of His humble birth in the stable of Bethlehem. St. Michael is the guardian angel of the Church, and for good reason he is also considered the guardian angel of France, seeing the special interventions of St. Michael over the centuries for the good of the kingdom of France. This great prince of Paradise even wished to have a place in this kingdom specially consecrated to him, in the diocese of Avranches, called Mont Saint Michel."[50]

The bishop of Avranches, St. Aubert, was doubtful at the first apparition of St. Michael, coming to ask that special rites of devotion be rendered to him on Mount Tomb. The angel appeared a second time with a severe look on his face and asked that a church be built on the mountain in his honor. St. Aubert was affected by this new angelic intervention and could not go back to sleep. He prayed fervently for the rest of the night and fasted on the days following, asking for enlightenment. In a third apparition, the great archangel looked at him very severely and scolded

---

[50] Fr. H.-M. Boudon, *Devotion to the Holy Angels*, pp. 239-240.

him for doubting. The angel struck the bishop's head with his finger and the mark he left never disappeared. The poor bishop, trembling, asked St. Michael where he wanted the church to be built. The angel told him that he would find a bull on the spot where the church should be, and that the area trampled by the hooves of the animal would show the dimensions of the future sanctuary. A year later, in 709, a chapel in the form of a circular crypt was raised on the place that had been indicated.

In the next century, Charlemagne chose St. Michael as the patron of his empire. Many other rulers came in pilgrimage to Mont St. Michel. The basilica of St. Gervaise in Avranches still conserves the skull of St. Aubert, marked by the finger of the archangel St. Michael, a mark unexplained by science.

St. Michael confirmed his special protection over the kingdom of France during his apparitions to St. Joan of Arc. Let us pray to him fervently, for the Church and for our own country.

Prayer

St. Michael, powerful archangel, help us in battle! Help us fight our enemy, who is the enemy of Christ and His Immaculate Mother.
— H.E. Bishop Théophile Louvard, PL, 1934

Or else:

Holy Angel, my savior in all danger, pray for us.
— Litany of the Holy Guardian Angels

Thoughts

- St. Michael is the standard-bearer of salvation; he marches victorious into battle with the redemptive cross. Let us follow him!
— H.E. Bishop Théophile Louvard, PL, 1934

- Every valiant act is accomplished with the help of St. Michael. According to Scripture, the protection of St. Michael will be greater still and his intervention more powerful when the end times come upon us.
— Adapted from St. Gregory the Great, SG, p. 446

Resolutions

1. To recite the Litany of the Holy Guardian Angels for our country (see page 269).

2. To read an episode from history about the intervention of angels in the destiny of nations.

3. To make a sacrifice for the conversion of someone who has given himself over to the devil. (See the prayer to St. Michael on page 266.)

FAITH IN ANGELS

Saturday of the 20th Week after Pentecost

GOD SPEAKS TO US:

"My Father, if You will, remove this chalice from Me; nonetheless, not My will but Thine be done." Then an angel appeared to Him to strengthen Him.

St. Luke 22:42-43

MEDITATION

Let us think of all the benefits that angels can call down upon us, but let us not be envious of those who have had the grace of seeing their angel with their eyes. Certain privileged souls, like Padre Pio, have been able to see their guardian angel. But in certain cases, a difficulty arises: discerning whether it is really the guardian angel who is appearing or a devil disguised as an angel of light. St. Gemma Galgani, who lived at the end of the 19th century and the beginning of the 20th, found herself in this complicated situation. At first, her confessor, Fr. Germano, gave her the rule of making her angel repeat after her, "Long live Jesus! Blessed be Mary!" When it was the devil appearing, he just said, "Long live... Blessed..." and fled. Unfortunately, this strategy was not enough to keep him from returning. Then the priest told Gemma, "From now on, when the devil comes back, spit in his face and treat him like a disgusting insect." Which is what she did. In general, she recognized very quickly that it was the devil and would spit in his face and make him flee. But one day Gemma had a doubt. She wondered who was there before her. It certainly looked like her guardian angel, but what if it was the devil! Very hesitantly, she looked him straight in the face. All he did was smile, as though he found the situation amusing. The poor girl did not find it amusing at all; she was not at all sure what to do. "Do I spit, do I not spit?" she asked herself. Finally, she decided to spit in his face... But to her great astonishment the angel did not move an inch, did not burst into anger like devils would. Blushing and embarrassed, Gemma bowed her head and saw a white rose there on the floor, where her saliva had fallen. On the petals of the rose were inscribed in gold the words, "Every gift of love is welcome!" Gemma died at the age of 25, in 1903, and these words had been the rule of her life. May this story help us have greater devotion to our guardian angel.

O my good angel, I promise to call upon you especially in difficulties, temptations and trials.

Prayer

Angel of the heavens, whom God has given me as my guardian, for my good: enlighten me, protect me, guide me, rule over me. Amen.

— St. Vincent Ferrer

Or else:

O angels! You whose affections are greater and stronger than my own, sustain my weakness. Adore the glory of my God for me, with the deepest adoration that you can offer.

— St. Francis de Sales, TD, September 29

Thoughts

- Our guardian angel is ready with a good thought to put in the mind of the one he has charge over, from the moment that person awakes.
— St. Vincent de Paul, TD2, October 2
- Our guardian angel is always at our side to incline us toward good and to defend us against the bad angels that are constantly lurking around us to incline us toward evil.
— Curé of Ars, TD2, October 2

Resolutions

1 To read the propers of the Mass of October 2.
2 To invoke St. Gemma Galgani several times over the course of the day, asking for the same submission to Providence.
3 To thank our guardian angel for the graces received over the course of our life.

DIVINE MERCY

21st Sunday after Pentecost

God speaks to us:

The master of that servant, taking pity on him, set him free and forgave his debt.

Gospel: St. Luke 18:27

Meditation

Forgiveness is the most beautiful flower of Christianity and of Paradise; it grows in no other field.

Nonetheless, we all have a natural repugnance toward forgiving others. What can we do to conquer this instinctive repugnance to forgiving the wrongs that our neighbor has done us? Our Lord invites us to reflect on the way God treats us, we who are sinners. Yes: even if it does not seem to us that we are guilty of many sins, we must never forget that every sin offends the divine majesty, our God who is so great, so holy, so good. Toward Him, we are indebted beyond what we could possibly pay. This is what Jesus willed to teach us in the parable which the Church offers us in the Gospel of this Sunday. Here we have an image of the mercy which God showers upon us. Indeed, God is infinitely merciful. The first of all miseries is nothingness, if we can even call it a misery, since every misery supposes some degree of being. And so, Creation was the first act of God's mercy. Left to itself, any creature would fall immediately back into nothingness. And behold, God maintains all creatures in existence. More than that, He has raised creation to the level of grace by communicating supernatural life to us. Yet this was not enough for His love. God is the goal of our life, and He willed also to be the way. Our earth has contemplated Him; His voice echoed in the air of this world; men witnessed Him passing from the cradle to the cross, from the cross to the altar, from the altar to our hearts.

"Calvary! A God nailed to the redemptive cross! A God avenging on Himself the iniquities which we committed, through a death which astonishes the divine majesty, disarms divine justice, and rains down on guilty humanity a forgiveness with no limits in time or in space or even in the gravity of crime—this is the last word of divine mercy, perpetually offended."[51] But just as we benefit from His mercy, God expects us to forgive in our turn those who have offended us.

Thank you, Lord, for Your great mercy. I in turn wish to imitate You by forgiving from the bottom of my heart anyone who has offended Me.

Prayer

Teach me, O Lord, the secrets of Your mercy, that I may fully profit by them.

— Fr. Gabriel, DI, p. 684

Or else:

Most merciful Father, for what merits of mine, what grace of mine, did it please Your Majesty to create me? …Give me then the grace to be grateful, O You who have created me out of nothing!

— Fr. Gabriel, ID, pp. 684-5

Thoughts

- The good God will forgive a repentant sinner faster than a mother will pull her child out of the fire.
  — Curé of Ars, TD2, March 12
- My weakness and my misery would cause me sadness, but Your mercy, O God, reassures me.
  — Curé of Ars, TD2, March 31

Resolutions

1 To sing a *Magnificat*, blessing God for His great mercy toward us.
2 To recite attentively during Mass the prayers that call upon the divine mercy: *Kyrie, Gloria, Agnus Dei…*
3 To show mercy toward those who irritate us or do things that frustrate us.

---

[51] H.E. Bishop Joseph Rumeau, *Pastoral Letter*, 1934.

THE BANKRUPT SERVANT

Monday of the 21st Week after Pentecost

GOD SPEAKS TO US:

The servant, going out, met one of his companions who owed him a hundred denarii; seizing him, he throttled him, saying, "Give what you owe me."

Gospel of Sunday: St. Matthew 18:28

MEDITATION

Sunday's parable brings home to us man's duty to forgive his fellow man. To show what human malice really is, the parable brings before our eyes the portrait of a heartless Catholic. The steward in the parable had wasted a large part of the fortune confided to him: ten thousand talents. That is an enormous amount of money, and it is obvious that the man will never manage to pay his debt. The sentence was immediate. The king decided to sell the man as a slave, along with his children. At that time, among the Jews as well as among the Romans, the law gave such total power to a creditor over his insolvent debtors.

Faced with this perspective, the thief was devastated. The only path open to him was to try to win time. So, he went down on his knees before the king and promised him, weeping, to pay his debt if he would only give him a little time. Perhaps he hoped to win the lottery… or else he counted on his master changing his mind after his first anger had fallen. Whatever the case may be, the sight of his servant begging softened the king, and he took pity on the man; in an extraordinary gesture of compassion and magnanimity, the king no longer demanded any payment but simply forgave the man his entire debt. "That's it," he said, "it's over, let's not mention it anymore. We will forget it this time. Go in peace." The steward was overwhelmed; he could not get over it. How could his master have been so generous toward him? Consoled, as though set free, with a light heart, he turns toward home, when he meets on his path, by chance, a person who owed him the modest sum of one hundred denarii. A hundred denarii is an insignificant amount of money, ridiculously small in comparison to the ten thousand talents that he owed his master. We have every reason to believe that he will leave his own debtor in peace without asking that he repay the modest amount which he owes. But not at all! Not only does he demand his money, but he goes so far as to have the man thrown into prison until he repaid him completely.

Lord Jesus, by this example, I understand the need to forgive all those who have done me any wrong.

Prayer

My God, do I have any right to be pitiless toward others, I who have such need of Your pity?
— *Friend of the Parish Clergy*, 1902, p. 693

Or else:

Lord, may I forget the slight offenses that are done to me, so that You might forgive me my offenses.
— *Friend of the Parish Clergy*, 1902, p. 693

Thoughts

- O my soul, you have an enormous debt toward God. He has loved you with such a love! He has showered you with so many graces! His love has always been so vigilant to do you good! He has surrounded you with such tenderness!
  — Fr. Emmanuel, M, p. 330

- May the thought of our sins make us gentle, tolerant, indulgent toward others, full of hope for the conversion and the sanctification of any soul, whoever it may be.
  — Charles de Foucauld, TD, October 3

Resolutions

1 Never to go to sleep with anger in our heart, but to recite an *Our Father* from the bottom of our heart to uproot from our soul any

negative feelings that we have toward those who have made us suffer.

2 To reread last Sunday's Gospel.

3 To spend a few minutes thinking back over all of the times that we have benefitted from the mercy of God over the course of our life, so as to be indulgent toward our neighbor.

THE FORGIVENESS OF INJURIES

Tuesday of the 21st Week after Pentecost

God speaks to us:

Pray therefore in this way: …Forgive us our trespasses as we forgive those who have trespassed against us.

St. Matthew 6:9, 12

Meditation

Already in the Old Testament God by His inspiration gave to man the law of forgiveness. Thus in the book of Ecclesiasticus we read, "Forgive thy neighbor if he hath hurt thee: and then shall thy sins be forgiven to thee when thou prayest. Man to man reserveth anger, and doth he seek remedy of God? He hath no mercy on a man like himself, and doth he entreat for his own sins? He that is but flesh, nourisheth anger, and doth he ask forgiveness of God? Who shall obtain pardon for his sins?" (Ecclus 28:2-5).

In the Sermon on the Mount, which contains in summary the entire New Law, Jesus establishes the forgiveness of offenses as the condition for the forgiveness of our own sins. "If you forgive men their offenses toward you, your heavenly Father will also forgive your sins against Him; but if you do not forgive men anything, your Father will not forgive your sins, either" (Mt. 6:14-15). This precept is so important that Jesus told us He would refuse even the offerings that we make at His altar as long as we are not reconciled with our brothers. And so, when we ourselves remain inflexible toward those who have done us wrong, God will not let Himself be moved in our favor. St. James reminds us of this fact in his Epistle: "No mercy for those who have not been merciful" (Jas. 2:13).

In the Lord's Prayer, we find this same teaching. The prayer of the Our Father, which our Lord Himself taught us, is brief but contains all our duties. We ask God to have toward us the same indulgence that we have toward our neighbor. This is the meaning of the fifth petition of the *Pater*: *Forgive us our trespasses, as we forgive those who trespass against us.* These passages from Holy Scripture lead us to say to ourselves, "It is our Lord who is speaking. It is God who is speaking." We therefore need to forgive our neighbor because God Himself commanded us to.

Prayer

Lord, You alone can close the wounds which a prideful sensibility has caused in my heart, every time I have fostered unlawful hatred.
— *Friend of the Parish Clergy*, 1902, p. 693

Or else:

Our Father, who art in Heaven, …forgive us our trespasses, as we forgive those who trespass against us.
— *Our Father*

Thoughts

- How can we obtain a grace if we are loaded down with offenses that are not yet forgiven, and how can our offenses be forgiven if we ourselves do not forgive those who owe us so much less?
  — Charles de Foucauld, TD, February 1
- How many souls will reproach us on Judgment Day because they would now be in Heaven, if only we had only answered their insults with goodness and charity.
  — Curé of Ars, TD2, September 17

Resolutions

1 To recite five *Our Fathers* slowly, with the desire to forgive from the bottom of our heart those who have done us wrong.

2 To recite a decade of the rosary for all those who have made us suffer over the course of our life and to avoid thinking back and mulling over a disagreement.

3 To offer a sacrifice that those who are victims of rank injustice might bring themselves to forgive, and to ask for the grace to imitate them.

A DIFFICULT LAW

Wednesday of the 21st Week after Pentecost

God speaks to us:

If you do not forgive men, neither will your Father forgive you your offenses.

St. Matthew 6:15

Meditation

The forgiveness of injuries is difficult. Justified reproaches are not easy to accept. Our self-love generally tends to balk, push back or dig in its heels when someone puts his finger on one of our weaknesses. But it is even harder when those reproaches are totally unjustified. Bourdaloue affirmed that "forgiving sincerely and in good faith is the most arduous trial of charity."[52] There is still a well of pride deep in our heart which bubbles to the surface when our neighbor injures us in some way. It is hard for us to forgive, to forgive always, to forgive everyone, and to forgive from the depths of our heart. And yet, even though the forgiveness of injuries is difficult, it is not optional, but a formal command of God.

Unfortunately, many Catholics invent a thousand excuses so as not to make that effort. We need to take care and resist the deceptive charm of false reasonings which we create to justify our hardness of heart. "To forgive truly, from the bottom of our heart, is too hard," we tell ourselves; "it isn't possible; it is beyond the power of nature." There we are right. But the Christian life is not a life according to nature, but a life according to grace. Our Lord desires to give us the strength to forgive from the bottom of our heart. It is up to us to let ourselves be shaped by Him. It is up to us to dominate the reticence of the old man, the man of sin. If we are able to do so, we have the sign that God is truly in our heart. By what

---

[52] Bourdaloue, *Complete Works*, II, p. 398.

right does our Lord require of us such a submission, such a self-denial, such a renunciation? He requires it as Master and Judge. Our Lord is our Master. Consequently, the simple fact that He commands us ought to be enough for us to submit. Jesus also asks us to forgive insofar as He is our Judge, as it is written, *"Mihi vindictam et ego retribuam,"* "Vengeance is Mine; I will repay, says the Lord" (Rom. 12:19).

Prayer

Lord, make possible for me by grace what is impossible to me by nature.

— *Imitation of Christ*, III, ch. 19

Or else:

I pray You, [Lord,] make every trial lovely and desirable to me for Your Name's sake, since suffering and affliction for Your sake is so profitable to the health of my soul.

— *Imitation of Christ*, III, ch. 19

Thoughts

- Once I have forgiven, and forgiven with the thought of God and for love of God, I can be as sure of the forgiveness of my own sins as I am sure of God's infallibility and His inviolable fidelity.
  — Bourdaloue, CW, II, p. 403

- As sinners, we are in infinite need of God's forgiveness. Let us forgive, and hope for all things from His mercy in time and in blessed eternity.
  — Bourdaloue, CW, II, p. 408

Resolutions

1 To recite one of the sorrowful mysteries, begging for the forgiveness of our sins.

2 To meditate for ten minutes on the Last Judgment so as to have the courage to forgive injuries.

3 To avoid rash judgments, hasty conclusions, putting people in a category, tale bearing, character assassination, or anything of the sort.

THE IMITATION OF JESUS CHRIST

Thursday of the 21st Week after Pentecost

God speaks to us:

Father, forgive them, for they do not know what they are doing.
St. Luke 23:34

Meditation

Catholic morality is a morality of imitation. Let us therefore follow our Lord. How did He act in face of His enemies? Did He curse them? Did He chastise them on the spot? We know very well that He did no such thing! As He endured the most excruciating torments, hanging between two thieves, He had blasphemers at His feet who were full of hatred and crying out against Him. Nonetheless, far from cursing them, He addressed to God, His Father, this word of mercy: *Father, forgive them, for they do not know what they are doing.* Thus, our Lord Himself put into practice this law of forgiveness. These are even the first words that He uttered from the cross.

That we might bring ourselves to forgive from the bottom of our heart, when the evil to be forgiven seems to us to be insurmountable or when we feel ourselves weak, let us turn toward our Lord on the cross. Let us hear Him forgive those who inflict evil upon Him. "I love My enemies and I forgive them," our Lord tells us. "Meditate on My Passion. You see all that I have endured—flagellation, crowning with thorns, crucifixion in the midst of insults and blasphemies, and above all you see how I reacted. Remember the first word I spoke in the hearing of those who were crucifying Me: *Father, forgive them, for they do not know what they are doing.*" This gaze upon the crucifix will allow us to grant others complete and genuine forgiveness, with no afterthought and nothing held back.

So, we have to be merciful first of all because God commands it of us; then because we ought to act toward others as we would have them act toward us; and finally, because we ought to imitate Jesus, who followed this law of forgiveness Himself. Our Lord also points to His Father as our example: "Be merciful, even as your heavenly Father is merciful." (Lk. 6:36)

Lord Jesus, help me to forgive from the bottom of my heart, without looking at myself, because I will thereby obtain mercy and be able one day to enter the blessed eternity of Heaven.

Prayer

O Lord, we beseech Thee, with steady kindness keep Thy household safe: that, through Thy protection, it may be free from all adversities, and devoutly given to good works for the glory of Thy name. Through our Lord Jesus Christ.

— Collect of Sunday Mass

Or else:

Show unto us, O Lord, Thy mercy. And grant us Thy salvation.

— Ordinary of the Mass

Thoughts

- The perfect life consists in imitating Jesus inwardly and outwardly: inwardly, by making our soul like His; outwardly, by leading a life according to His example.

  — Charles de Foucauld, TD, June 28

- May our heart drink from the heart of God so much charity that it reaches even to our worst enemies.

  — H.E. Bishop Joseph Rumeau, PL, 1934

Resolutions

1. To meditate for a few minutes in front of a crucifix, thinking of the mercy of Jesus.
2. To imitate Jesus by showing gentleness to our neighbor and by keeping all harshness from our tone and all disdain from our eyes when we have to correct someone.
3. To pray for the conversion of an atheist.

THE EXAMPLE OF A SAINT

Friday of the 21st Week after Pentecost

God speaks to us:

Put on, therefore, as God's chosen ones, holy and beloved, a heart of mercy.

Epistle of St. Paul to the Colossians 3:12

Meditation

St. Jeanne de Chantal, foundress of the order of the Visitation along with St. Francis de Sales, was born in Dijon, France. She married the Baron de Chantal in 159She had been married for eight years and already had six children, two of whom died at a young age, when her husband went hunting one day with a kinsman. The baron had put on a fawn-colored jacket. His cousin saw him through the undergrowth, took him for a deer and wounded him by mistake. The Baron de Chantal realized that he would not recover and said to his kinsman, "I am as good as dead, my friend. It is by lack of prudence that you have done this, and I forgive you from the bottom of my heart." The Baron de Chantal had a priest called so that he might receive the last sacraments, and he died a few days later from his wound. He had forgiven his friend spontaneously, but it was harder for the baroness. St. Jeanne de Chantal, who was only 28 at the time, could not bring herself to forgive the murderer of her husband. It took the intervention of St. Francis de Sales to help her to take that step, and he wrote to her, "It is not necessary that you look for a day or an opportunity to meet the man who killed your husband; but if he appears before you, I want you to bear a gentle, gracious and compassionate heart toward him. I know that without a doubt your heart will be moved and overcome, that your blood will boil, but what does that matter? So also did the heart of our dear Lord at the death of Lazarus and at the thought of His Passion. Yes, but at both times He raised His eyes to Heaven. You see, my daughter: God makes you realize through these emotions how much we are flesh and blood. *A Dieu*, my child. Remain at peace."53 The saint acted on this advice, but she later admitted that the words of forgiveness which then came to her lips had cost her more than all the work of her sanctification. A few years later she even accepted to be the godmother of a child of this former friend who had killed her husband.

St. Jeanne de Chantal, following your example, I, too, wish to pardon those who have wronged me over the course of my life.

Prayer

Almighty and merciful God, who didst endow blessed Jane Frances, ever burning with love for Thee, with wondrous strength of soul…: grant through her merits and prayers, that we, who know our own weakness and trust only in Thy power, may, by the help of Thy heavenly grace, overcome all adversity.

— Collect of the Mass of St. Jeanne de Chantal

Or else:

O Holy Spirit, make my heart merciful in imitation of the heart of Jesus.

— Fr. Gabriel, DI, p. 890

Thoughts

- The Holy Spirit wishes to chisel the features of Jesus in us, transforming us into living images of the Savior; therefore, He gently and unceasingly urges us to be merciful.

  — Fr. Gabriel, DI, p. 892

- How can one who is really convinced of his own frailty, weakness, and inconstancy, dare to condemn others?

  — Fr. Gabriel, DI, p. 891

Resolutions

1. To say a decade of the rosary for those in our country, more and more numerous, who are victims of aggression.
2. To recite several times today the first prayer, above.
3. To resolve never to mull over an old argument.

---

[53] Msgr. François Trochu, *Saint François de Sales*, vol. II, pp. 113-114.

BLESSED ARE THE MERCIFUL

Saturday of the 21st Week after Pentecost

God speaks to us:

Blessed are the merciful, for they shall obtain mercy.

St. Matthew 5:7

Meditation

Jesus opened the Sermon on the Mount with eight beatitudes, among which we find that of mercy: *Blessed are the merciful, for they shall obtain mercy.* The essential condition for God to have mercy on us, is that we be merciful toward our neighbor. We have already presented the reasons that ought to encourage us to observe this law. To close this chapter, we are going to look for some preventative remedies that we can use to keep bitterness from taking root in us.

Let us follow the advice which St. Benedict gave to his monks, and which Pope Pius XII repeated to young couples. St. Benedict very wisely recommends that we never go to sleep angry. If we forgive day by day from the bottom of our heart, evil will never take root in us, and we will be able more easily to remove bitterness when it comes.

After that, let us not be too demanding of others. Let us not ask of creatures what God alone can give us. Disappointments often come from our leaning too much on certain people. When they do not live up to what we expected of them, we close off our heart, we become bitter, we mull over their lack of attention toward us, and we focalize on their weaknesses.

Let us be attentive to the good qualities in our neighbor rather than his defects and let us be clear-sighted about our own weaknesses; the more we realize our own misery, the more we will be indulgent toward others.

Finally, may we nourish ourselves on the Holy Eucharist: Jesus Christ present in the host has compassion on the miseries of man and He brings

Saturday of the 21st Week after Pentecost

the remedy. At communion, our Lord comes with the same saving influence as He brought in the time of the Gospel. He did not just feel sorry for the suffering or the guilty, and leave it at that. He helped them, nourished them, healed them. He does the same today.

O Jesus in the host, purify me, sanctify me, save me.

Prayer

O Lord, may the consideration of Your infinite mercy dilate my heart, that I may learn how to treat others mercifully.
— Fr. Gabriel, DI, p. 769

Or else:

Deign to pardon us, [Lord,] but only by Your mercy!
— Fr. Gabriel, DI, p. 771

Thoughts

- Charity soars to marvelous heights when it lets itself be mercifully drawn down to the miseries of our neighbor; and the lower it descends out of love toward the weak, the more strength it has to continue its rise to the summit.
— St. Gregory the Great, TD, August 20

- Let us maintain vast treasuries of indulgence for those whose failings we have to endure, or for those who may have done us some wrong; treasuries of thoughtfulness for those who misunderstand us; treasuries of love for those who hate us.
— H.E. Bishop Joseph Rumeau, PL, 1934

Resolutions

1. To recognize the qualities of people who try our patience so as not to nourish our negative feelings toward them, and to ask God for the grace to endure that in them which irritates or bothers us.
2. Not to take offense at slights or forgetfulness from the people with whom we live or work.
3. To make a spiritual communion (see page 260).

A TRICK QUESTION

22nd Sunday after Pentecost

God speaks to us:

Is it lawful to give tribute to Caesar, or not?
Gospel: St. Matthew 22:17

Meditation

In today's Gospel, the Pharisees are trying to catch our Lord in His words.

To draw Jesus into their trap, the Pharisees start by flattering Him. "Master," they say, "we know that Thou art truthful, and that Thou teachest the way of God in truth and that Thou carest naught for any man; for Thou dost not regard the person of men" (Mt. 22:16). At first glance, these words appear as magnificent praise, corresponding exactly to reality. Our Lord, who is Truth itself, can only teach the truth. But on the lips of the Pharisees, it is not praise at all. It is a trap they are setting for Him, pure and simple. The next words show this clearly.

The Pharisees continue their statement by asking Jesus, *Is it lawful to give tribute to Caesar, or not?* This is a wily question. If our Lord answers in the negative, as the Pharisees hope, they will be able to deliver Him straight to Pontius Pilate as an enemy of the local ruler. If He answers *yes*, He will offend national feeling, and many Jews will cease to follow Him. If He refuses to answer, His silence will damage His reputation for frankness.

Thus, whatever He does, whatever He says, our Lord will be caught in the trap. However, Jesus is completely unfazed and begins very calmly by reproaching the Pharisees for their bad faith. "Why do you test Me, you hypocrites?" (Mt. 22:18). Why are you drawing Me onto the shifting sands of politics? Then He shows them the image of Caesar stamped on the denarius which they hold out to Him, and says, "Render to Caesar the things that are Caesar's, and to God the things that are God's" (Mt. 22:21). In a few words, He turns the situation around and then gives a clear definition of the virtue of justice: to render to God, to the State and to our neighbor what is due to each.

On the strength of Your words, Lord Jesus, I wish to live up to Your expectations by rendering to You what is Your due, without failing to render to the State and to my neighbor what I owe to them.

Prayer

Teach me, O Lord, to fulfill all my duties in homage to Your sovereign majesty.

— Fr. Gabriel, DI, p. 1002

Or else:

Give me, O God, a strong efficacious desire for justice, that I may draw near to You, O infinite Justice.

— Fr. Gabriel, DI, p. 808

Thoughts

- To God your Creator and Your Redeemer you owe all that you are and all that you have. Render to God what is God's: to God, supreme Beauty, you owe all your love, all your thoughts, all your aspirations, and all your consideration.

   — St. Vincent de Paul, TD1, May 25

- Every Christian is bound to fulfill all the duties of a good citizen, and, consequently, must obey political authority, unless its orders are opposed to the law of God; for, in this case, it would no longer represent divine authority.

   — Fr. Gabriel, DI, pp. 1003-4

Resolutions

1. To fulfill our duties in the social and political domain with prudence and wisdom.
2. To avoid using flattery and deception to draw on us the approval or the good graces of our neighbor.
3. To render today to God what is God's, by sanctifying our Sunday through prayer and by paying particular attention to the members of our family.

THE VIRTUE OF JUSTICE

Monday of the 22nd Week after Pentecost

God speaks to us:

Render to Caesar the things that are Caesar's.
Gospel of Sunday: St. Matthew 22:21

Meditation

Let us meditate today on the command of Jesus: *Render to Caesar the things that are Caesar's*; in other words, let us render to our neighbor whatever we owe him.

It is not easy to be exempt from all reproach in the domain of justice. Human nature being what it is, we can tend to focus on our own profit or to downplay the need to give back what does not belong to us.

Already St. John Chrysostom said in his day that nothing is easier than to find ourselves unthinkingly in possession of what belongs to someone else, because of our own cupidity and the continual occasions in which we find ourselves to take away the good of our neighbor. Highway robbers are not the only ones guilty of theft.

Thus, we can steal by not repaying our debts. This is the case for a business owner who does not pay his employees on time, or does not that pay them just wages, that is, wages proportionate to their work. It is the case likewise for an employee who does not work as much as he should or who abuses the goods of the business for his own private use. It is also the case for those who fail to support the Church by their donations or who do not pay their school tuition but then go and spend their money on other, frivolous things.

Theft also slips into other actions like the sale of products.

For example, we can steal by fraudulent sales if we lie during negotiations. False declarations to our insurance company or attempts to deprive our neighbor of his just inheritance, or else theft by artificially inflating prices through organized bidding between sellers, are all ways of falling into the guilt of theft in our modern society.

To avoid this guilt, let us remember that we should act toward others as we would like others to act toward us.

O our Lady, mirror of justice, help me to see today if I still owe any debt to my neighbor, so that I may promptly restore his goods to him.

Prayer

Teach me, O Lord, to love justice and to hate all that is opposed to it.
— Fr. Gabriel, DI, p. 805

Or else:

Remember me, O God, and lead me in the right way to Your Kingdom.
— *Imitation of Christ*, III, ch. 58

Thoughts

- Justice is the perpetual and constant will to render to each one his right.
— St. Thomas Aquinas, IIa-IIæ, q. 58, a. 1

- In your trade and in commercial transactions, allow yourself no dishonesty; remember the story of Ananias and Saphira[54]; they were punished by bodily death.
— St. Benedict, TD, September 28

Resolutions

1 To make a serious examination of conscience to know where we stand as regards the virtue of justice.

2 To make a specific resolution to be more faithful in this domain.

3 To show ourselves constantly trustworthy in our profession.

---

[54] Ananias and Saphira had made a false declaration by disordered love of money and suffered the immediate justice of God.

THE RESTITUTION OF DEBTS

Tuesday of the 22nd Week after Pentecost

GOD SPEAKS TO US:

Render to Caesar the things that are Caesar's.

Gospel of Sunday: St. Matthew 22:21

MEDITATION

Each time we harm our neighbor in his goods, we must restore what we have unduly kept from him. *Render to Caesar the things that are Caesar's.* Sadly, there are many who neglect this duty! Already in his time, St. Augustine (+430) said, "Those who retain the goods of others come to prostrate themselves before the altars, their eyes bathed in tears, hearts full of bitterness and regret. They accuse themselves, they condemn themselves, and it seems that they wish to reconcile themselves perfectly with God. But when one speaks to them of restitution, they begin to go back on what they have said and change their way of speaking. Up until then they listen to the priest as to the representative of God; they submit themselves to him as to their judge; they obey him as a shepherd and doctor of their souls: whatever he demands of them and orders them to do, all seems light to them. Yet let him require of them a restitution, they seek to correct him, and when they fail to gain him to their way of thinking, they look for another, less troublesome [confessor], one who will deceive them and damn himself along with them."[55] Forgiveness is not something independent of reparation; on the contrary, it demands reparation. If a person steals an object from us and comes to ask our forgiveness, it is to be hoped that we accept to forgive him, but we also require the restitution of our goods. The duty of restitution applies likewise to us and is to be found in every case of theft, whether direct or indirect, visible or

---

[55] St. Augustine, quoted by Bourdaloue, in *Complete Works*, II, p. 415.

hidden. Certain people admit the principle of restitution but seek to be exempted from it by claiming that it is impossible. There exist particular cases of people in truly inextricable situations, but the analysis of such cases is beyond the scope of this booklet. What God asks of us today is to acknowledge any past transgression against the seventh and ninth commandments and to take effective means to repair the wrong we have done to our neighbor. To do so, let us stir up in ourselves a true desire to repair the damage that we have caused and then find fitting solutions.

Lord Jesus, I resolve to do all I can to pay my debts toward my neighbor, and to pay those that I owe to You.

Prayer

O Lord, You who are just and love what is just, teach me how to practice justice perfectly.

— Fr. Gabriel, DI, p. 810

Or else:

May it be Your pleasure, my God, that the time may come when I shall be able to pay at least a small part of the immense debt I owe You.

— Fr. Gabriel, DI, p. 175

Thoughts

- Now we receive, and later we will be brought before the Master to pay Him all of our past debts, that is, to render Him an account of all the things which He has confided to us.

   — St. Augustine, XIV, p. 49

- You cannot serve God and mammon.

   — Mt. 6:24

Resolutions

1. To make an examination of conscience to determine whether we owe a debt to anyone, and then to pay it as soon as possible, setting ourselves a no-later-than date.
2. To acquire the habit of not delaying before paying our debts.
3. To meditate for a few minutes on the benefits which God has granted us, and then rendering Him thanks.

LYING

Wednesday of the 22nd Week after Pentecost

God speaks to us:

Master, we know that Thou art truthful, and that Thou teachest the way of God in truth and that Thou carest naught for any man; for Thou dost not regard the person of men.

Gospel of Sunday: St. Matthew 22:16

Meditation

The flattery which the Pharisees employ in speaking to Jesus in last Sunday's Gospel is a disguised form of lying. For the Pharisees to say the contrary of what they are thinking in order to draw Jesus into their trap, is miserably dishonest. This sin of lying is unfortunately very widespread still today and is at the origin of much injustice.

The first form of lying is the pernicious lie, uttered with the intention of doing harm. This sin includes all forms of slander and extends also to those who bear false tales. Every time we spread words that harm someone's reputation without reason and without proof, we are participating in the lie of the one who began the slander. This form of lying is particularly grave.

Sometimes lies are used to get us out of difficult situations, such as falsified tax returns, medical records, or insurance information.

Without going to that extent, other forms of lying do exist. Certain people lie to boost their image, systematically exaggerating the facts they recount in order to make themselves seem like the heroes of the story. The consequences are less serious, but still, it is not permitted.

There is also the officious lie, which we employ in order to be of service to someone else. A given person who works in a large company exaggerates the qualities of a friend, lying about him and thereby undercutting someone who is in fact more deserving. So, there are various forms of lies.

On the other hand, it is not because we can never lie, that we are obliged always to tell the truth. We are not obliged to answer indiscreet questions, for example. The truth should be spoken in the right time and the right place. The virtue of prudence will indicate the proper action in every circumstance.

O Holy Ghost, give me such a love for the truth that I never turn to lies under any pretext.

Prayer

O God, who are Truth itself, teach us to serve You in truth!

— Fr. Emmanuel, M, p. 235

Or else:

Grant, we beseech Thee, O almighty God, that the splendor of Thy brightness may shine forth upon us, and the light of Thy Light may, by the illumination of the Holy Ghost, confirm the hearts of those who have been born again by Thy grace.

— Collect for the Vigil of Pentecost

Thoughts

- The devil is a liar and the father of lies.

  — Jn. 8:44

- Be on guard against equivocation, ambiguity, or dissimulation. While it is not always advisable to say all that is true, it is never permissible to speak against the truth.

  — St. Francis de Sales, *Introduction to the Devout Life*, bk. III, ch. 30

Resolutions

1 To examine our conscience to see whether we have anything to reproach ourselves with in the domain of lying, and if necessary to end with an act of contrition.

2 To consider the circumstances which could lead us to lie, and then resolve on a strategy to avoid falling.

3 To develop the virtue of discretion in order to avoid sins of the tongue, without failing to offer our opinion to others when it could be of service.

MAN IN THE IMAGE OF GOD

Thursday of the 22nd Week after Pentecost

God speaks to us:

Whose are this image and the inscription?
Gospel of Sunday: St. Matthew 22:20

Meditation

Whose are this image and the inscription? These questions which our Lord asks the Jews who had tried to trap Him will be asked of every soul by God on the Day of Judgment. On that day, some will reflect the image of God, while others show forth the image of the devil. That we might keep from being placed in this second category, let us render to Caesar that which is Caesar's, but let us also render to God that which is God's. In the words of St. Augustine, "We must renew in ourselves that image which God has imprinted on our soul at its creation... It is in loving the truth that this image, which God imprinted on our soul in creating us, is renewed, and that we render to our Caesar [that is, to God] the coin which belongs to Him."[56] The book of Genesis teaches us that, in the beginning, God created us in His image. "God said, 'Let us make man to Our image and likeness: and let him have dominion over the fishes of the sea...' And God created man to His own image: to the image of God He created him: male and female He created them" (Gen. 1:26-27). Notice that God did not say that man *was* His image, but that he was *to* His image. This means that God created us on the model of His image, on the model of a perfect creature, a creature without equal. He created us on the model of our Lord Jesus Christ—our Lord, who is the man *par excellence*.

---

[56] St. Augustine, *Complete Works*, XVII, 9, Sermon 90, p. 62.

Thursday of the 22nd Week after Pentecost

Created in the image of God, man enjoyed a happiness beyond description. His body was totally subject to his soul, and his soul was in turn subject to God. All creatures respected in him the image and the seal of the Creator. Unfortunately, by sin, the image of God was deformed, altered, damaged, not only in Adam, but in all his descendants.

Lord Jesus, Your image was partially restored in me on the day of my baptism, but it remains tarnished and dim. And so, I humbly ask You: shape my soul and model it to Your image and Your likeness.

Prayer

O my God, since I am Yours for so many reasons, and have so many obligations to serve You, permit no longer that sin, or Satan, or the world, usurp, even in the slightest degree, that which is entirely Yours.

— Fr. Gabriel, DI, p. 1004

Or else:

Here I am, O my God, I give myself entirely to You.

— Fr. Gabriel, DI, p. 1004

Thoughts

- God created us in His image. What ought to be our ambition, if not to reflect in our souls and in our lives something of His infinite goodness?

  — H.E. Bishop Joseph Rumeau, PL, 1934

- Is it not the greatest gift of God, that as He teaches us to imitate Him, He also stirs up in us His own likeness, the gift of self?

  — Pauline Jaricot, PD, March 9

Resolutions

1. To meditate for ten minutes on the beauty of a soul in the state of grace.
2. To identify what most troubles us at the idea of appearing today before God, and to make a fitting resolution.
3. To see in my neighbor a creature of God and to respect him as such, even if the image of God has been deformed in him.

JESUS, OUR MODEL

Friday of the 22nd Week after Pentecost

GOD SPEAKS TO US:

Put on the Lord Jesus Christ.

Epistle of St. Paul to the Romans 13:14

MEDITATION

If we wish to grow spiritually, if we desire God to see in us the image of His Son, we must look at the exemplar, the model, the archetype. The genuine archetype of man created and then created anew, is our Lord. Splendor of the Father's glory and imprint of His substance, Jesus is truly the image of God, an image so perfect that He could say in all truth, "He who sees Me sees also the Father." (Jn. 14:9)

Let us meet His gaze of love so that our one object may be to love God and to make Him loved. In a heart to heart with God, in prayer, may we let ourselves be sought out by God, loved by God, led by God. And every day of our lives, let us work to reproduce in ourselves His divine features. In this way we will prove that we really are children of God and brothers of Jesus Christ.

Let us understand the place which our Lord desires to hold in our life. The Catholic religion is more than a standard of morality and more even than a doctrine; it is first a profound adhesion to a person, a living Person who loves us, who is right here beside us, and who has only one desire: that of uniting Himself to us in order to transform us into Him. That union is the heart of our Lord's teaching, which we find also in the Apostles. Let us remember what St. Paul said: *Put on the Lord Jesus Christ*. Yes, on the Day of Judgment, those only will be admitted into Heaven who are a faithful image of our Lord Jesus Christ.

Is this not the time to ask ourselves, "Do I reflect our Lord Jesus Christ by my demeanor? Does God see in me the image of His Son? What ought

I to do, that this image might shine more perfectly in me?" Certainly, our Lord is so perfect a model that we will never be able to imitate Him in all His virtues, but we must express certain virtues if we are to prove that we are truly members of His family, and not men of the world.

O sweet Virgin, sculpt our soul that we might become, like you, a living image of your divine Son.

Prayer

Ah! Lord, draw us after You and grant us the grace to enter the practice of Your example, which brings us to seek the Kingdom of God and abandon ourselves to Him.

— St. Vincent de Paul, TD2, July 7

Or else:

O Lord, let Your grace always lead and follow me, and keep me ever intent on good works, through Your Son Jesus Christ. Amen.

— *Imitation of Christ*, III, ch. 55

Thoughts

- The more our actions resemble those of Jesus Christ on earth, and the more our sufferings are united to His, the more both are pleasing to God.

  — St. Vincent de Paul, TD2, April 17

- Happy the soul which has taken Jesus Christ for its guide, its model and its beloved.

  — Curé of Ars, TD2, January 14

Resolutions

1. To recite the prayer *Soul of Christ* (page 283) and meditate on the plea, "in Your wounds, hide me!"
2. To meditate for a few minutes on a scene from the Gospel, trying to discern what Jesus expects of us.
3. To reproduce today a virtue of Jesus. Specify which one.

JESUS, OUR KING

Saturday of the 22nd Week after Pentecost

God speaks to us:

Render to Caesar that which is Caesar's, and to God that which is God's.

Gospel of Sunday: St. Matthew 22:21

Meditation

By these words, our Lord is marking the distinction between the temporal power and the spiritual power. He is showing that these two powers are not mixed but very distinct from one another. There is a domain proper to the Church and another proper to the State.

A first pitfall would be to want to absorb civil society into religious society, as we see in Islam. The Moslem religion treats not only the relations between man and God, but goes so far as to govern political and social life as well. Islam is in fact a religion of laws, which leaves nothing to the decision of the initiative of the believer. Thus, *sharia*, which is the canon law of Islam, dictates family custom, penal law, national and international law, and relations with non-Moslems. So, the religious society totally absorbs civil society.

On the contrary, another pitfall consists in wanting to absorb the religious society into civil society, to the point of recognizing no other sovereign master than the State. This is the pitfall of secularism, which is our daily experience in modern nations and whose bitter fruits we realize more every day. According to this idea, the State should in no way refer to the Church in the establishment of its laws. These, then, are the two pitfalls to be avoided in the relations between Church and State.

In his encyclical *Quas Primas*, Pope Pius XI expressed in a few words the Catholic vision of the relations which ought to exist between Church and State: The kingship of our Lord, he writes, "demands that the State should take account of the commandments of God and of Christian principles, both in making laws and in administering justice, and also in providing for the young a sound moral education."[57] In the moral domain, the temporal power is supposed to be subject to the spiritual power, so that the State might not be an obstacle for its citizens on the path to heavenly beatitude, but that it might on the contrary be a strong ally of the holy Church.

O Lord Jesus, deign to receive once again in society the place that is due to You. I wish for my part to do all I can to make You reign in my life and in what depends on me.

Prayer

Prince of all ages, Christ, King of nations, we acknowledge You as the sole Ruler of our minds and hearts.
— Vespers hymn for the Feast of Christ the King

Or else:

May the rulers of nations render You public homage; may courts and judges honor You; may laws and the arts proclaim You.
— Vespers hymn for the Feast of Christ the King

Thoughts

- The Lord is our Judge, the Lord is our Lawgiver, the Lord is our King; He will save us.
  — Antiphon for Vespers of the Feast of Christ the King

- See, our King advances in the vanguard, and will fight for us! Let us follow like men; no terrors shall daunt us.
  — *Imitation of Christ*, III, ch. 56

---

[57] Pius XI, *Quas Primas*, §32. Translation from the Vatican website.

Resolutions

1 To recite a rosary so that Jesus may receive again the place He deserves in civil society.

2 To read the encyclical *Quas Primas* of Pius XI.

3 To defend the Catholic vision of Church-State relations when the opportunity arises, showing the terrible consequences of the two pitfalls described in the meditation: neither sharia, nor secularism.

THE FAITH OF THE WOMAN WITH THE FLOW OF BLOOD

23rd Sunday after Pentecost

God speaks to us:

[The woman with a flow of blood] said to herself, "If I touch but His cloak I shall be healed."

Gospel: St. Matthew 9:21

Meditation

As Jesus made His way to the home of Jairus, the ruler of the synagogue, a woman who for twelve years had been suffering from hemorrhage came and touched the tassel of His cloak, saying, "If I can only reach Him, if I have the happiness of touching even the tassel of His garment, it will be enough; I will soon experience the effects of that divine power. I will be saved. Yes, *If I touch but His cloak, I shall be healed.*" This is the first woman in the Gospel who comes to find Jesus in public. Out of humility, she does not dare to present herself before Him, but is content merely to touch Him from the crowd, behind Him. In fact, her illness was considered to be something impure. Seeking our Lord, she was not disappointed in her hopes. Jesus fully responded to her expectation. He healed her and healed her totally.

Nonetheless, our Lord, who is God, knows what has happened near Him and He says out loud, "Who touched Me?" (Lk. 8:45) We can well imagine the panic of this woman. "The woman came up trembling, and falling down at His feet, declared in the presence of all the people why she had touched Him, and how she had been healed instantly" (Lk. 8:47). Our Lord says to her, "Take courage, daughter; thy faith has saved thee" (Mt. 9:22). Our Lord calls this poor woman "my daughter" because she believed in Him. It is by faith that this woman became His daughter. Jesus called attention to her in this way in order that her faith might serve as an example, and likewise in order to enliven the faith of the ruler of the synagogue.

If the mere garments of our Lord had such power, what are we to think of the efficacy of a good communion, communion received with a spirit of faith? In communion, we do not merely touch the cloak of our Lord, but we receive Him in person. And we receive Him not simply as we welcome a friend into our home; we receive Him into us, we possess Him in the deepest regions of our soul. And He comes into us whole and entire, with His body, His blood, His soul, and His divinity.

Lord Jesus, increase my faith, especially as I approach You in holy communion.

Prayer

I do believe, Lord! Help my unbelief.

— Mk. 9:23

Or else:

Lord, appease the hunger of this, Your beggar; warm my coldness by the fire of Your love, and lighten my blindness by the light of Your presence.

— *Imitation of Christ*, IV, ch. 16

Thoughts

- Discouragement is never justified... A soul who has faith in God, who is sure of its God, well knows how to find a way to escape from these straits, and makes use of its own impotence and difficulties as a springboard to plunge into God by a strong, determined act of faith.

  — Fr. Gabriel, DI, pp. 705-6

- Jesus never said, "My omnipotence has saved you, has cured you," but *your faith*, as if to make us understand that faith is the indispensable condition that He requires if we are to benefit from His omnipotence.

  — Fr. Gabriel, DI, p. 705

Resolutions

1. To recite the Act of Faith in asking for the grace to believe in the power of prayer to touch the heart of Jesus (see page 263).

2. To read attentively the Gospel of today's Mass.

3. To conquer our moodiness by chasing negative thoughts and admiring the graces which we have received, blessing God for them.

RAISING OF A CHILD FROM THE DEAD

Monday of the 23rd Week after Pentecost

GOD SPEAKS TO US:

[Jesus] went in and took her by the hand; and the girl arose. And the report of this spread throughout all that district.

Gospel of Sunday: St. Matthew 9:25-26

MEDITATION

After healing the woman with an issue of blood, Jesus continues His way toward the home of Jairus, the ruler of the synagogue. In the meantime, someone informs Him that He need not bother going on to the house because Jairus' daughter, who was gravely ill, has just died. But Jesus continues His path, unaffected. When He reaches the house of Jairus, He tells the flute players and the crowd of mourners to leave. He takes as witnesses only the parents of the child and three Apostles. He then draws near the corpse of the child, takes her hand and says to her, "Girl, arise!" (Lk. 8:55). And immediately the girl sits up. Then, to emphasize the reality of the miracle, He commands the parents to give the child something to eat.

Before leaving, our Lord asks the witnesses of the miracle to speak of it to no one, in this way showing how we should flee pride and vainglory.

This miracle of Jesus gave St. John Chrysostom an opportunity to strengthen the virtue of hope in parents affected by the death of their children. He said to them, "Today, it is a truth more brilliant than the sun that death is but a sleep. This time, you will tell me, [Jesus] did not raise my daughter from the dead! True! But He will raise her much more glorious. The child whom He raised had to die a second time; but your daughter, once she is called back to life, will never again know death... Christ has conquered death...

"If your child dwelt in a palace, it would be enough for you to know that he is happy and you would not ask to see him; and now that he is in possession of a much higher felicity, your courage fails you for a few days of separation... Do not weep over an event which will earn for you your crown, which will merit your reward... Oh! If you knew what the present life is, and what the life to come is; if you knew that one is but a spider's web and a vain shadow, whereas the goods of the other life are all immutable and eternal, you would need no more convincing."[58]

Lord Jesus, help me to accept the sorrow of separation from those whom I have known and loved, and who have already passed through the gates of eternity.

Prayer

O Lord, show me the path I must follow to reach You.
— Fr. Gabriel, DI, p. 577

Or else:

When shall I see You, O precious, long-desired, amiable Lord? When shall I appear before Your face? When shall I be satiated with Your beauty?
— Fr. Gabriel, DI, p. 407

Thoughts

- We have not here a lasting dwelling, but we seek a future city, for our homeland is in heaven.
 — Fr. Gabriel, DI, p. 407

- How sweet and gentle death is for souls who have loved only Him.
 — Elizabeth of the Trinity, L 278

---

[58] St. John Chrysostom, *Complete Works*, VI, pp. 371-374.

Monday of the 23rd Week after Pentecost

Resolutions

1 To recite the Act of Hope, meditating on its meaning (see page 264).

2 To think of those we know who have left this earth during the past year, to pray for them and also to better realize the shortness of life on earth.

3 To avoid building ourselves up in the eyes of others, so as not to lose the merits of our good actions.

THE SCHOOL OF THE SAINTS

Tuesday of the 23rd Week after Pentecost

GOD SPEAKS TO US:

Wisdom showed the just man the kingdom of God, and gave him the knowledge of holy things.

Wisdom 10:10

MEDITATION

Last Sunday's Gospel recounted the episode of Jesus raising the daughter of Jairus. Jesus there described death as a *sleep*. "The girl is asleep, not dead," He told the crowd (Mt. 9:24). In this way He also wanted to help us to long with all our being for the true life, the life which never ends, the blessed life of Heaven.

We are made for Heaven and to conquer it we must acquire the knowledge that saints have. In the Old Testament, Holy Scripture tells us that God gave to the patriarch Jacob *the knowledge of holy things*, that is, the knowledge of sanctity. This is the knowledge which we must seek. Indeed, to reach Heaven, it is not enough to want to be saints; we also have to know how to be one. Whoever desires the end, desires the means. And so let us place ourselves in the school of the saints in order to reach holiness.

We see three characteristics in the life of the saints. First of all, saints did not seek holiness in any other place than where God had put them by circumstances, by the action of His Providence. Everyone can therefore say: Among the saints who are today in Heaven, there are some who attained holiness in a state of life like mine. So, there is no reason why I in turn cannot reach holiness in the family situation and the social conditions where I am today. If I want to be a saint, I must not dream of another life than my own; rather, it is here where I am that I have to sanctify myself.

Tuesday of the 23rd Week after Pentecost

Next, to reach holiness, the saints used their religious convictions to sanctify their condition, that is, to avoid the disorders inherent to their duty of state and to fulfill all their duties, including those which pleased them least.

Finally, the saints turned difficulties into opportunities by using their duty of state to draw nearer to God, because "for those who love God all things work together unto good" (Rom. 8:28), that is, everything we go through, whether pleasant or painful, can and should serve our sanctification.

Lord Jesus, help me to acquire *the knowledge of holy things*, so that I might reach the blessed eternity of Heaven.

Prayer

Grant, we beseech Thee, O Lord, that Thy faithful people may ever rejoice in honoring all Thy Saints, and may be defended by their unceasing prayers.

— Postcommunion for the Mass of All Saints

Or else:

Apostles and prophets, beg that the rigorous Judge forgive those who sincerely weep for their sins.

— Vespers hymn for All Saints

Thoughts

- The paths of holiness are paths of return to God by footsteps of love.
  — Fr. Calmel, 365 D, March 1

- Oh! How sweet it is to love on earth as souls love in Heaven; and to learn to love each other in this world, as we will love eternally in the next!
  — St. Francis de Sales, TD, July 26

Resolutions

1 To better appreciate our duty of state and turn toward our holiness the various circumstances of our life, pleasant or unpleasant.

2 To put all our effort into doing well our duty of state.

3 To bless God several times over the course of the day, in difficulties as in happier moments, remembering that everything is grace.

THE EXISTENCE OF PURGATORY

Wednesday of the 23rd Week after Pentecost

GOD SPEAKS TO US:

Amen I say to thee, thou wilt not come out from it until thou hast paid the last penny.

St. Matthew 5:26

MEDITATION

The Old and the New Testament both let us glimpse the existence of purgatory. In the Old Testament, Judas Maccabees undertakes a collection in order to offer expiatory sacrifices for the solace of souls who had died in combat. He collects twelve thousand silver drachmas and sends them to Jerusalem. And the sacred writer concludes by writing, "It is therefore a holy and wholesome thought to pray for the dead, that they may be loosed from sins" (II Mac. 12:46). The New Testament contains several references to Purgatory. Our Lord affirms that "whoever speaks against the Holy Spirit, it will not be forgiven him, either in this world or in the world to come" (Mt. 12:32). Certain sins will therefore be forgiven in the world to come. Elsewhere, our Lord threatens the sinner with prison when He says, *Amen I say to thee, thou wilt not come out from it until thou hast paid the last penny.* These words mean that we will have to stay in purgatory until we have expiated all our sins. St. Paul writes in turn, "The fire will assay the quality of everyone's work… If his work burns he will lose his reward, but himself will be saved, yet so as through fire" (I Cor. 3:13, 15). These passages in Holy Scripture assume the existence of purgatory.

The Fathers of the Church used these texts to confirm the existence of an intermediary place between Heaven and hell, like hell in its sufferings but like Heaven by the love which unites souls to God. Several councils and popes have made it their duty to remind Catholics of this truth of our religion. The Second Council of Lyon, in 1274, declared that the souls which have been separated from their bodies in charity and repentance are purified after their death by cleansing pains.[59] Pope Eugene IV, in 1439, solemnly defined the existence of purgatory in these terms: "In the name of the Holy Trinity, of the Father, and of the Son, and of the Holy Spirit… We define that this truth of faith be believed and accepted by all Christians… that, if those truly penitent have departed in the love of God, before they have made satisfaction by the worthy fruits of penance for sins of commission and omission, the souls of these are cleansed after death by purgatorial punishments."[60] The voice of the Church has spoken, and so it is no longer possible to deny this dogma without falling into heresy.

Lord Jesus, I believe firmly in the existence of purgatory and desire to expiate my sins in this life.

Prayer

Turn away Thy face from my sins, and blot out all my iniquities. Create a clean heart in me, O God: and renew a right spirit within my bowels. Cast me not away from Thy face; and take not Thy holy spirit from me.
— Ps. 50:11-13

Or else:

O tender Lord Jesus, give them eternal rest.

— *Dies Irae*

Thoughts

- In all thy works remember thy last end, and thou shalt never sin.
  — Ecclus. 7:40

- If now we are not generous in suffering, if here on earth we do not know how to accept suffering, pure and unmitigated, as Jesus did on the Cross, our purification will of necessity have to be completed in purgatory.

  — Fr. Gabriel, DI, p. 1135

---

[59] DZ 856 (464), *The Church Teaches*, p. 348.
[60] DZ 1300 and 1304 (691 and 693), *The Sources of Catholic Dogma*, p. 219.

Resolutions

1. To meditate for a few minutes on purgatory and to make a concrete resolution for the day.
2. To visit a cemetery and pray for those buried there.
3. To offer in the morning all the sufferings of the day to come, in a spirit of expiation for our sins.

THE SUFFERINGS OF PURGATORY

Thursday of the 23rd Week after Pentecost

God speaks to us:

"The fire will assay the quality of everyone's work... If his work burns he will lose his reward, but himself will be saved, yet so as through fire."

1st Epistle of St. Paul to the Corinthians 3:13, 16

Meditation

When Jesus was on earth, His divine attributes were disdained or blasphemed. His wisdom was often misunderstood, His providence not acknowledged, His will not followed. The souls in Purgatory now participate in His sufferings, seeing how they themselves disdained the divine attributes in refusing to recognize them, or at least to submit to them. In contemplating God in the light of the faith, they perceive that He is essentially Father. And they have so badly loved this Father who is so loving! For God, the venial sins of His children are in a certain way more wounding than the mortal insults of His enemies. What then must be the cry of souls in Purgatory who see through the love of Jesus for His Father the ingratitude of their entire life!

"For God so loved the world that He gave His only-begotten Son... that the world might be saved through Him" (Jn. 3:16-17), and we too often forget this love of God for us, or else we doubt it. The Sacred Heart complained of this ingratitude to St. Margaret Mary in terms which have a divine fullness but even more an ineffable human accent: "I feel the ingratitude of souls more than all that I suffered during My Passion. If only they would make Me some return for My Love, I should think but little of all I have done for them and would wish, were it possible, to suffer still more. But the sole return they make for all My eagerness to do them good is to reject Me and treat Me with coldness."[61] These

---

[61] Third revelation, 1674.

words are the more poignant when we meditate on them at the foot of the cross, contemplating the agony of Jesus in body and soul. Think then how keenly the souls in Purgatory must realize their ingratitude toward their heavenly Father and toward Jesus, who suffered so much for them.

O Jesus, I will to make reparation for my ingratitude and compensate my failures to love by leading from now on a more fervent, more generous life.

Prayer

O holy souls in purgatory, beloved of God and loving Him, who adore with such love the hand that strikes you, may God give you rest, light and peace!

— Fr. Emmanuel, M, p. 400

Or else:

O Lord, rebuke me not in Thy indignation, nor chastise me in Thy wrath.

— Ps. 6:2

Thoughts

- What sufferings there are in purgatory! What agonies! What regret! There, we must do rigorous penance! There, all is punished! There, nothing is forgotten, not even a useless word. O justice of God!
  — Fr. Emmanuel, M, p. 400

- Nonetheless, in purgatory, everyone is subject to God, no one rebels, no one murmurs, and everyone suffers, as everyone awaits relief, light, rest, peace!
  — Fr. Emmanuel, M, p. 400

Resolutions

1. To meditate for ten minutes on the sufferings of the souls in purgatory in the light of the divine attributes: God's wisdom, His power, His justice, His mercy.
2. To mark every hour of the day with the prayer, "Eternal rest grant unto them, O Lord."
3. To have a Mass celebrated for the souls in Purgatory who are most forgotten, and to assist at that Mass if possible.

THE SILENCE OF THE SOULS IN PURGATORY

Friday of the 23rd Week after Pentecost

God speaks to us:

Jesus kept silence.

St. Matthew 26:63

Meditation

St. Catherine of Genoa wrote that, "The participation of Himself that God grants the soul" in purgatory, "however slight it be, keeps it so wholly taken up with His majesty that it can think of nothing else; everything to do with self passes away; it neither sees, speaks, nor knows loss or pain of its own."[62] This silence is the shadow of God in the human soul. Thus, the soul in purgatory does not live folded in on itself; on the contrary, it is entirely aimed toward God. And this divine shadow which engulfs it is so impressive that the soul admires it in silence, as we savor in silence a majestic landscape which we are contemplating.

But the silence in purgatory is also that of a soul which has offended God. Sin can find no justification before the eternal Judge. During His Passion, bearing the weight of our sins, *Jesus kept silence; Jesus autem tacebat*. It is the same with the souls in purgatory.

The silence of the soul in purgatory is the silence of a contemplative soul, the silence of a soul still tainted, and it is also the silence of a soul which abandons itself totally to God, submitting itself to Him entirely. As astonishing as it may seem, the justice of God awakens in the soul a reaction of pure love. The soul perfectly accepts its fate. It yields with all its being, embracing its chastisement to glorify the holiness of God. Even if it were possible for the soul to escape its condemnation, it would not consent. It is ready to seize upon any suffering, any agony which

---

[62] St. Catherine of Genoa, *Treatise on Purgatory*, ch. 17, pp. 51-52.

could render to God some compensation for His glory, even if it is too late. The glory of God must be recognized, if not in this life, then at least after death. The soul knows this and perfectly conforms to it. And in this acceptance, it imitates Jesus in His Passion.

Help me, Lord Jesus, to submit myself totally to You, as do the souls in purgatory.

Prayer

Hear, O Lord, my prayer: give ear to my supplication in Thy truth: hear me in Thy justice. And enter not into judgment with Thy servant: for in Thy sight no man living shall be justified.

— Ps. 142:1-2

Or else:

My soul is troubled exceedingly: but Thou, O Lord, how long? Turn to me, O Lord, and deliver my soul: O save me for Thy mercy's sake.

— Ps. 6:4-5

Thoughts

- It is good to wait with silence for the salvation of God.

  — Lam. 3:26

- Good souls in purgatory, I do not dare to call you *holy* because you are not quite holy yet, but you will be one day, and I rejoice at the thought, and wish this day would come soon... How pure is your love! You desire only the glory of God, only His will.

  — Charles de Foucauld, TD, November 2

Resolutions

1. To meditate for a few minutes on the silence which reigns in purgatory and to see how to use our times of silence to live today closer to God.

2. To acquiesce perfectly to the will of God, without complaining about anything.

3. To meditate on a few of the Stations of the Cross, thinking of the silence of Jesus in His ascent to Calvary, ill-treated and covered with insults.

PRAYER FOR OUR DEAR DEPARTED

Saturday of the 23rd Week after Pentecost

God speaks to us:

It is a holy and wholesome thought to pray for the dead, that they may be loosed from sins.

2nd Book of Maccabees 12:46

Meditation

It is good for us to fulfill our debt of friendship and gratitude toward our departed loved ones, by begging the mercy of God for them.

Let us therefore lift up to Heaven the wishes and desires that arise spontaneously in our hearts. It is a duty of charity to pray for our parents and for our departed friends, because we can never be certain that they are in Heaven. St. Monica said to her son St. Augustine, "All I ask of you is that, wherever you may be, you should remember me at the altar of the Lord."[63] Let us therefore pray to God with all our heart that the souls of the faithful departed might rest in peace.

Most of all let us make our own the words that the Church holds out to us in Her liturgy, that prayer which God always hears. The Church has just the right tone when She makes us pray. She is filled with hope for our departed, but at the same time Her prayers have a certain gravity. The Church reminds us of the seriousness of life, which will end with a happy eternity for some, unhappy for others.

Let us therefore pray and let us visit cemeteries for the solace and deliverance of our departed loved ones. Let us also think to attend the holy sacrifice of the Mass, to have Masses offered for the departed, and let us add our small daily sacrifices to the sacrifice of our Lord.

---

[63] *Confessions*, Bk IX, ch. 11, p. 199.

When we have less courage for saying the rosary, let us think to offer it for our departed.

When a sacrifice presents itself which costs something of our nature, whether a service someone asks of us, an act of obedience which is painful, or some vexation, let us learn to offer it for the solace of our dear departed. When a soul in a state of grace deprives itself of something, accepts a trial, or freely endures some suffering, that action has a value of satisfaction for sin, which means it can bring solace to the soul in purgatory for whom we offer it. In this way we can shorten the purgatory of those dear to us and allow them to enjoy the beatific vision sooner.

Prayer

Grant, O Lord, eternal rest to the souls of the departed; and may the thought of death spur me on to greater generosity.

— Fr. Gabriel, DI, p. 1133

Or else:

Out of the depths I have cried to Thee, O Lord: Lord, hear my prayer.

— *Alleluia* of Sunday Mass

Thoughts

- After prayer for the conversion of sinners, the practice of prayer for the deliverance of the souls in purgatory is the most pleasing to God.

  — Curé of Ars, TD2, November 23

- In working toward the deliverance of suffering souls by performing works of mercy, we are living the spirit of Jesus Christ in its fullness.

  — Curé of Ars, TD2, November 24

Resolutions

1. To recite and meditate on the *De Profundis* for our dear departed (see page 280).
2. To read the proper of the funeral Mass, praying for the departed within our family.
3. To accept the trials of the day and offer their value of satisfaction for the deliverance of a soul in purgatory who is close to us.

THE DESTRUCTION OF JERUSALEM

24th Sunday after Pentecost

God speaks to us:

There shall be then great tribulation, such as hath not been found from the beginning of the world until now.

Gospel: St. Matthew 24:21

Meditation

In this last Sunday of the liturgical year, the Church offers to our meditation the passage from the Gospel of St. Matthew which speaks of the unprecedented catastrophes which are to fall upon our poor humanity.

In hearing this discourse, we are tempted to think that our Lord is speaking of events that are in the past, since He concludes by saying, "This generation will not pass away till all these things have been accomplished" (Mt. 24:34).

In reality our Lord is foretelling both the destruction of Jerusalem, which occurred a few decades after His death, and the destruction of the world, which will take place at the end of time. Indeed, the destruction of Jerusalem is an image, a figure, an anticipated representation of what will unfold at the end of the world, which is why these two events are described in a single discourse. Our Lord had said, *"There shall be then great tribulation, such as hath not been found from the beginning of the world until now."*

"Jerusalem endured the horrors of a two-year siege, during which the unhappy Jews fell to destroying one another; mothers ate the flesh of their children. After such horror the city was burned, and with it a great number of its inhabitants; the Temple was destroyed, fulfilling the prophecy of our Lord."[64]

---

[64] Fr. Emmanuel, *Meditations*, p. 316.

Fortunately, our Lord also prophesied that the days of the siege of Jerusalem would be shortened on account of the elect (Mt. 24:22). Our Lord had pity on the Jews who had converted to Catholicism, who would also have been affected by the persecution if it had lasted longer. To protected them, our Lord put an end to His vengeance upon the deicide nation.

These are the details in today's Gospel which concern the destruction of Jerusalem, and which give us a glimpse of what is going to take place at the end of the world, no longer for a single city, but for the whole world.

Lord Jesus, this terrifying description makes me realize what Your justice means. Have mercy on me!

Prayer

Lord Jesus Christ, Who… hast deigned to make Thy mother the Reconciliatrix of sinners, grant, we beseech Thee, that by the pious intercession of the same most blessed Virgin Mary we might attain forgiveness for our sins.

— Collect for the Mass of Our Lady of La Salette

Or else:

Be mindful, O Virgin Mother of God, when thou standest in the sight of the Lord, to speak good things for us, and to turn away His anger from us.

— Offertory for the Mass of Our Lady of La Salette

Thoughts

- Jesus left the Temple… and said to them, "Amen I say to you, there will not be left here one stone upon another that will not be thrown down."

    — St. Matthew 24:1-2

- "Daughters of Jerusalem, do not weep for Me, but weep for yourselves and for your children. For behold, days are coming in which men will say, 'Blessed are the barren.'"

    — St. Luke 23:28-29

Resolutions

1 To read attentively today's Gospel, letting penetrate the reality of God's justice.

2 To invoke several times during the day our Lady of La Salette, Reconciliatrix of sinners.

3 To say a rosary begging for the conversion of sinners and to end with the invocation, "Our Lady of Holy Hope, convert us."

SIGNS AND PRECURSORS

Monday of the 24th Week after Pentecost

GOD SPEAKS TO US:

When the Son of Man comes, will He find, do you think, faith on the earth?

St. Luke 18:8

MEDITATION

Our Lord told us the signs by which to recognize the coming of the end of the world. He spoke of a corruption of doctrine by false teachers. "False christs and false prophets will arise…" (Mt. 24:24) The principal sign which Jesus gives us is therefore the corruption of the faith, and a corruption so widespread that it could reach the elect themselves if God did not intervene. St. Paul in turn would say to the Thessalonians, "The day of the Lord will not come unless the apostasy comes first, and the man of sin is revealed, the son of perdition, who opposes and is exalted above all that is called God… and gives himself out as if he were God" (II Thess. 2:2-4). Apostasy means the abandoning of the faith by those who once embraced it. A great apostasy is therefore a massive abandoning of the faith. Jesus Himself predicted it explicitly: *When the Son of Man comes, will He find, do you think, faith on the earth?*

Our Lord continues His description, indicating the attitude which Catholics should have in these circumstances. They must not listen to false teachers, for their power of deception will be such that even going to see them would mean running the risk of adopting their ideas.

Our Lord has also given other signs of the end of time: "You shall hear of wars and rumors of wars… Nation will rise against nation, and kingdom against kingdom; and there will be pestilences and famines and earthquakes in various places. But all these things are the beginning of sorrows" (Mt. 24:6-8). "There will be signs in the sun and moon and stars, and upon the earth distress of nations bewildered by the roaring of sea and waves; men fainting for fear and for expectation of the things that are coming on the world" (Lk. 21:25-26). Troubles and terrors exist in every age, but at the end of time they will appear with greater violence and intensity.

Lord Jesus, in this troubled period through which we are passing, I trust in You.

Prayer

Lord, I believe, but give me a more solid faith. Mary, my mother, enlighten me.

— St. Alphonsus Liguori, HDD, p. 324

Or else:

O my Jesus, tell me what I must do to remedy the disorders in my life; I am ready for anything. And you, O Mary! Help me to do so, whatever the cost.

— St. Alphonsus Liguori, HDD, p. 100

Thoughts

- May the spectacle of the misfortunes of our time never turn our heart from eternity—not, of course, that we would cease to work within time, to build and to struggle, but that we struggle and build, remaining strong in every trial; that we work in view of pleasing the Lord.

  — Fr. Calmel, 365 D, October 30

- Nature, which is ordinarily the exterior radiance and the instrument of the goodness of the Creator toward man, enters the general chaos and becomes the manifestation of the anger of the sovereign King of the world and the instrument of His punishment of sinners.

  — Fr. Hugueny, PC, IV, p. 124

Resolutions

1. To see cataclysms as warnings from God, to bring men to repentance.
2. To nourish our faith by daily spiritual reading.
3. To support works of apostolate and to be ourselves witness to our faith with humility and conviction, when the opportunity arises.

THE DESTRUCTION OF THE UNIVERSE

Tuesday of the 24th Week after Pentecost

God speaks to us:

The heavens that now are, and the earth, by that same word have been stored up, being reserved for fire against the day of judgment and destruction of ungodly men.

2nd Epistle of St. Peter 3:7

Meditation

The world suffered the chastisement of the Flood in the days of Noah and will perish by fire at the end of time. St. Peter says on this subject, "First you must know, that in the last days there will come deceitful scoffers, men walking according to their own lusts... For of this they are willfully ignorant, that the world that then was, deluged with water, perished. But *the heavens that now are, and the earth, by that same word have been stored up, being reserved for fire against the day of judgment and destruction of ungodly men*" (II Pet. 3:3-7). On the day of Judgment, flames will go before our Lord because He will devastate the surface of the earth with fire and will purify it, purifying all that needs purifying in good souls, and will at last bury the wicked in hell. On commenting this verse from Psalm 96, "A fire shall go before Him, and shall burn His enemies round about" (96:3), St. Robert Bellarmine explains, "The Prophet is saying that only the impious will be burned by this fire, for they alone have their treasure on this earth and so they alone will suffer, whereas the just have nothing to suffer from the loss of these goods."[65]

This description gives rise to a holy fear in us. Nonetheless, the perspective of the end of the world should also fill us with hope and even with joy, as we see in these verses (11-13) of Psalm 95: "Let the heavens rejoice,

---

[65] *The Four Last Things in the Psalms*, pp. 77-78.

and let the earth be glad, let the sea be moved, and the fulness thereof: the fields and all things that are in them shall be joyful. Then shall all the trees of the woods rejoice before the face of the Lord, because He cometh: because He cometh to judge the earth. He shall judge the world with justice, and the people with His truth." St. Robert Bellarmine gives the following explanation: "The Second Coming, although it is often related in Scripture as something dark and terrifying, is sometimes also described in consoling tones, as in this verse of our psalm, on account of the joy of the elect which will radiate to the heavens, over the earth and over the sea, now destined to take on a superior form."[66]

Lord Jesus, seeing that the world is destined to perish one day by fire, I understand the need to avoid attaching myself to it in a disordered way.

Prayer

O righteous Awarder of punishment, my prayers deserve not to be heard; but Thou art good: grant, in Thy kindness, that I may not burn in the unquenchable fire.

— *Dies Irae*

Or else:

My God, I beg You, may I escape this dreadful fire! Deign to enkindle in my soul the fire of Your love.

— Fr. Emmanuel, M, p. 347

Thoughts

- Fire is a beautiful creation of God; it will serve to purify all material creation that has been in the service of sin.

  — Fr. Emmanuel, M, p. 347

- This fire will reduce to ashes the good and the wicked; but with a significant difference. The good will only suffer from this fire to the extent that they must endure a purgatory; the wicked, on the contrary, will taste the beginning of their hell.

  — Fr. Emmanuel, M, p. 347

---

[66] *Ibid.*, p. 83.

Resolutions

1 To recite the prayer *Come Holy Ghost* (see page 264) in praying that our heart may burn with the fire of divine love.

2 To reflect for a few minutes on today's meditation.

3 To respect nature and see there the work of God, without forgetting that it participates today in our state of sin.

THE GENERAL RESURRECTION

Wednesday of the 24th Week after Pentecost

God speaks to us:

My flesh also shall rest in hope.

Psalm 15:9

Meditation

After the destruction of the universe will come the general resurrection.

Bossuet has explained why it is fitting that our flesh know corruption. "The flesh is bound for corruption because it has been an attraction to evil, a source of wicked desires—in the words of the holy Apostle, a 'sinful flesh' (Rom. 8:3). This flesh must be destroyed, even that of the elect, because in its sinful state, it does not deserve to be reunited to a soul which is now blessed, nor to enter the kingdom of God: 'Flesh and blood can obtain no part in the kingdom of God' (I Cor. 15:50). This first form of our flesh must therefore be changed so as to be renewed; it must lose all of its first being, that it might receive another from the hand of God... O Christian soul, what do you dread at the approach of death? ...Perhaps that in seeing your house fall you fear having no refuge? Yet listen to the words of the divine Apostle: 'We know that if the earthly house in which we dwell be destroyed, we have a building from God, a house not made by human hands, eternal in the heavens' (2 Cor. 5:1)."[67] We express this truth in the *Credo*: "I believe in the resurrection of the body." God drew our body from nothing and will have no difficulty reuniting it to our soul. The trumpet blast resounding even to the tomb will gather all the dead before the throne of the Lord. What a difference will there be then among the resurrected! The bodies of the just will be

---

[67] Bossuet, *Oratorical Works*, 4th Week of Lent, 1662.

radiant, agile, magnificent, perfect, while those of the impious will be ugly, heavy, frightful, hideous, horrible to see. Indeed, it is fitting that our body, which has been the seat of our virtues as of our sins, should contribute to the joy or the pain of our soul. May this perspective fill the just with consolation and stir up salutary remorse in the sinner!

O Lord Jesus, help me to respect my body here below, since it is the temple of the Holy Ghost. May I never profane this body, so that it might one day share in the joy of my soul in the blessed eternity of Heaven.

Prayer

Lord, give me a place among Thy sheep, separating me from the goats and setting me on Thy right hand.

— *Dies Irae*

Or else:

Prostrate in supplication I implore Thee, with a heart contrite as though crushed to ashes; oh! have a care of my last hour!

— *Dies Irae*

Thoughts

- The resurrection will be a great work of God, just like creation. In creation, God drew being from nothingness; now, He will draw all bodies from the ashes, rendering to each soul precisely and exactly its own body, whole and entire.

  — Fr. Emmanuel, M, pp. 347-48

- The bodies of the damned will rise to suffer, and to suffer fire, and to suffer it eternally without ever being consumed. The bodies of the blessed, on the contrary, will be transfigured by the glory of their soul.

  — Fr. Emmanuel, M, p. 348

Resolutions

1. To avoid all excessive care of our body, since it is soon destined to be the food of worms.
2. Negatively, to avoid looking in the mirror too often; and positively, to accept the physical imperfections that we have from birth or that come with aging.
3. To respect our body by dressing decently and to keep watch over our eyes, especially in front of screens.

THE GLORIOUS RETURN OF JESUS

Thursday of the 24th Week after Pentecost

God speaks to us:

Then shall all the tribes of the earth... see the Son of Man coming in the clouds of heaven with much power and majesty.

Gospel of Sunday: St. Matthew 24:30

Meditation

After listing the signs of the end of the world, our Lord describes His glorious return. Our Lord uses the image of lightning to help us understand that this return will be unexpected. Lightning has no need for an introduction; it appears out of nowhere and is visible everywhere. And so Jesus Christ will appear suddenly and will be seen by all. Our Lord adds, "Wheresoever the body shall be, there shall the eagles also be gathered together" (Mt. 24:28). Whereever shall be the body of our Lord, there also shall be the eagles, that is, the angels and saints who gather for the Last Judgment. Our Lord tells us, *Then shall all the tribes of the earth... see the Son of Man coming in the clouds of heaven with much power and majesty.* Dread and terrible will be that Day of Judgment. On that day "the sun shall be darkened" (Mt. 24:29). In fact, the sun will be eclipsed by the radiance of our Lord, "light of the world."

Then will appear the sign of the Son of Man. This sign is the cross. The cross was the instrument of our salvation, and it will remind us of what our Lord did for us. It will be a source of joy for the just, but of terror for the reprobate. Behind the cross we will see our Lord *coming in the clouds of heaven with much power and majesty.* He will appear in glory. We will not see Him in His divinity, but in His glorified humanity. The vision of God is reserved for the elect, as our Lord tells us: "Blessed are the clean of heart, for they shall see God" (Mt. 5:8). As much as His first coming was discreet, hidden, humble, so now will this second coming be radiant, majestic, glorious. All men, good and wicked, will see Him, but with very different impressions. What a consolation for the just to witness the triumph of our Lord! But what confusion for sinners!

Lord Jesus, at the thought of Your glorious return, I realize the necessity to submit myself humbly to Your will.

Prayer

O sweet Jesus, detach us every year more and more from this world, whose fashion passeth away, with its vain toils, its false glories, and its lying pleasures.

— Dom Guéranger, LY, II, p. 493

Or else:

Come, Lord Jesus! Come, and perfect us in love, by eternal union, unto the glory of the Father, and of Thyself the Son, and of the Holy Ghost, forever and ever!

— Dom Guéranger, LY, II, p. 494

Thoughts

- Since we are certain that the Lord will come and that we are moving toward our encounter with Him in Paradise, let us live in a way worthy of meeting Him!
  — Fr. Calmel, 365 D, November 16
- Recompense is set aside for those who await the coming of God and who await it with love, because we could never await with love the coming of the Judge unless we know our own case is strong.
  — St. Gregory the Great, TD, December 1

Resolutions

1. Over the course of the day to make our sign of the cross with attention and devotion.
2. To reflect for a few minutes on the glorious triumph of Jesus in order to endure with patience the miseries of this life.
3. To put on our desk or on our computer screen a beautiful picture of Jesus to help us confide our thoughts to Him over the course of the day.

THE LAST JUDGMENT

Friday of the 24th Week after Pentecost

God speaks to us:

I saw the dead, the great and the small, standing before the throne, and scrolls were opened…; and the dead were judged out of those things that were written in the scrolls, according to their works.

Apocalypse 20:12

Meditation

Behold now all men raised from the dead, standing at the feet of the sovereign Judge.

Our Lord is there. His divine mother is at His right hand. His glorious cross is carried by the noblest of the heavenly spirits. His sacred wounds shine like suns. He is seated majestically on His throne of glory, incorruptible judge, whom nothing could turn from justice; infinitely wise judge, whom nothing could lead into error; sovereignly enlightened judge, who reads in the depths of hearts; judge whose sentence is without appeal and will be executed for eternity. All men are there, at His feet. Open before Him is the book wherein is written all that will serve for the judgment of the world.

All that was most hidden will appear in full light. This book contains in detail all the acts of virtue accomplished, and the evil committed, as well as the evil we have caused to be committed, and the evil that we have not hindered when we ought to have done so, and finally the good which we accomplished badly. For the glory of the good and the confusion of the wicked, all will be brought into the light of day, even those things most secretly concealed.

After this manifestation of consciences, which will happen in the blink of an eye, the double sentencing will occur before all generations of all nations and of all times. To those at His right, Jesus will say, "Come, blessed of My Father," and to those at His left, "Depart from Me, accursed ones, into the everlasting fire" (Mt. 25:34, 41). The *Dies Irae* affirms that no crime will go unpunished. These are indeed grave considerations which give us much food for reflection!

Let us add that our Lord, in His goodness and His mercy, has Himself given us the secret for appearing before Him with confidence at the Last Judgment. Let us hear Him: "Watch, then, praying at all times, that you may be accounted worthy to escape all these things that are to be, and to stand before the Son of Man" (Lk. 21:36).

Lord Jesus, touched by Your warning, I promise You to make real efforts to avoid the snares of the devil and to be more prayerful.

Prayer

O Jesus, my Savior and my Judge, grant me forgiveness; do not wait for the day when You will come to judge me.

— St. Alphonsus Liguori, HDD, p. 130

Or else:

On that day [of the Last Judgment], You will call me, my God, You will take me by the hand, raise me from the earth and place me before the sovereign Judge. I beg You, my God, place me at His right hand.

— Fr. Emmanuel, M, p. 346

Thoughts

- In the light of eternity the soul sees things as they really are. Oh! how empty is all that has not been done for God and with God!

  — Elizabeth of the Trinity, L 333

- O my soul, what will be your place on that great day? Love God now, and you will not fear that day!

  — Fr. Emmanuel, M, p. 350

Resolutions

1. To recite the *Confiteor* slowly (see page 263), regretting especially those sins that most wounded the Heart of Jesus.

2. To meditate for ten minutes on the Last Judgment and to draw consequences for the day to come.

3. To spend this day as if it were the last day of our life, so as to apply ourselves better to our duty of state and to our personal life.

THANKSGIVING

Saturday of the 24th Week after Pentecost

God speaks to us:

Joyfully render thanks to the Father, who has made us worthy to share the lot of the saints in light.

Epistle of Sunday: St. Paul to the Colossians 1:12

Meditation

Today the liturgical year draws to a close. Today therefore marks the end of another chapter in the history of our life, and it is for us an opportunity to give thanks to God, as St. Paul invited us to do in last Sunday's Epistle.

This duty of gratitude is so important that our Lord Himself willed to give us the example. Jesus never attributed any merit to Himself. He constantly renders thanks to His Father: "I praise Thee, Father, Lord of Heaven and earth, that Thou didst hide these things from the wise and prudent, and didst reveal them to little ones" (Lk. 10:21). In this way our Lord by His example teaches us to give thanks.

What is gratitude, in fact? It is a virtue by which we hold onto the memory of benefits received. The soul that is grateful to God holds onto the memory of His gifts and is animated by deep and ardent sentiments of affection toward Him. The soul blesses God, wishes Him all kinds of goods, as though He lacked any, and strives to repay Him in all the measure possible.

Our good God expects this gratitude from us. It is something necessary at every moment, and something we should fulfill especially here at the end of a liturgical year. And so let us thank God for the graces of light and strength which allowed us to overcome temptations; let us thank Him for the joyful moments, and even for the trials endured over the course of the year gone by.

Let us also thank God for the graces received through the sacraments of Penance and the Eucharist. Every fervent communion is a grace and a source of new graces. May the Blessed Virgin be our model in this gratitude. What is the *Magnificat*, that canticle which she left to us, if not her song of thanksgiving to the good God?

O our Lady, give me a grateful soul, a soul filled with love of God for all that He has done for me, until the day that I will be able to sing forever with you the mercies of God in the blessed eternity of Heaven. Amen.

Prayer

My soul doth magnify the Lord, and my spirit rejoices in God, my Savior.

— *Magnificat*

Or else:

I will bless the Lord at all times, His praise shall be always in my mouth.

— Ps. 33:2

Thoughts

- Let us ask God for fidelity and gratitude. Let us often tell ourselves, and tell God in prayer, this double story of our sins and His mercies. Let us often place this double image before our eyes. And may the sight of it stir up three sentiments in us: humility, gratitude, and a realization of our great duties after having received so much.
  — Charles de Foucauld, TD, October 14

- When the soul is touched by gratitude, it opens to the light.
  — Pauline Jaricot

Resolutions

1. To think back over the year gone by, thanking God for the graces received.
2. To recite or sing a *Magnificat* (see page 272).
3. To teach the children this duty of gratitude by pointing out to them the graces which they receive from God every day.

THE FEAST OF CHRIST THE KING

The Last Sunday of October

God speaks to us:

Pilate therefore said to Jesus, "Thou art then a king?" Jesus answered, "Thou sayest it; I am a king."

Gospel: St. John 18:37

Meditation

That Jesus Christ is king is proclaimed in every page of Holy Scripture. Our Lord is still in His cradle in Bethlehem and already the Magi seek the king of the Jews. And right up to His death, Jesus affirms His royalty, so that Pilate asks Him the question, "Art Thou the king of the Jews?" (Jn. 18:33) And to this question our Lord answers clearly, *Thou sayest it; I am a king.*

Jesus is indeed a king, and He draws His kingship both from His divinity and from His humanity. In the prologue to his Gospel, St. John affirms, "All things were made by Him and without Him was made nothing that has been made." (Jn. 1:3) Not only were all things created by Him at the origin, in the beginning of the world, but still today our Lord continues to uphold us in existence. Were He to cease for a single instant His action on the world and immediately all things would disappear into nothingness.

Our Lord is therefore king because He is God, but as man He is king, and doubly so. The bond which unites the humanity of Jesus to the Word gives this humanity an unparalleled dignity, an incomparable grandeur. His hypostatic union again elevates Jesus to the dignity of a king. From this point of view, our Lord again appears as king of all men, and even of angels. He presents Himself as the firstborn, as the archetype, the model, the exemplar of every creature.

Our Lord is therefore king because He is God; He is also king by His humanity by the unique, intimate bond which unites Him to the divinity.

But there is still a third foundation of His kingship. This title of King which our Lord possesses by His divine nature and which He holds by His hypostatic union, He also willed to merit. He conquered it by His cross, by His blood, by His sacrifice. We sing this truth in the *Vexilla Regis*: "*Regnavit a ligno Deus*" — "God has reigned from the wood." Sin enters the world through a tree. Salvation was given to us in the same way. The tree of the knowledge of good and evil gives way to the tree of the cross. In this way our Lord conquered His title as king.

Lord Jesus, King of all hearts, reign over me.

Prayer

Almighty and everlasting God… grant that all the families of nations now kept apart by the wound of sin, may be brought under the sweet yoke of His rule.

— Collect of the Mass

Or else:

We beg, Lord, that we who are proud to fight under the banner of Christ our King, may reign with Him forever in His realm above.

— Postcommunion of the Mass

Thoughts

- As for us, my very dear brethren, who are already instructed on the eternal joys, through the death and Resurrection of our Redeemer and His Ascension into Heaven, let us long ardently for our King.
  — St. Gregory the Great, TD, October 30

- If, therefore, the rulers of nations wish to preserve their authority, to promote and increase the prosperity of their countries, they will not neglect the public duty of reverence and obedience to the rule of Christ.
  — Pius XI, *Quas Primas*

Resolutions

1 To read attentively the propers of the Mass.

2 To sing three times, *Christus vincit, Christus regnat, Christus imperat.*

3 To submit to Jesus all the important decisions of our life, not only on a personal level but also on a social and political level.

THE FEAST OF ALL SAINTS

November 1st

God speaks to us:

I saw a great multitude which no man could number, of all nations and tribes and peoples and tongues, standing before the throne and in sight of the Lamb.

Epistle: St. John's Apocalypse 7:9

Meditation

The great feast of All Saints, which we celebrate today, naturally turns our hearts toward Heaven.

This feast carries our heart toward those ranks of martyrs, confessors, doctors, and virgins and we rejoice to see how the good God rewards those who love Him.

This feast of All Saints is not of Apostolic institution, but it dates far back in antiquity.

In 836, Pope Gregory IV on a visit to France urged King Louis the Fair to have this feast celebrated in his lands. The prince willingly agreed.

The feast was soon universally adopted and bore such fruits of spirituality and was so sweet to Christian hearts and so fostered piety, that it became a law of the Church.

In this way the feast of All Saints took its place in our calendar.

This feast answers a real need.

The limited number of days in the year make it impossible to celebrate individually the feast of every saint in Heaven recognized by the Church.

Moreover, many fervent Catholics led so virtuous a life in the world or in the cloister that they went straight to Heaven. We do not know them all, but they deserve our veneration, and it is eminently fitting that we honor them worthily. These are the primary aims of the feast of All Saints.

Yet beyond this duty of gratitude, the feast of All Saints places before our eyes our own glorious destiny. It shows us the crowns of gold that shine on the heads of the elect, the palms of triumph that they hold in their hands, and it tells us, "You, too, are called to share the destiny of the saints." This is very encouraging for us.

Saints of Paradise, men and women, you who look upon us from Heaven and count on us to carry on your virtues, uphold us in our combat so that we might deserve to join you in blessed eternity.

Prayer

All ye holy Saints of God, intercede for us.

— Litany of the Saints

Or else:

Deign, O Lord, to grant Your faithful people always to rejoice in the veneration of Your saints and to be protected by their constant supplication.

— Pauline Jaricot, TD, October 1

Thoughts

- Consider the nobility, the beauty and the multitude of the citizens and inhabitants of paradise. O how blessed is that number! The least of them is more beautiful than all the world. They sing always the sweet canticle of eternal love.

  — St. Francis de Sales, TD, November 1

- We are loved by God, loved by the friends of God. Let us therefore love them and let us long with all our heart to be joined to them. They call to us; they are waiting for us. Let us call them to our assistance.

  — Fr. Emmanuel, M, p. 399

Resolutions

1. To arrive early enough for Mass to be able to prepare ourselves to attend, and to avoid futile conversations after Mass.
2. To visit a cemetery in order to gain an indulgence for our dear departed.
3. To invoke our favorite saint over the course of the day, so as to call down on ourselves the blessings of God.

Addenda

From the Assumption to Advent

Spiritual Communion

Spiritual communion consists in an ardent desire to receive Jesus in the Blessed Sacrament, and in an act of love such as one would make if one had received Him sacramentally.[68] The Council of Trent strongly praises spiritual communion and encourages the faithful to practice it.[69]

To make a good spiritual communion, St. Alphonsus Liguori recommends the following act:

> My Jesus, I believe that Thou art Present in the Blessed Sacrament. I Love Thee above all things, and I desire Thee in my Soul. Since I cannot now receive Thee sacramentally, come at least spiritually into my heart. As though Thou wert already there, I embrace Thee and unite myself wholly to Thee; permit not that I should ever be separated from Thee.[70]

Depending on the circumstances, if one needs a shorter prayer, or if one prefers a simpler form, the same saint proposes that we very simply say:

> O Jesus, I believe that You are present in the Blessed Sacrament; I love You and desire You. Come into my heart. I embrace You. Please never leave me.[71]

---

[68] St. Thomas Aquinas, *Summa Theologica*, IIIa, q. 80, a. 1, *ad* 3.
[69] Council of Trent, Session XIII, Decree Concerning the Sacrament of the Eucharist, ch. 8, in DZ 1648-1649.
[70] St. Alphonsus Liguori, *Visits to the Blessed Sacrament*, Apôtre du Foyer, 2000, p. 13.
[71] *Ibid.*, p. 14.

The Mysteries of the Rosary

Joyful Mysteries

First mystery: the Annunciation of the Angel Gabriel to the Virgin Mary; fruit of this mystery: humility

Second mystery: the Visitation of our Lady to her cousin Elizabeth; fruit of this mystery: fraternal charity

Third mystery: the birth of Jesus in the stable at Bethlehem; fruit of this mystery: the spirit of poverty

Fourth mystery: the Presentation of the child Jesus in the Temple; fruit of this mystery: obedience

Fifth mystery: the finding of the child Jesus in the Temple; fruit of this mystery: the seeking of God in all things.

Sorrowful Mysteries

First mystery: the agony of Jesus in the Garden of Olives; fruit of this mystery: contrition for our sins

Second mystery: the scourging of our Lord at the pillar; fruit of this mystery: the mortification of the senses

Third mystery: the crowning with thorns; fruit of this mystery: the mortification of pride

Fourth mystery: the carrying of the cross; fruit of this mystery: patience and perseverance in trials

Fifth mystery: the crucifixion and death of Jesus on the cross; fruit of this mystery: a greater love of God and of souls.

Glorious Mysteries

First mystery: the Resurrection of our Lord; fruit of this mystery: faith

Second mystery: the Ascension of Jesus into Heaven; fruit of this mystery: hope

Third mystery: the descent of the Holy Ghost on the Blessed Virgin and the Apostles; fruit of this mystery: missionary zeal

Fourth mystery: the Assumption of our Lady into Heaven; fruit of this mystery: the grace of a happy death

Fifth mystery: the crowning of Mary as queen of Heaven and earth; fruit of this mystery: a great devotion to the Blessed Virgin.

Creed

I believe in God, the Father Almighty, Creator of Heaven and earth;

and in Jesus Christ, His only son, our Lord,

who was conceived of the Holy Ghost, was born of the Virgin Mary,

suffered under Pontius Pilate, was crucified, died, and was buried;

He descended into hell, and on the third day He rose again from the dead;

He ascended into Heaven and is seated at the right hand of God, the Father Almighty,

from whence He shall come to judge the living and the dead.

I believe in the Holy Ghost,

the Holy Catholic Church, the Communion of Saints,

the forgiveness of sins,

the resurrection of the body,

and life everlasting. Amen.

Confiteor

I confess to almighty God, to blessed Mary ever Virgin, to blessed Michael the Archangel, to blessed John the Baptist, to the holy Apostles Peter and Paul, and to all the Saints, that I have sinned exceedingly in thought, word and deed: through my fault, through my fault, through my most grievous fault.

Therefore, I beseech blessed Mary ever Virgin, blessed Michael the Archangel, blessed John the Baptist, the holy Apostles Peter and Paul, and all the Saints, to pray to the Lord our God for me.

Glory Be to the Father

Glory be to the Father, and to the Son, and to the Holy Ghost, as it was in the beginning, is now, and ever shall be, world without end. Amen.

Act of Faith

O my God, I firmly believe that Thou art one God in three divine Persons, the Father, the Son, and the Holy Ghost; I believe that Thy divine Son became man and died for our sins, and that He will come to judge the living and the dead. I believe these and all the truths which the holy Catholic Church teaches, because Thou hast revealed them, who canst neither deceive nor be deceived.

Act of Hope

O my God, relying on Thy infinite goodness and promises, I hope to obtain pardon of my sins, the help of Thy grace, and life everlasting, through the merits of Jesus Christ, my Lord and Redeemer.

Act of Charity

O my God, I love Thee above all things, with my whole heart and soul, because Thou art all good and worthy of all my love. I love my neighbor as myself for love of Thee. I forgive all who have injured me and ask pardon of all whom I have injured.

Act of Contrition

O my God, I am heartily sorry for having offended Thee, and I detest all my sins because I dread the loss of heaven and the pains of hell, but most of all because they offend Thee, my God, who art all good and deserving of all my love. I firmly resolve, with the help of Thy grace, to confess my sins, to do penance, and to amend my life.

Prayer to the Holy Ghost

Come, Holy Ghost, and fill the hearts of Thy faithful, and enkindle in them the fire of Thy love.
V. Send forth Thy Spirit and they shall be created.
R. And Thou shalt renew the face of the earth.
Let us pray: O God, who didst instruct the hearts of the faithful by the light of the Holy Ghost, grant that by the same Spirit we may be truly wise, and ever rejoice in Thy consolation, through Christ, our Lord. Amen.

Act of Confidence in God

St. Claude de la Colombière

My God, I am so convinced that You keep watch over those who hope in You, and that we can want for nothing when we look for all from You, that I am resolved in the future to live free from every care, and to turn all my anxieties over to You. "In the peace I find in Thee I will sleep, and I will rest: for Thou, O Lord, hast singularly settled me in the hope I have of Thy divine goodness" (Ps. 4:9-10). Men may deprive me of possessions and of honor; sickness may strip me of strength and the means of serving You; I may even lose Your grace by sin; but I shall never lose my hope. I shall keep it until the last moment of my life; and at that moment all the demons in Hell shall strive to tear it from me in vain. "In the peace I find in Thee I will sleep and I will rest…" Others may look for happiness from their wealth or their talents; others may rest on the innocence of their life, or the severity of their penance, or the amount of their alms, or the fervor of their prayers; "for Thou, O Lord, hast singularly settled me in hope." As for me, Lord, all my confidence is my confidence itself. This confidence has never deceived anyone. No one, no one has hoped in You, Lord, and has been confounded (Ecclus. 2:11).

I am sure, therefore, that I shall be eternally happy, since I firmly hope to be, and because it is from You, O God, that I hope for it. "In Thee, O Lord, have I hoped, let me never be confounded" (Ps. 30:2). I know, alas I know only too well, that I am weak and unstable. I know what temptation can do against the strongest virtue. I have seen the stars of heaven fall, and the pillars of the firmament; but that cannot frighten me. So long as I continue to hope, I shall be sheltered from all misfortune; and I am sure of hoping always, since I hope also for this unwavering hopefulness.

Finally, I am sure that I cannot hope too much in You, and that I cannot receive less than I have hoped for from You. So I hope that You will hold me safe on the steepest slopes, that You will sustain me against the most furious assaults, and that You will make my weakness triumph over my most fearful enemies. I hope that You will love me always, and that I too shall love You without ceasing. To carry my hope once and for all as far as it can go, I hope from You to possess You, O my Creator, in time and in Eternity. Amen.

Prayer to St. Michael Archangel

Saint Michael, the Archangel, defend us in battle; be our protection against the wickedness and the snares of the devil. May God rebuke him, we humbly pray: and do thou, O Prince of the heavenly host, by the power of God, cast into hell Satan and all the evil spirits who wander about the world seeking the ruin of souls. Amen.

Invocations to St. Michael the Archangel

Saint Michael the Archangel, by thy radiance enlighten us.
Saint Michael the Archangel, beneath thy wings protect us.
Saint Michael the Archangel, with thy sword defend us.

Litany of the Sacred Heart

Lord, have mercy on us. *Lord, have mercy on us.*
Christ, have mercy on us. *Christ, have mercy on us.*
Lord, have mercy on us. *Lord, have mercy on us.*
Christ, hear us. Christ, *graciously hear us.*
God the Father of Heaven, *have mercy on us.*
God the Son, Redeemer of the world,
God the Holy Ghost,
Holy Trinity one God,
Heart of Jesus, Son of the Eternal Father,
Heart of Jesus, formed by the Holy Ghost in the womb of the Virgin Mother,
Heart of Jesus, united hypostatically to the Word of God,
Heart of Jesus, infinite in Majesty,
Heart of Jesus, holy temple of God,
Heart of Jesus, tabernacle of the Most High,
Heart of Jesus, house of God and gate of Heaven,
Heart of Jesus, glowing furnace of charity,
Heart of Jesus, abode of justice and love,
Heart of Jesus, full of kindness and love,
Heart of Jesus, abyss of all virtues,
Heart of Jesus, most worthy of all praise,
Heart of Jesus, King and center of all hearts,
Heart of Jesus, wherein are all the treasures of wisdom and knowledge,
Heart of Jesus, wherein abides the fullness of Divinity,
Heart of Jesus, in which the Father was well pleased,
Heart of Jesus, of whose fullness we have all received,
Heart of Jesus, desire of the everlasting hills,
Heart of Jesus, patient and abounding in mercy,
Heart of Jesus, rich unto all that call upon Thee,
Heart of Jesus, source of life and holiness,
Heart of Jesus, atonement for our sins,
Heart of Jesus, glutted with reproaches,
Heart of Jesus, wounded for our crimes,
Heart of Jesus, made obedient unto death,

Heart of Jesus, pierced by the lance, *have mercy on us.*
Heart of Jesus, source of all consolation,
Heart of Jesus, our life and resurrection,
Heart of Jesus, our peace and reconciliation,
Heart of Jesus, Victim of sin,
Heart of Jesus, salvation of all who trust in Thee,
Heart of Jesus, hope of all who die in Thee,
Heart of Jesus, delight of all the saints,

Lamb of God, who takest away the sins of the world,
    spare us, O Lord.
Lamb of God, who takest away the sins of the world,
    graciously hear us, O Lord.
Lamb of God, who takest away the sins of the world,
    have mercy on us.

V. Jesus, meek and humble of heart,
R. Make our hearts like unto Thine.

Let us pray: Almighty and eternal God, look upon the Heart of Thy well-beloved Son, and upon the praise and satisfaction which He rendered to Thee on behalf of sinners; and, being thus appeased, grant them the pardon which they seek from Thy mercy, in the name of the same Jesus Christ, Thy Son, who liveth and reigneth with Thee, forever and ever. Amen.

Litany of the Holy Guardian Angels

Lord, have mercy on us. *Lord, have mercy on us.*
Christ, have mercy on us. *Christ, have mercy on us.*
Lord, have mercy on us. *Lord, have mercy on us.*
Christ, hear us. *Christ, hear us.*
Christ, hear us. *Christ, graciously hear us.*
God the Father of Heaven, *have mercy on us.*
God the Son, Redeemer of the world,
God, the Holy Ghost,
Holy Trinity, One God,
Holy Mary, Queen of the Angels, *pray for us.*
Saint Michael,
Saint Gabriel,
Saint Raphael,
Holy Choir of Seraphim,
Holy Choir of Cherubim,
Holy Choir of Thrones,
Holy Choir of Dominations,
Holy Choir of Principalities,
Holy Choir of Powers,
Holy Choir of Virtues,
Holy Choir of Archangels,
Holy Choir of Angels,
All the hierarchies of blessed spirits,
All the holy guardian angels,
My holy guardian angel,
Holy Angel, my counselor,
Holy Angel, my patron,
Holy Angel, my defender,
Holy Angel, my loving friend,
Holy Angel, my consoler,
Holy Angel, my brother,
Holy Angel, my witness,

Holy Angel, my helper,
Holy Angel, my vigilant guardian,
Holy Angel, my intercessor,
Holy Angel, to whom my path is entrusted,
Holy Angel, my sovereign,
Holy Angel, my guide,
Holy Angel, my savior in all danger,
Holy Angel, inspiring good thoughts,
Holy Angel, who will be with me at the hour of my death,

Lamb of God, who taketh away the sins of the world,
spare us, O Lord.
Lamb of God, who taketh away the sins of the world,
graciously hear us, O Lord.
Lamb of God, who taketh away the sins of the world,
have mercy on us, O Lord.

V. Holy guardian angels, pray for us.
R. That we may be made worthy of the promises of Christ.

Let us pray: Almighty and eternal God, who, by an ineffable design of Thy goodness have assigned to each of the faithful, from the womb of his mother, an angel to guard him in body and soul, grant me the grace to have such reverence and love for the one whom Thou in Thy mercy has given me, that, upheld by Thy grace and with his aid, I might deserve at last to contemplate with him and all the other holy angels the radiance of Thy glory in the blessed homeland. Through Jesus Christ Thy Son, who livest and reignest with Thee in the unity of the Holy Ghost, world without end. Amen.

Litany of Humility

O Jesus, meek and humble of heart, *hear me.*
From the desire of being esteemed, *deliver me, Jesus.*
From the desire of being loved,
From the desire of being extolled,
From the desire of being honored,
From the desire of being praised,
From the desire of being preferred to others,
From the desire of being consulted,
From the desire of being approved,
From the fear of being humiliated,
From the fear of being despised,
From the fear of suffering rebukes,
From the fear of being calumniated,
From the fear of being forgotten,
From the fear of being ridiculed,
From the fear of being wronged,
From the fear of being suspected,
That others may be loved more than I,
    Jesus, grant me the grace to desire it.
That others may be esteemed more than I,
That, in the opinion of the world, others may increase
    and I may decrease,
That others may be chosen and I set aside,
That others may be praised and I go unnoticed,
That others may be preferred to me in everything,
That others may become holier than I,
    provided that I may become as holy as I should,

From the Assumption to Advent

Latin Hymns

Magnificat

1. *Magnificat * anima mea Dominum.*

   My soul doth magnify the Lord:

2. *Et exsultavit spiritus meus * in Deo salutari meo.*

   And my spirit hath rejoiced in God my Savior.

3. *Quia respexit humilitatem ancillæ suæ: * ecce enim ex hoc beatam me dicent omnes generationes.*

   Because He hath regarded the humility of His handmaid; for behold from henceforth all generations shall call me blessed.

4. *Quia fecit mihi magna qui potens est: * et sanctum nomen eius.*

   For He that is mighty hath done great things to me: and holy is His name.

5. *Et misericordia eius a progenie in progenies * timentibus eum.*

   And His mercy is from generation to generations, to them that fear Him.

6. *Fecit potentiam in brachio suo: * dispersit superbos mente cordis sui.*

   He hath shown might in His arm: He hath scattered the proud in the conceit of their heart:

7. *Deposuit potentes de sede, * et exaltavit humiles.*

   He hath put down the mighty from their seat, and hath exalted the humble.

8. *Esurientes implevit bonis: * et divites dimisit inanes.*

   He hath filled the hungry with good things: and the rich He hath sent away empty.

9. *Suscepit Israël puerum suum, * recordatus misericordiæ suæ.*

   He hath received Israel His servant, being mindful of His mercy.

10. *Sicut locutus est ad patres nostros, * Abraham et semini eius in sæcula.*

    As He spoke to our fathers, to Abraham and to his seed forever.

11. *Gloria Patri et Filio, * et Spiritui Sancto.*

Glory be to the Father and to the Son and to the Holy Ghost.

12. *Sicut erat in principio, et nunc, et semper, * et in sæcula sæculorum. Amen.*

As it was in the beginning, is now, and ever shall be, world without end. Amen.

The Seven Penitential Psalms[72]

Psalm 6

Lord, when Thou dost reprove me, let it not be in anger; when Thou dost chastise me, let it not be in displeasure.

Lord, pity me; I have no strength left; Lord, heal me; my limbs tremble;

my spirits are altogether broken; Lord, wilt Thou never be content?

Lord, turn back, and grant a wretched soul relief; as Thou art ever merciful, save me.

When death comes, there is no more remembering Thee; none can praise Thee in the tomb.

I am spent with sighing; every night I lie weeping on my bed, till the tears drench my pillow.

Grief has dimmed my eyes, faded their lustre now, so many are the adversaries that surround me.

Depart from me, all you that traffic in iniquity; the Lord has heard my cry of distress.

Here was a prayer divinely heard, a boon divinely granted.

All my enemies will be abashed and terrified; taken aback, all in a moment, and put to shame.

Glory be to the Father, and to the Son, and to the Holy Ghost.

As it was in the beginning, is now, and ever shall be, world without end. Amen.

---

[72] The English translation of the seven penitential psalms is by Fr. Ronald Knox. Psalm 90 is from the Douay-Rheims translation.

Psalm 31

Blessed are they who have their faults forgiven, their transgressions buried deep;

blessed is the man who is not guilty in the Lord's reckoning, the heart that hides no treason.

While I kept my own secret, evermore I went sighing, so wasted my frame away,

bowed down day and night by Thy chastisement; still my strength ebbed, faint as in mid-summer heat.

At last I made my transgression known to Thee, and hid my sin no longer; Fault of mine, said I, I here confess to the Lord; and with that, Thou didst remit the guilt of my sin.

Let every devout soul, then, turn to Thee in prayer when hard times befall; rise the floods never so high, they shall have no power to reach it.

Thou art my hiding-place, when I am sore bestead; songs of triumph are all about me, and Thou my deliverer.

Friend, let me counsel thee, trace for thee the path thy feet should tread; let my prudence watch over thee.

Do not be like the horse and the mule, senseless creatures which will not come near thee unless their spirit is tamed by bit and bridle.

Again and again the sinner must feel the lash; he who trusts in the Lord finds nothing but mercy all around him.

Just souls, be glad, and rejoice in the Lord; true hearts, make your boast in Him.

Glory be to the Father, and to the Son, and to the Holy Ghost.

As it was in the beginning, is now, and ever shall be, world without end. Amen.

Psalm 37

Thy reproof, Lord, not Thy vengeance; Thy chastisement, not Thy condemnation!

Thy arrows pierce me, Thy hand presses me hard;

Thy anger has driven away all health from my body, never a bone sound in it, so grievous are my sins.

My own wrong-doing towers high above me, hangs on me like a heavy burden;

my wounds fester and rankle, with my own folly to blame.

Beaten down, bowed to the earth, I go mourning all day long,

my whole frame afire, my whole body diseased;

so spent, so crushed, I groan aloud in the weariness of my heart.

Thou, Lord, knowest all my longings, no complaint of mine escapes Thee;

restless my heart, gone my strength; the very light that shone in my eyes is mine no longer.

Friends and neighbours that meet me keep their distance from a doomed man; old companions shun me.

Ill-wishers that grudge me life itself lay snares about me, threaten me with ruin; relentlessly their malice plots against me.

And I, all the while, am deaf to their threats, dumb before my accusers;

mine the unheeding ear, and the tongue that utters no defence.

On Thee, Lord, my hopes are set; Thou, O Lord my God, wilt listen to me.

Such is the prayer I make, Do not let my enemies triumph over me, boast of my downfall.

Fall full well I may; misery clouds my view;

I am ever ready to publish my guilt, ever anxious over my sin.

Unprovoked, their malice still prevails; so many that bear me a grudge so wantonly,

rewarding good with evil, and for the very rightness of my cause assailing me.

Do not fail me, O Lord my God, do not forsake me;

hasten to my defence, O Lord, my only refuge.

Glory be to the Father, and to the Son, and to the Holy Ghost.

As it was in the beginning, is now, and ever shall be, world without end. Amen.

Psalm 50 (*Miserere*)

1. *Miserere mei, Deus * secundum magnam misericordiam tuam.*

Have mercy on me, O God, as Thou art ever rich in mercy;

2. *Et secundum multitudinem miserationum tuarum, * dele iniquitatem meam.*

in the abundance of Thy compassion, blot out the record of my misdeeds.

3. *Amplius lava me ab iniquitate mea: * et a peccato meo munda me.*

Wash me clean, cleaner yet, from my guilt, purge me of my sin,

4. *Quoniam iniquitatem meam ego cognosco: * et peccatum meum contra me est semper.*

the guilt which I freely acknowledge, the sin which is never lost to my sight.

5. *Tibi soli peccavi, et malum coram te feci: * ut justificeris in sermonibus tuis, et vincas cum judicaris.*

Thee only my sins have offended; it is Thy will I have disobeyed; Thy sentence was deserved, and still when Thou givest award Thou hast right on Thy side.

6. *Ecce enim in iniquitatibus conceptus sum: * et in peccatis concepit me mater mea.*

For indeed, I was born in sin; guilt was with me already when my mother conceived me.

7. *Ecce enim veritatem dilexisti: * incerta et occulta sapientiæ tuæ manifestasti mihi.*

But Thou art a lover of faithfulness, and now, deep in my heart, Thy wisdom has instructed me.

8. *Asperges me hyssopo, et mundabor: * lavabis me, et super nivem dealbabor.*

Sprinkle me with a wand of hyssop, and I shall be clean; washed, I shall be whiter than snow;

9. *Auditui meo dabis gaudium et lætitiam: * et exultabunt ossa humiliata.*

tidings send me of good news and rejoicing, and the body that lies in the dust shall thrill with pride.

The Seven Penitential Psalms

10. *Averte faciem tuam a peccatis meis: * et omnes iniquitates meas dele.*

Turn Thy eyes away from my sins, blot out the record of my guilt;

11. *Cor mundum crea in me, Deus: * et spiritum rectum innova in visceribus meis.*

my God, bring a clean heart to birth within me; breathe new life, true life, into my being.

12. *Ne projicias me a facie tua: * et spiritum sanctum tuum ne auferas a me.*

Do not banish me from Thy presence, do not take Thy holy spirit away from me;

13. *Redde mihi lætitiam salutaris tui: * et spiritu principali confirma me.*

give me back the comfort of Thy saving power, and strengthen me in generous resolve.

14. *Docebo iniquos vias tuas: * et impii ad te convertentur.*

So will I teach the wicked to follow Thy paths; sinners shall come back to Thy obedience.

15. *Libera me de sanguinibus, Deus, Deus salutis meæ: * et exsultabit lingua mea justitiam tuam.*

My God, my divine Deliverer, save me from the guilt of bloodshed! This tongue shall boast of Thy mercies;

16. *Domine, labia mea aperies: * et os meum annuntiabit laudem tuam.*

O Lord, Thou wilt open my lips, and my mouth shall tell of Thy praise.

17. *Quoniam si voluisses sacrificium, dedissem utique: * holocaustis non delectaberis.*

Thou hast no mind for sacrifice, burnt-offerings, if I brought them, Thou wouldst refuse;

18. *Sacrificium Deo spiritus contribulatus: * cor contritum et humiliatum, Deus, non despicies.*

here, O God, is my sacrifice, a broken spirit; a heart that is humbled and contrite Thou, O God, wilt never disdain.

19. *Benigne fac, Domine, in bona voluntate tua Sion: * ut ædificentur muri Jerusalem.*

Lord, in Thy great love send prosperity to Sion, so that the walls of Jerusalem may rise again.

20. *Tunc acceptabis sacrificium justitiæ, oblationes et holocausta: * tunc imponent super altare tuum vitulos.*

Then indeed Thou wilt take pleasure in solemn sacrifice, in gift and burnt-offering; then indeed bullocks will be laid upon Thy altar.

21. *Gloria Patri et Filio, * et Spiritui Sancto.*

Glory be to the Father and to the Son and to the Holy Ghost.

22. *Sicut erat in principio, et nunc, et semper, * et in sæcula sæculorum. Amen.*

As it was in the beginning, is now, and ever shall be, world without end. Amen.

Psalm 101

O Lord, hear my prayer, and let my cry come unto Thee.

Do not turn Thy face away from me, but lend me Thy ear in time of affliction; give me swift audience whenever I call upon Thee.

See how this life of mine passes away like smoke, how this frame wastes like a tinder!

Drained of strength, like grass the sun scorches, I leave my food untasted, forgotten;

I am spent with sighing, till my skin clings to my bones.

I am no better than a pelican out in the desert, an owl on some ruined dwelling;

I keep mournful watch, lonely as a single sparrow on the house top.

Still my enemies taunt me, in their mad rage make a by-word of me.

Ashes are all my food, I drink nothing but what comes to me mingled with my tears;

I shrink before Thy vengeful anger, so low Thou hast brought me, who didst once lift me so high.

Like a tapering shadow my days dwindle, wasting away, like grass in the sun!

Lord, Thou endurest forever, Thy name, age after age, is not forgotten;

surely Thou wilt bestir Thyself, and give Sion redress! It is time, now, to take pity on her, the hour has come.

See how Thy servants love her even in ruin, how they water her dust with their tears!

Will not the heathen learn reverence, Lord, for Thy glorious name, all those monarchs of the earth,

when they hear that the Lord has built Sion anew; that He has revealed himself there in glory,

has given heed to the prayer of the afflicted, neglects their appeal no more?

Such legend inscribe we for a later age to read it; a new people will arise, to praise the Lord;

the Lord, who looks down from His sanctuary on high, viewing earth from heaven,

who has listened to the groans of the prisoners, delivered a race that was doomed to die.

There will be talk of the Lord's name in Sion, of His praise in Jerusalem,

when peoples and kings meet there to pay Him their homage.

Here, on my journey, He has brought my strength to an end, cut short my days.

What, my God, wilt Thou snatch me away, my life half done? Age after age Thy years endure;

it was Thou, Lord, that didst lay the foundations of earth when time began, it was Thy hand that built the heavens.

They will perish, but Thou wilt remain; they will all be like a cloak that grows threadbare, and Thou wilt lay them aside like a garment, and exchange them for new;

Thou art unchanging, Thy years can never fail.

The posterity of Thy servants shall yet hold their lands in peace, their race shall live on in Thy keeping.

Glory be to the Father, and to the Son, and to the Holy Ghost.

As it was in the beginning, is now, and ever shall be, world without end. Amen.

Psalm 129 (*De Profundis*)

1. *De profundis clamavi ad te, Domine: * Domine, exaudi vocem meam.*

   Out of the depths I cry to Thee, O Lord; Master, listen to my voice;

2. *Fiant aures tuæ intendentes, * in vocem deprecationis meæ.*

   Let but Thy ears be attentive to the voice that calls on Thee for pardon.

3. *Si iniquitates observaveris, Domine: * Domine, qui sustinebit?*

   If Thou, Lord, wilt keep record of our iniquities, Master, who has strength to bear it?

4. Quia apud te propitiatio est: * et propter legem tuam sustinui te, Domine.

   Ah, but with Thee there is forgiveness; be Thy name ever revered. I wait for the Lord,

5. *Sustinuit anima mea in verbo ejus: * speravit anima mea in Domino.*

   for His word of promise my soul waits; patient my soul waits,

6. *A custodia matutina usque ad noctem: * speret Israël in Domino.*

   as ever watchman that looked for the day. Patient as watchman at dawn, for the Lord Israel waits,

7. *Quia apud Dominum misericordia: * et copiosa apud eum redemptio.*

   the Lord with whom there is mercy, with whom is abundant power to ransom.

8. *Et ipse redimet Israël * ex omnibus iniquitatibus ejus.*

   He it is that will ransom Israel from all his iniquities.

9. *Requiem æternam * dona eis, Domine.*

   Eternal rest grant unto them, O Lord,

10. *Et lux perpetua *luceat eis.*

    and let perpetual light shine upon them.

Psalm 142

Listen, Lord, to my prayer; give my plea a hearing, as Thou art ever faithful; listen, Thou who lovest the right.

Do not call Thy servant to account; what man is there living that can stand guiltless in Thy presence?

See how my enemies plot against my life, how they have abased me in the dust, set me down in dark places, like the long-forgotten dead!

My spirits are crushed within me, my heart is cowed.

And my mind goes back to past days; I think of all Thou didst once, dwell on the proofs Thou gavest of Thy power.

To Thee I spread out my hands in prayer, for Thee my soul thirsts, like a land parched with drought.

Hasten, Lord, to answer my prayer; my spirit grows faint. Do not turn Thy face away from me, and leave me like one sunk in the abyss.

Speedily let me win Thy mercy, my hope is in Thee; to Thee I lift up my heart, show me the path I must follow;

to Thee I fly for refuge, deliver me, Lord, from my enemies.

Thou art my God, teach me to do Thy will; let Thy gracious spirit lead me, safe ground under my feet.

For the honour of Thy own name, Lord, grant me life; in Thy mercy rescue me from my cruel affliction.

Have pity on me, and scatter my enemies; Thy servant I; make an end of my cruel persecutors.

Glory be to the Father, and to the Son, and to the Holy Ghost.

As it was in the beginning, is now, and ever shall be, world without end. Amen.

Psalm 90

He that dwelleth in the aid of the most High, shall abide under the protection of the God of Jacob.

He shall say to the Lord: Thou art my protector, and my refuge: my God, in Him will I trust.

For He hath delivered me from the snare of the hunters: and from the sharp word.

He will overshadow thee with His shoulders: and under His wings thou shalt trust.

His truth shall compass thee with a shield: thou shalt not be afraid of the terror of the night.

Of the arrow that flieth in the day, of the business that walketh about in the dark: of invasion, or of the noonday devil.

A thousand shall fall at thy side, and ten thousand at thy right hand: but it shall not come nigh thee.

But thou shalt consider with thy eyes: and shalt see the reward of the wicked.

Because Thou, O Lord, art my hope: thou hast made the most High thy refuge.

There shall no evil come to thee: nor shall the scourge come near thy dwelling.

For He hath given his angels charge over thee; to keep thee in all thy ways.

In their hands they shall bear thee up: lest thou dash thy foot against a stone.

Thou shalt walk upon the asp and the basilisk: and thou shalt trample under foot the lion and the dragon.

Because he hoped in Me I will deliver him: I will protect him because he hath known My name.

He shall cry to Me, and I will hear him: I am with him in tribulation, I will deliver him, and I will glorify him.

I will fill him with length of days; and I will show him My salvation.

Glory be to the Father, and *to* the Son, and to *the Holy Ghost*.

As it *was in the beginni*ng, is now, and ever shall be, world without end. Amen.

Salve Regina

Salve, Regina, Mater misericordiæ: vita, dulcedo et spes nostra, salve.
  Ad te clamamus, exsules filii Hevæ.
  Ad te suspiramus, gementes et flentes in hac lacrimarum valle.

  Eia ergo, advocata nostra, illos tuos misericordes oculos ad nos converte.
  Et Jesum, benedictum fructum ventris tui, nobis post hoc exsilium ostende.
  O clemens, o pia, o dulcis Virgo Maria!

  Hail, holy Queen, Mother of Mercy, our life, our sweetness and our hope.
  To thee do we cry, poor banished children of Eve.
  To thee do we send up our sighs, mourning and weeping in this valley of tears.
  Turn then, most gracious advocate, thine eyes of mercy towards us.
  And after this our exile show unto us the blessed fruit of thy womb, Jesus.
  O clement, O loving, O sweet Virgin Mary!

Soul of Christ (*Anima Christi*)

Anima Christi, sanctifica me.
Corpus Christi, salva me.
Sanguis Christi, inebria me.
Aqua lateris Christi, lava me.

Passio Christi, conforta me.
O bone Iesu, exaudi me.
Intra tua vulnera absconde me.
Ne permittas me separari a te.

Ab hoste maligno defende me.

In hora mortis meæ voca me,
et jube me venire ad te,
ut cum Sanctis tuis laudem te

In sæcula sæculorum. Amen.

Soul of Christ, sanctify me.
Body of Christ, save me.
Blood of Christ, inebriate me.
Water from the side of Christ, wash me.

Passion of Christ, strengthen me.
O good Jesus, hear me.
In Thy wounds, hide me.
Permit me not to be separated from Thee.

From the malicious enemy, defend me.

At the hour of my death, call me and bid me come to Thee,
that with Thy saints I may praise Thee,
for ever and ever. Amen.

From the Assumption to Advent

Hymn *Soul of My Savior*

Soul of my Savior, sanctify my breast,
Body of Christ, be Thou my saving guest,
Blood of my Savior, bathe me in Thy tide,
Wash me with waters gushing from Thy side.

    Strength and protection may Thy Passion be;
    O blessèd Jesus, hear and answer me;
    Deep in Thy wounds, Lord, hide and shelter me,
    So shall I never, never part from Thee.

Guard and defend me from the foe malign,
In death's dread moments make me only Thine;
Call me and bid me come to Thee on high
Where I may praise Thee with Thy saints for ay.

Bibliography

Holy Scripture[73]

Acts:	Acts of the Apostles
Apoc.:	Book of the Apocalypse
Col.:	Epistle of St. Paul to the Colossians
Cant.:	Canticle of Canticles
Ecclus.:	Book of Ecclesiasticus
Eph.:	Epistle of St. Paul to the Ephesians
Ex.:	Book of Exodus
Ez.:	Book of the Prophet Ezechiel
Gal.:	Epistle of St. Paul to the Galatians
Gen.:	Book of Genesis
Heb.:	Epistle of St. Paul to the Hebrews
Is.:	Book of the Prophet Isaias
Jas.:	Epistle of St. James
Jer.:	Book of the Prophet Jeremias
Jn.:	Gospel according to St. John
Lam.:	Book of the Lamentations of Jeremy
Lk.:	Gospel according to St. Luke
Mk.:	Gospel according to St. Mark
Mt.:	Gospel according to St. Matthew
Os.:	Book of the Prophet Osee (Hosea)
Ph.:	Epistle of St. Paul to the Philippians
Ps.:	Psalm
Rom.:	Epistle of St. Paul to the Romans
Tob.:	Book of Tobias
I Cor.:	First Epistle of St. Paul to the Corinthians
I Jn.:	First Epistle of St. John
I Kings:	First Book of Kings
I Pet.:	First Epistle of St. Peter
I Thess.:	First Epistle of St. Paul to the Thessalonians
II Mac.:	Second Book of Maccabees
II Pet.:	Second Epistle of St. Peter
II Thess.:	Second Epistle of St. Paul to the Thessalonians
II Tim.:	Second Epistle of St. Paul to Timothy
III Kings:	Third Book of Kings
IV Kings:	Fourth Book of Kings

---

[73] As a general rule, passages from the Old Testament are taken from the Douay-Rheims translation and passages from the New Testament are taken from the translation of the Confraternity of Christian Doctrine or from *The Roman Catholic Daily Missal* (Angelus Press). The translation of the penitential psalms is from the Knox Bible.

Bibliography

St. Alphonsus Liguori

GM: *The Glories of Mary*, P.J. Kenedy, 1888.

HDD: *Holiness Day by Day [La sainteté au jour le jour]*, Clovis, 2014.

Instructions on the Commandments and Sacraments, St. Athanasius Press, 2016.

Visits to the Blessed Sacrament [Visites au Saint-Sacrement], Saint-Paul, 1990.

St. Ambrose

Commentary on the Gospel of St. Luke [Traité sur l'Evangile de saint Luc], Sources Chrétiennes, Le Cerf, 1965.

St. Augustine

"Homily on the First Epistle of St. John," in *Nicene and Post-Nicene Fathers, First Series,* vol. VII, The Christian Literature Company, 1888, translated by H. Browne.

The Confessions, Dorset Press, NY, 1961, from the translation of R.S. Pine-Coffin.

CW: *Complete Works [Œuvres complètes]*, Louis Vivès, 1870, vol. V, XIV, XVII.

St. Basil of Caesarea

Against Eunomius, The Catholic University Press, 2011, translated by Mark DelCogliano and Andrew Radde-Gallwitz.

St. Benedict

TD: *Thought for the Day [Une Pensée par jour]*, texts selected by Véronique Dupont, O.S.B., Médiaspaul, 2007.

Fr. Calmel

365 D: *365 Days with Fr. Calmel [365 jours avec le père Calmel]*, manuscript, May 2014.

St. Catherine of Genoa

Treatise on Purgatory, Burns & Oates, Ltd., 1858.

St. Catherine of Siena

D: *Dialogue*, Kegan Paul, Trench, Trubner & Co., Ltd., 1907, translat by Algar Thorold.

R: *The Rosary: Texts of Saint Catherine of Siena [Le rosaire, textes de sainte Catherine de Sienne]*, Monastery of Chambarand.

Charles de Foucauld

TD: *Thought for the Day [Une Pensée par jour]*, texts selected by Patrice Mahieu, O.S.B., Médiaspaul, 2010.

St. Claude de la Colombière

Spiritual Writings [Ecrits spirituels], Desclée de Brouwer, 1982.

Clement XI

Universal Prayer, "Thanksgiving after Mass," in *Diurnale romanum*, 1960.

Curé of Ars

R: *The Rosary: Texts of the Curé of Ars [Le rosaire, textes du saint curé d'Ars]*, Monastery of Chambarand.

Select Thoughts of the Curé of Ars [Pensées choisies du saint cure d'Ars], ed. J. Frossard, Téqui, 1961.

TD1: *Thought for the Day [Une pensée par jour]*, Clovis, 2006.

TD2: *Thought for the Day*, texts selected by Claudine Fearon, Médiaspaul, 2010.

Elizabeth of the Trinity

The Complete Works, Vol. 1: I Have Found God, Institute of Carmelite Studies, 2014, translation by Sr. Aletheia Kane, O.C.D.

L: Letters translated in *The Complete Works, Vol. 2: Letters from Carmel*, Institute of Carmelite Studies, 2014, translation by Anne Englund Nash.

Where the French edition is referenced, passages are translated directly from Elisabeth de la Trinité, Œuvres *complètes*, Cerf, 1991. Passages from the Diary *[Journal]*, 1899-1900, from the Personal Notes *[Notes Intimes]* and from the poems are translated from the French edition.

TD: *Thought for the Day [Une Pensée par jour]*, texts selected by the Carmelites of Dijon, Médiaspaul, 2006.

Bibliography

Fr. Emmanuel

M: Fr. Emmanuel, O.S.B., *Meditations for Every Day of the Liturgical Year [Méditations pour tous les jours de l'année liturgique]*, Dismas, 1987.

St. Francis de Sales

Introduction to the Devout Life, Image Books, 1966, translated by John K. Ryan.

Works of St. Francis de Sales [Œuvres de saint François de Sales], Annecy, 1895, vol. VI.

TD: *Thought for the Day [Une pensée par jour]*, texts gathered by Sr. Marie-Christophe (Monastery of the Visitation, Voiron), Médiaspaul, 2008.

St. Francis of Assisi

Thomas de Celano, *Life of St. Francis of Assisi [Vie de saint François d'Assise]*, Editions Franciscaines, 1952.

St. Gregory the Great

D: *Dialogues of St. Gregory the Great [Dialogues de saint Grégoire le Grand]*, Alfred Marne et fils, 1875.

SG: *Sermons on the Gospels [Homélies sur les Évangiles]*, Sainte-Madeleine, 2000.

TD: *Thought for the Day [Une pensée par jour]*, texts selected by Jacqueline Martin-Bagnaudez, Médiaspaul, 2012.

St. John Chrysostom

Complete Works, [Œuvres complètes], Louis Vivès, 1868, vol. I-VI.

Pauline Jaricot

TD: *Thought for the Day [Une pensée par jour]*, texts selected by *Pontifical Missionary Works* (Lyon, France), Médiaspaul, 2008.

Padre Pio

TD2: *Thought for the Day [Une pensée par jour]*, texts selected by Fr. Gerardo Di Flumeri, O.F.M. Cap., Médiaspaul, 2010.

St. Pius X

"Our Apostolic Mandate" (Letter on the Sillon), August 25, 1910. Translation from *The Great Papal Encyclicals* series, *Angelus Press*; republished in part in *The Angelus* Magazine, May-June 2021.

Pius XI
    Encyclical *Quas Primas,* December 11, 1925. Translation from the Vatican website.

Pius XII
    Encyclical *Mystici Corporis,* June 29, 1943. Translation from the Vatican website.

St. Teresa of Avila

TD: *Thought for the Day*, texts gathered by Martine Loriau, Médiaspaul, 2009.

WP: *The Way of Perfection*, Thomas Baker, London, 1919, translated by the Benedictines of Stanbrook.

St. Thomas Aquinas

Catena Aurea: Commentary on the Four Gospels, Collected out of the Works of the Fathers by St. Thomas Aquinas, Commentary on the Four Gospels Collected out of the Works of the Fathers, vol. I, Part I, St. Matthew, Oxford, John Henry Parker, 1841, and *vol. III, part I, St. Luke,* John Henry Parker, Oxford, 1843.

Summa Theologica, Christian Classics, Westminster, MD, 1981, translated by the Fathers of the English Dominican Province.

St. Vincent de Paul

TD1:   *Thought for the Day, [Une pensée par jour]*, Clovis, 2006.

TD2:   *Thought for the Day*, texts gathered by Fr. Jean-Yves Ducourneau, Médiaspaul, 2007.

R: *The Rosary: Texts of St. Vincent de Paul [Le rosaire, textes de saint Vincent de Paul]*, Monastery of Chambarand.

Other Authors

OW: Bossuet, *Oratorical Works [Œuvres oratoires]*, Desclée de Brouwer, Paris, 1892.

    Fr. Henri-Marie Bourdon, *Devotion to the Holy Angels [La devotion aux saints anges]*, Clovis, 1998.

CW: Bourdaloue, *Complete Works [Œuvres complètes]*, II, L. Guérin, 1864.

Bibliography

        Fr. Bernard Bro, O.P., *Saint Thérèse of Lisieux: Her Family, Her God, Her Message*, Ignatius Press, 2003, translated by Anne Englund Nash.

VH: H.E. Bishop Chevrot, *The Little Virtues of the Home [Les petites vertus du foyer]*, Le Laurier, 2001.

        Geneviève Esquier, *Men Who Believed in Heaven [Ceux qui croyaient au Ciel]*, L'Escalade, 1985.

DI: Fr. Gabriel of St. Mary Magdalen, O.C.D., *Divine Intimacy*, TAN, 1996.

LY: Dom Guéranger, O.S.B., *The Liturgical Year: Time after Pentecost*, bk. II, Loreto Publications, 2000, translated by Dom Laurence Shepherd. English versions of liturgical hymns are generally taken from *The Liturgical Year*.

PC: Fr. Hugueny, O.P., *Psalms and Canticles [Psaumes et Cantiques]*, Action Catholique, 1927, IV.

Thomas À Kempis, *The Imitation of Christ*, Penguin Classics, 1952, translated by Leo Sherley-Price.

Cardinal Mercier, *Christian Mortification [Mortification chrétienne]*, Editions du Sel, 2020.

        Blaise Pascal, *Pascal's Pensées*, E.P. Dutton & Co., Inc., New York, 1958, introduction by T.S. Eliot.

        Fr. Paul-Marie, *The Apparition and the Secret of La Salette [L'apparition et le secret de La Salette]*, Hovine, 1982.

        Cardinal Pie, *Works of His Excellency the Bishop of Poitiers [Œuvres de Monseigneur l'évêque de Poitiers]*, III, H. Oudin & Co., 1884.

Fr. François Trochu, *The Curé d'Ars*, TAN Books, 1977, translated by a monk of Buckfast Abbey, and *Saint François de Sales*, Librairie Catholique Emmanuel Vitte, 1946.

Pastoral Letters

        H.E. Bishop Jules de Carsalade du Pont, Archbishop of Perpignan, *Pastoral Letter*, 1902.

        H.E. Bishop Jean Chesnelong, Archbishop of Sens, *Pastoral Letter*, 1921.

        H.E. Bishop Maurice Clément, Bishop of Monaco, *Pastoral Letter*, 1934.

H.E. Bishop Marcel Dubois, Archbishop of Besançon, *Pastoral Letter*, 1957.

H.E. Bishop Olivier de Durfort de Civrac de Lorge, Bishop of Poitiers, *Pastoral Letter*, 1932.

H.E. Bishop André Fauvel, Bishop of Quimper, *Pastoral Letter*, 1957.

H.E. Bishop Alphonse Gaudron, Bishop of Évreux, *Pastoral Letter*, 1949.

H.E. Bishop Cosme Jorcin, Bishop of Digne, *Pastoral Letter*, 1926.

H.E. Bishop Théophile Louvard, Bishop of Coutances and Avranches, *Pastoral Letter*, 1934.

H.E. Bishop Pierre Marceillac, Bishop of Pamiers, *Pastoral Letter*, 1918.

H.E. Bishop Joseph Rumeau, Bishop of Angers, *Pastoral Letter*, 1934.

Other Works

Catechism of the Council of Trent, Joseph F. Wagner, Inc., 1943, translated by John A. McHugh, O.P., and Charles J. Callan, O.P.

The Church Teaches, by Jesuit Fathers of St. Mary's College, TAN Books, 1973.

DZ: Denzinger-Schönmetzer, *Enchiridion Symbolorum, Definitionum et Declarationum*, Herder, 1976. Church documents are listed by number, with the numbering from Denzinger's original edition given in parentheses.

DS: *Dictionary of Spirituality [Dictionnaire de spiritualité]*, published under the direction of Marcel Viller, S.J., Gabriel Beauchesne et ses fils, 1932, I; 1933, II.

Friend of the Parish Clergy [L'ami du clergé paroissial], Imprimerie Maitrier et Courtot, 1902, XIV.

The Guardian Angel [L'Ange gardien], July 1895. Review of the Archconfraternity of the Holy Guardian Angels, based near Lyon, France, published from 1891 to 2021.

Patrologia Latina, Ed. J.-P. Migne, 1854, vol. 172.

Bibliography

The Roman Catholic Daily Missal, Angelus Press, 2004, for the translation of prayers and texts of Masses.

The Sources of Catholic Dogma, Henry Denzinger, Loreto Publications, 1955, translated by Roy J. DeFerrari.

By the same Author

From Advent to Epiphany	Angelus Press, 2018
From Epiphany to Lent	Angelus Press, 2020
Toward Easter	Angelus Press, 2020
Eastertide Day by Day	Angelus Press, 2020
From Trinity Sunday to the Assumption	Angelus Press, 2022
The Catholic Family Vol. 1	Angelus Press, 2020
The Catholic Family Vol. 2	Angelus Press, 2021
The Catholic Family Vol. 3	Angelus Press, 2021
The Rosary with Archbishop Lefebvre	Angelus Press, 2018

Compiled by the Author

The Mass of All Time—Sermons, Classes and Notes by Archbishop Marcel Lefebvre	Angelus Press, 2018
The Spiritual Life—Writings of Archbishop Marcel Lefebvre	Stas Editions, 2014.